Full-Stack Vue.js 2 and Laravel 5

Bring the frontend and backend together with Vue, Vuex, and Laravel

Anthony Gore

BIRMINGHAM - MUMBAI

Full-Stack Vue.js 2 and Laravel 5

First published: December 2017

Production reference: 1261217

Published by Packt Publishing Ltd.
Livery Place
35 Livery Street
Birmingham
B3 2PB, UK.
ISBN 978-1-78829-958-9

www.packtpub.com

Credits

Author
Anthony Gore

Reviewer
Ashley Menhennett

Commissioning Editor
Kunal Chaudhari

Acquisition Editor
Siddharth Mandal

Content Development Editor
Mohammed Yusuf Imaratwale

Technical Editor
Harshal Kadam

Copy Editor
Safis Editing

Project Coordinator
Hardik Bhinde

Proofreader
Safis Editing

Indexer
Tejal Daruwale Soni

Graphics
Tania Dutta

Production Coordinator
Shantanu Zagade

About the Author

Anthony Gore is a full-stack web developer from Sydney, Australia. He loves to share knowledge about web technologies, with a particular passion for JavaScript.

Anthony is the founder of Vue.js Developers, the largest online community of Vue enthusiasts, and he curates the weekly *Vue.js Developers Newsletter*. He is also a frequent blogger and the author of *Ultimate Vue.js Developers Video Course*.

Besides web development, Anthony is a keen musician and is often traveling abroad and working remotely.

I would like to thank my parents, Graeme and Paula, for encouraging me to follow my interests and passions and for their love and support while I worked on this book.

About the Reviewer

Ashley Menhennett is a developer from South Australia, with 6 years of experience in web and software development, thriving on solving real-world problems through the application of software engineering processes. Ashley has recently accepted an offer of a graduate position in platform engineering, with plans to continue future study in the field of computer science. Ashley enjoys spending time with family and his Jack Russell, Alice.

With thanks to my friends and family for their support.

www.PacktPub.com

For support files and downloads related to your book, please visit `www.PacktPub.com`. Did you know that Packt offers eBook versions of every book published, with PDF and ePub files available? You can upgrade to the eBook version at `www.PacktPub.com` and as a print book customer, you are entitled to a discount on the eBook copy. Get in touch with us at `service@packtpub.com` for more details.

At `www.PacktPub.com`, you can also read a collection of free technical articles, sign up for a range of free newsletters and receive exclusive discounts and offers on Packt books and eBooks.

`https://www.packtpub.com/mapt`

Get the most in-demand software skills with Mapt. Mapt gives you full access to all Packt books and video courses, as well as industry-leading tools to help you plan your personal development and advance your career.

Why subscribe?

- Fully searchable across every book published by Packt
- Copy and paste, print, and bookmark content
- On demand and accessible via a web browser

Customer Feedback

Thanks for purchasing this Packt book. At Packt, quality is at the heart of our editorial process. To help us improve, please leave us an honest review on this book's Amazon page at https://www.amazon.com/dp/1788299582.

If you'd like to join our team of regular reviewers, you can e-mail us at customerreviews@packtpub.com. We award our regular reviewers with free eBooks and videos in exchange for their valuable feedback. Help us be relentless in improving our products!

Table of Contents

Preface

The year is 2014 and the war of **Single-Page Application** (SPA) solutions is truly raging. There are many rivals: Angular, React, Ember, Knockout, and Backbone, to name but a few. However, the battle being most closely watched is between Google's Angular and Facebook's React.

Angular, the SPA king until this point, is a full-fledged framework that follows the familiar MVC paradigm. React, the unlikely challenger seems quite odd in comparison with its core library only dealing with the view layer and markup written entirely in JavaScript! While Angular holds the bigger market share, React has caused a seismic shift in how developers think about web application design and has raised the bar on framework size and performance.

Meanwhile, a developer named Evan You was experimenting with his own new framework, Vue.js. It would combine the best features of Angular and React to achieve a perfect balance between simplicity and power. Your vision would resonate so well with other developers that Vue would soon be among the most popular SPA solutions.

Despite the fierce competition, Vue gained traction quickly. This was partly thanks to Taylor Otwell, the creator of Laravel, who tweeted in early 2015 about how impressed he was with Vue. This tweet generated a lot of interest in Vue from the Laravel community.

The partnership of Vue and Laravel would become further entwined with the release of Laravel version 5.3 in September 2016, when Vue was included as a default frontend library. This was a perfectly logical alliance for two software projects with the same philosophy: simplicity and an emphasis on the developer experience.

Today, Vue and Laravel offer an immensely powerful and flexible full-stack framework for developing web applications, and as you'll find throughout this book, they're a real treat to work with.

What this book covers

Building a full-stack app requires a wide variety of knowledge, not just about Vue and Laravel, but also Vue Router, Vuex, and Webpack, not to mention JavaScript, PHP, and web development in general.

As such, one of the biggest challenges for me as the author was deciding what should and shouldn't be included. The topics I ultimately settled upon arose as answers to one of the two following questions:

- What are the essential features, tools, and design patterns that the reader will use in all, or most, of their Vue.js apps?
- What are the key issues of designing and building *full-stack* Vue.js apps as opposed to other architectures?

Here's how the chosen topics are distributed across the chapters of the book:

Chapter 1, *Hello Vue - An Introduction to Vue.js*, presents an overview of Vue.js, and the book's case-study project, *Vuebnb*.

Chapter 2, *Prototyping Vuebnb, Your First Vue.js Project*, provides a practical introduction to the essential features of Vue.js, including installation, template syntax, directives, lifecycle hooks and so on.

Chapter 3, *Setting Up a Laravel Development Environment*, shows how to set up a new Laravel project for inclusion in a full-stack Vue.js app.

Chapter 4, *Building a Web Service with Laravel*, is about laying the foundations of the backend of our case-study project, by setting up the database, models, and API endpoints.

Chapter 5, *Integrating Laravel and Vue.js with Webpack*, explains how a sophisticated Vue app will require a build step, and introduces Webpack for bundling project assets.

Chapter 6, *Composing Widgets with Vue.js Components*, teaches how components are an essential concept of modern UI development and one of the most powerful features of Vue.js.

Chapter 7, *Building a Multi-Page App with Vue Router*, introduces Vue Router and shows how we can add virtual pages to a frontend app.

Chapter 8, *Managing Your Application State with Vuex*, explains how state management is a must-have feature for managing complex UI data. We introduce the Flux pattern and Vuex.

Chapter 9, *Adding a User Login and API Authentication With Passport*, focuses on one of the trickiest aspects of full-stack apps—authentication. This chapter shows how to use Passport for secure AJAX calls to the backend.

Chapter 10, *Deploying a Full-Stack App to the Cloud*, describes how to build and deploy our completed project to a cloud-based server and use a CDN for serving static assets.

What you need for this book

Before you begin development on the case-study project, you must ensure that you have the correct software and hardware.

Operating system

You can use a Windows or Linux-based operating system. I'm a Mac guy though, so any Terminal commands used in this book will be Linux commands.

Note that we'll be using the Homestead virtual development environment, which includes the Ubuntu Linux operating system. If you SSH into the box and run all your Terminal commands from there, you can use the same commands as me, even if you have a Windows host operating system.

Development tools

Downloading the project code will require Git. If you haven't got Git installed already, follow the directions in this guide: `https://git-scm.com/book/en/v2/Getting-Started-Installing-Git`.

To develop a JavaScript application you'll need Node.js and NPM. These can be installed from the same package; see the instructions here: `https://nodejs.org/en/download/`.

We'll also be using Laravel Homestead. Instructions will be given in Chapter 3, *Setting Up a Laravel Development Environment*.

Browser

Vue requires ECMAScript 5, which means you can use a recent version of any major browser to run it. I recommend you use Google Chrome, though, as I'll be giving debugging examples for Chrome Dev Tools, and it will be easier for you to follow along if you're using Chrome as well.

When choosing your browser, you should also consider compatibility with Vue Devtools.

Vue Devtools

The Vue Devtools browser extension makes debugging Vue a breeze, and we'll be using it extensively in this book. The extension is made for Google Chrome, but will also work in Firefox (and Safari, with a bit of hacking.)

See the following link for more information and installation instructions: `https://github.com/vuejs/vue-devtools`

IDE

You will, of course, need a text editor or IDE for developing the case-study project.

Hardware

You'll need a computer with specs sufficient for installing and running the software just mentioned. The most resource-intensive program will be VirtualBox 5.2 (or VMWare or Parallels), which we'll be using to set up the Homestead virtual development environment.

You'll also need an internet connection for downloading the source code and project dependencies.

Who this book is for

This book is for Laravel developers who are seeking a practical and best-practice approach to full-stack development with Vue.js and Laravel.

Any web developer interested in the topic can successfully use this book, though, so long as they meet the following criteria:

Topic	Level
HTML and CSS	Intermediate knowledge
JavaScript	Intermediate knowledge
PHP	Intermediate knowledge
Laravel	Basic knowledge
Git	Basic knowledge

Note that readers will not need any prior experience with Vue.js or other JavaScript frameworks.

Conventions

In this book, you will find a number of text styles that distinguish between different kinds of information. Here are some examples of these styles and an explanation of their meaning.

Code words in text, database table names, folder names, filenames, file extensions, pathnames, dummy URLs, user input, and Twitter handles are shown as follows: "For example, here I've created a custom element, `grocery-item`, which renders as a `li`."

A block of code is set as follows:

```
<div id="app">
  <!--Vue has dominion within this node-->
</div>
<script>
  new Vue({
    el: '#app'
  });
</script>
```

Any command-line input or output is written as follows:

```
$ npm install
```

New terms and **important words** are shown in bold. Words that you see on the screen, for example, in menus or dialog boxes, appear in the text like this: "This is not permitted by Vue and if you attempt it you will get this error: **Do not mount Vue to <html> or <body> - mount to normal elements instead**."

Warnings or important notes appear in a box like this.

Tips and tricks appear like this.

Reader feedback

Feedback from our readers is always welcome. Let us know what you think about this book-what you liked or disliked. Reader feedback is important for us as it helps us develop titles that you will really get the most out of.

To send us general feedback, simply e-mail feedback@packtpub.com, and mention the book's title in the subject of your message.

If there is a topic that you have expertise in and you are interested in either writing or contributing to a book, see our author guide at www.packtpub.com/authors.

Customer support

Now that you are the proud owner of a Packt book, we have a number of things to help you to get the most from your purchase.

Downloading the example code

You can download the example code files for this book from your account at http://www.packtpub.com. If you purchased this book elsewhere, you can visit http://www.packtpub.com/support and register to have the files e-mailed directly to you.

You can download the code files by following these steps:

1. Log in or register to our website using your e-mail address and password.
2. Hover the mouse pointer on the **SUPPORT** tab at the top.
3. Click on **Code Downloads & Errata**.
4. Enter the name of the book in the **Search** box.
5. Select the book for which you're looking to download the code files.
6. Choose from the drop-down menu where you purchased this book from.
7. Click on **Code Download**.

You can also download the code files by clicking on the **Code Files** button on the book's webpage at the Packt Publishing website. This page can be accessed by entering the book's name in the **Search** box. Please note that you need to be logged in to your Packt account.

Once the file is downloaded, please make sure that you unzip or extract the folder using the latest version of:

- WinRAR / 7-Zip for Windows
- Zipeg / iZip / UnRarX for Mac
- 7-Zip / PeaZip for Linux

The code bundle for the book is also hosted on GitHub at `https://github.com/PacktPublishing/Full-Stack-Vue.js-2-and-Laravel-5`. We also have other code bundles from our rich catalog of books and videos available at `https://github.com/PacktPublishing/`. Check them out!

Errata

Although we have taken every care to ensure the accuracy of our content, mistakes do happen. If you find a mistake in one of our books-maybe a mistake in the text or the code-we would be grateful if you could report this to us. By doing so, you can save other readers from frustration and help us improve subsequent versions of this book. If you find any errata, please report them by visiting `http://www.packtpub.com/submit-errata`, selecting your book, clicking on the **Errata Submission Form** link, and entering the details of your errata. Once your errata are verified, your submission will be accepted and the errata will be uploaded to our website or added to any list of existing errata under the Errata section of that title.

To view the previously submitted errata, go to `https://www.packtpub.com/books/content/support` and enter the name of the book in the search field. The required information will appear under the **Errata** section.

Piracy

Piracy of copyrighted material on the Internet is an ongoing problem across all media. At Packt, we take the protection of our copyright and licenses very seriously. If you come across any illegal copies of our works in any form on the Internet, please provide us with the location address or website name immediately so that we can pursue a remedy.

Please contact us at `copyright@packtpub.com` with a link to the suspected pirated material.

We appreciate your help in protecting our authors and our ability to bring you valuable content.

Questions

If you have a problem with any aspect of this book, you can contact us at `questions@packtpub.com`, and we will do our best to address the problem.

1

Hello Vue – An Introduction to Vue.js

Welcome to *Full-Stack Vue.js 2 and Laravel 5*! In this first chapter, we'll take a high-level overview of Vue.js, getting you familiar with what it can do, in preparation for learning how to do it.

We'll also get acquainted with *Vuebnb*, the main case-study project featured in this book.

Topics this chapter covers:

- Basic features of Vue, including templates, directives, and components
- Advanced features of Vue including single-file components and server-side rendering
- Tools in the Vue ecosystem including Vue Devtools, Vue Router, and Vuex
- The main case-study project that you'll be building as you progress through the book, *Vuebnb*
- Instructions for installing the project code

Introducing Vue.js

At the time of writing in late 2017, Vue.js is at version 2.5. In less than four years from its first release, Vue has become one of the most popular open source projects on GitHub. This popularity is partly due to its powerful features, but also to its emphasis on developer experience and ease of adoption.

The core library of Vue.js, like React, is only for manipulating the view layer from the MVC architectural pattern. However, Vue has two official supporting libraries, Vue Router and Vuex, responsible for routing and data management respectively.

Vue is not supported by a tech giant in the way that React and Angular are and relies on donations from a small number of corporate patrons and dedicated Vue users. Even more impressively, Evan You is currently the only full-time Vue developer, though a core team of 20 more developers from around the world assist with development, maintenance, and documentation.

The key design principles of Vue are as follows:

- **Focus**: Vue has opted for a small, focused API, and its sole purpose is the creation of UIs
- **Simplicity**: Vue's syntax is terse and easy to follow
- **Compactness**: The core library script is ~25 KB minified, making it smaller than React and even jQuery
- **Speed**: Rendering benchmarks beat many of the main frameworks, including React
- **Versatility**: Vue works well for small jobs where you might normally use jQuery, but can scale up as a legitimate SPA solution

Basic features

Let's now do a high-level overview of Vue's basic features. If you want, you can create an HTML file on your computer like the following one, open it in your browser, and code along with the following examples.

If you'd rather wait until the next chapter, when we start working on the case-study project, that's fine too as our objective here is simply to get a feel for what Vue can do:

```html
<!DOCTYPE html>
<html lang="en">
<head>
  <meta charset="utf-8">
  <meta http-equiv="X-UA-Compatible" content="IE=edge">
  <title>Hello Vue</title>
</head>
<body>
  <!--We'll be adding stuff here!-->
</body>
</html>
```

Installation

Although Vue can be used as a JavaScript module in more sophisticated setups, it can also simply be included as an external script in the body of your HTML document:

```html
<script src="https://unpkg.com/vue/dist/vue.js"></script>
```

Templates

By default, Vue will use an HTML file for its template. An included script will declare an instance of Vue and use the el property in the configuration object to tell Vue where in the template the app will be mounted:

```html
<div id="app">
  <!--Vue has dominion within this node-->
</div>
<script>
  new Vue({
    el: '#app'
  });
</script>
```

We can bind data to our template by creating it as a `data` property and using the mustache syntax to print it in the page:

```
<div id="app">
  {{ message }}
  <!--Renders as "Hello World"-->
</div>
<script>
  new Vue({
    el: '#app',
    data: {
      message: 'Hello World'
    }
  });
</script>
```

Directives

Similar to Angular, we can add functionality to our templates by using **directives**. These are special properties we add to HTML tags starting with the v- prefix.

Say we have an array of data. We can render this data to the page as sequential HTML elements by using the v-for directive:

```
<div id="app">
  <h3>Grocery list</h3>
  <ul>
    <li v-for="grocery in groceries">{{ grocery }}</li>
  </ul>
</div>
<script>
  var app = new Vue({
    el: '#app',
    data: {
      groceries: [ 'Bread', 'Milk' ]
    }
  });
</script>
```

The preceding code renders as follows:

```
<div id="app">
  <h3>Grocery list</h3>
  <ul>
    <li>Bread</li>
    <li>Milk</li>
  </ul>
</div>
```

Reactivity

A key feature of Vue's design is its reactivity system. When you modify data, the view automatically updates to reflect that change.

For example, if we create a function that pushes another item to our array of grocery items after the page has already been rendered, the page will automatically re-render to reflect that change:

```
setTimeout(function() {
  app.groceries.push('Apples');
}, 2000);
```

Two seconds after the initial rendering, we see this:

```
<div id="app">
  <h3>Grocery list</h3>
  <ul>
    <li>Bread</li>
    <li>Milk</li>
    <li>Apples</li>
  </ul>
</div>
```

Components

Components extend basic HTML elements and allow you to create your own reusable custom elements.

For example, here I've created a custom element, `grocery-item`, which renders as a `li`. The text child of that node is sourced from a custom HTML property, `title`, which is accessible from within the component code:

```
<div id="app">
  <h3>Grocery list</h3>
  <ul>
    <grocery-item title="Bread"></grocery-item>
    <grocery-item title="Milk"></grocery-item>
  </ul>
</div>
<script>
  Vue.component( 'grocery-item', {
    props: [ 'title' ],
    template: '<li>{{ title }}</li>'
  });

  new Vue({
    el: '#app'
  });
</script>
```

This renders as follows:

```
<div id="app">
  <h3>Grocery list</h3>
  <ul>
    <li>Bread</li>
    <li>Milk</li>
  </ul>
</div>
```

But probably the main reason to use components is that it makes it easier to architect a larger application. Functionality can be broken into reuseable, self-contained components.

Advanced features

If you have been coding along with the examples so far, close your browser now until next chapter, as the following advanced snippets can't simply be included in a browser script.

Single-file components

A drawback of using components is that you need to write your template in a JavaScript string outside of your main HTML file. There are ways to write template definitions in your HTML file, but then you have an awkward separation between markup and logic.

A convenient solution to this is **single-file components**:

```
<template>
  <li v-on:click="bought = !bought" v-bind:class="{ bought: bought }">
    <div>{{ title }}</div>
  </li>
</template>
<script>
  export default {
    props: [ 'title' ],
    data: function() {
      return {
        bought: false
      };
    }
  }
</script>
<style>
  .bought {
    opacity: 0.5;
  }
</style>
```

These files have the .vue extension and encapsulate the component template, JavaScript configuration, and style all in a single file.

Of course, a web browser can't read these files, so they need to be first processed by a build tool such as Webpack.

Module build

As we saw earlier, Vue can be dropped into a project as an external script for direct use in a browser. Vue is also available as an NPM module for use in more sophisticated projects, including a build tool such as Webpack.

If you're unfamiliar with Webpack, it's a module bundler that takes all your project assets and bundles them up into something you can provide to the browser. In the bundling process, you can transform those assets as well.

Using Vue as a module and introducing Webpack opens possibilities such as the following:

- Single-file components
- ES feature proposals not currently supported in browsers
- Modularized code
- Pre-processors such as SASS and Pug

 We will be exploring Webpack more extensively in Chapter 5, *Integrating Laravel and Vue.js with Webpack*.

Server-side rendering

Server-side rendering is a great way to increase the perception of loading speed in full-stack apps. Users get a complete page with visible content when they load your site, as opposed to an empty page that doesn't get populated until JavaScript runs.

Say we have an app built with components. If we use our browser development tool to view our page DOM *after* the page has loaded, we will see our fully rendered app:

```
<div id="app">
  <ul>
    <li>Component 1</li>
    <li>Component 2</li>
    <li>
      <div>Component 3</div>
    </li>
  </ul>
</div>
```

But if we view the source of the document, that is, index.html, as it was when sent by the server, you'll see it just has our mount element:

```
<div id="app"></div>
```

Why? Because JavaScript is responsible for building our page and, ipso facto, JavaScript has to run before the page is built. But with server-side rendering, our index file includes the HTML needed for the browser to build a DOM before JavaScript is downloaded and run. The app does not load any faster, but content is shown sooner.

The Vue ecosystem

While Vue is a standalone library, it is even more powerful when combined with some of the optional tools in its ecosystem. For most projects, you'll include Vue Router and Vuex in your frontend stack, and use Vue Devtools for debugging.

Vue Devtools

Vue Devtools is a browser extension that can assist you in the development of a Vue.js project. Among other things, it allows you to see the hierarchy of components in your app and the state of components, which is useful for debugging:

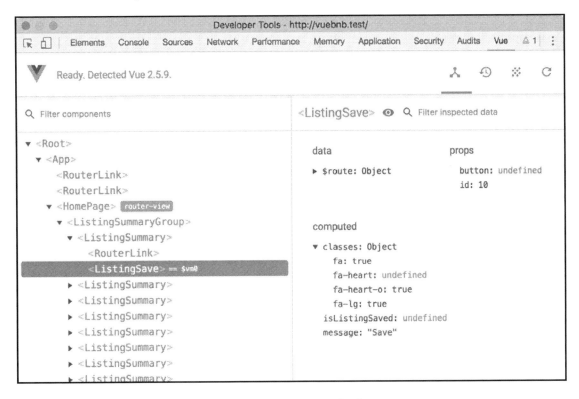

Figure 1.1. Vue Devtools component hierarchy

We'll see what else it can do later in this section.

Vue Router

Vue Router allows you to map different states of your SPA to different URLs, giving you virtual pages. For example, `mydomain.com/` might be the front page of a blog and have a component hierarchy like this:

```
<div id="app">
  <my-header></my-header>
  <blog-summaries></blog-summaries>
  <my-footer></my-footer>
</div>
```

Whereas `mydomain.com/post/1` might be an individual post from the blog and look like this:

```
<div id="app">
  <my-header></my-header>
  <blog-post post-id="id">
  <my-footer></my-footer>
</div>
```

Changing from one page to the other doesn't require a *reload* of the page, just swapping the middle component to reflect the state of the URL, which is exactly what Vue Router does.

Vuex

Vuex provides a powerful way to manage the data of an application as the complexity of the UI increases, by centralizing the application's data into a single store.

We can get snapshots of the application's state by inspecting the store in Vue Devtools:

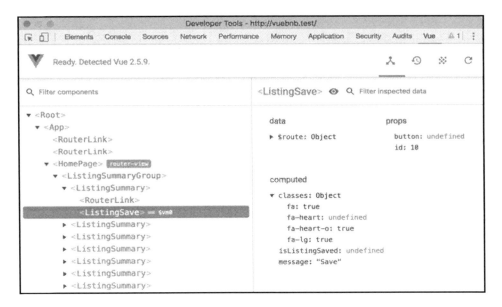

Figure 1.2. Vue Devtools Vuex tab

The left column tracks changes made to the application data. For example, say the user saves or unsaves an item. You might name this event `toggleSaved`. Vue Devtools lets you see the particulars of this event as it occurs.

We can also revert to any previous state of the data without having to touch the code or reload the page. This function, called *Time Travel Debugging*, is something you'll find very useful for debugging complex UIs.

Case-study project

After a whirlwind overview of Vue's key features, I'm sure you're keen now to start properly learning Vue and putting it to use. Let's first have a look at the case-study project you'll be building throughout the book.

Vuebnb

Vuebnb is a realistic, full-stack web application which utilizes many of the main features of Vue, Laravel, and the other tools and design patterns covered in this book.

From a user's point of view, Vuebnb is an online marketplace for renting short-term lodgings in cities around the world. You may notice some likeness between Vuebnb and another online marketplace for accommodation with a similar name!

You can view a completed version of Vuebnb here: `http://vuebnb.vuejsdevelopers.com`.

If you don't have internet access right now, here are screenshots of two of the main pages. Firstly, the home page, where users can search or browse through accommodation options:

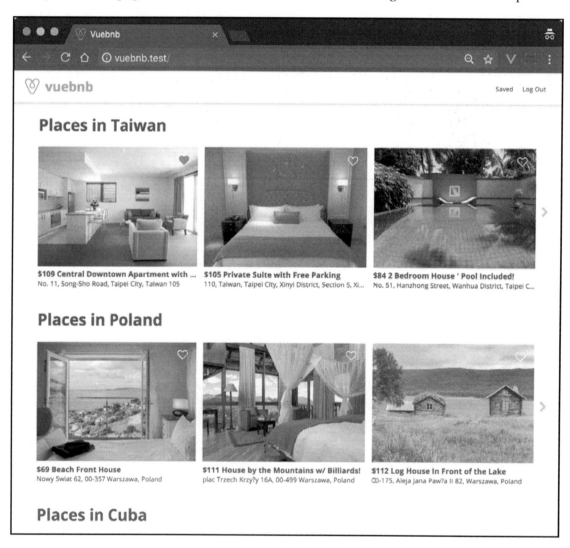

Figure 1.3. Vuebnb home page

Secondly, the listing page, where users view information specific to a single lodging they may be interested in renting:

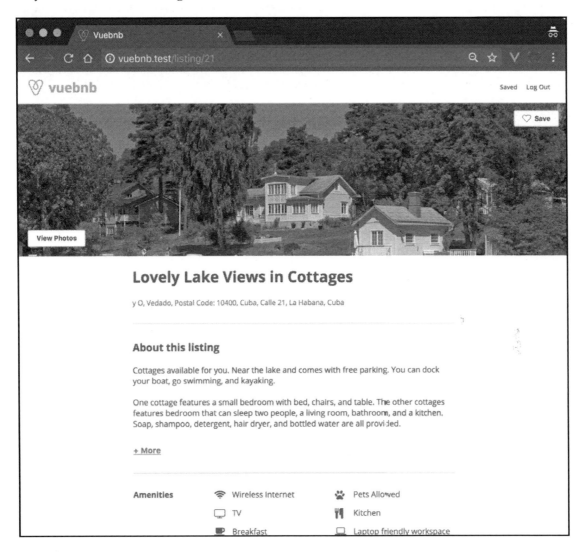

Figure 1.4. Vuebnb listing page

Code base

The case-study project runs through the entire duration of this book, so once you've created the code base you can keep adding to it chapter by chapter. By the end, you'll have built and deployed a full-stack app from scratch.

The code base is in a GitHub repository. Download it in whatever folder on your computer that you normally put projects in, for example, `~/Projects`:

```
$ cd ~/Projects
$ git clone
https://github.com/PacktPublishing/Full-Stack-Vue.js-2-and-Laravel-5
$ cd Full-Stack-Vue.js-2-and-Laravel-5
```

Rather than cloning this repository directly, you could first make a *fork* and clone that. This will allow you to make any changes you like and save your work to your own remote repository. Here's a guide to forking a repository on GitHub: `https://help.github.com/articles/fork-a-repo/`.

Folders

The code base contains the following folders:

```
● ● ●                    Full-Stack-Vue.js-2-and-Laravel-5 — -bash — 87×6
Anthonys-MacBook-Pro:Full-Stack-Vue.js-2-and-Laravel-5 anthonygore$ ls
Chapter02              Chapter06                  Chapter10
Chapter03              Chapter07                  images
Chapter04              Chapter08                  vuebnb
Chapter05              Chapter09                  vuebnb-prototype
Anthonys-MacBook-Pro:Full-Stack-Vue.js-2-and-Laravel-5 anthonygore$ ▌
```

Figure 1.5. Code base directory contents

Here's a rundown of what each folder is used for:

- `Chapter02` to `Chapter10` contains the *completed state* of the code for each chapter (excluding this one)
- The *images* directory contains sample images for use in Vuebnb. This will be explained in `Chapter 4`, *Building a Web Service with Laravel*
- *vuebnb* is the project code you'll use for the main case-study project that we begin work on in `Chapter 3`, *Setting Up a Laravel Development Environment*
- *vuebnb-prototype* is the project code of the Vuebnb prototype that we'll build in `Chapter 2`, *Prototyping Vuebnb, Your First Vue.js Project*

Summary

In this first chapter, we did a high-level introduction to Vue.js, covering the basic features such as templates, directives, and components, as well as advanced features such as single-file components and server-side rendering. We also had a look at the tools in Vue's ecosystem including Vue Router and Vuex.

We then did an overview of Vuebnb, the full-stack project that you'll be building as you progress through the book, and saw how to install the code base from GitHub.

In the next chapter, we'll get properly acquainted with Vue's basic features and starting putting them to use by building a prototype of Vuebnb.

2

Prototyping Vuebnb, Your First Vue.js Project

In this chapter, we will learn the basic features of Vue.js. We'll then put this knowledge into practice by building a prototype of the case-study project, Vuebnb.

Topics this chapter covers:

- Installation and basic configuration of Vue.js
- Vue.js essential concepts, such as data binding, directives, watchers and lifecycle hooks
- How Vue's reactivity system works
- Project requirements for the case-study project
- Using Vue.js to add page content including dynamic text, lists, and a header image
- Building an image modal UI feature with Vue

Vuebnb prototype

In this chapter, we'll be building a prototype of Vuebnb, the case-study project that runs for the duration of this book. The prototype will just be of the listing page, and by the end of the chapter will look like this:

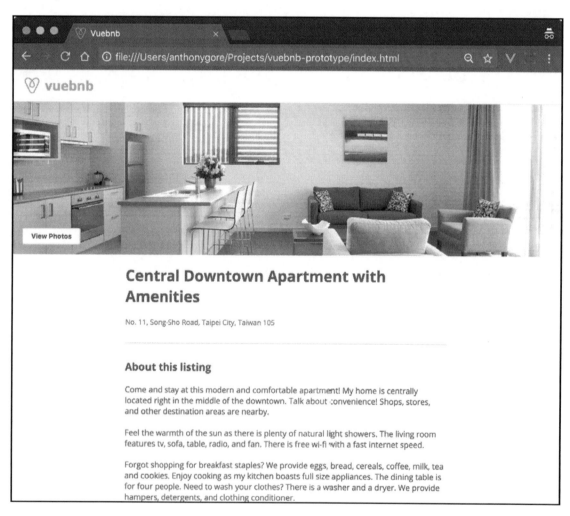

Figure 2.1. Vuebnb prototype

Once we've set up our backend in `Chapter 3`, *Setting Up a Laravel Development Environment*, and `Chapter 4`, *Building a Web Service with Laravel*, we'll migrate this prototype into the main project.

Project code

Before we begin, you'll need to download the code base to your computer by cloning it from GitHub. Instructions are given in the section *Code base* in `Chapter 1`, *Hello Vue - An Introduction to Vue.js*.

The folder `vuebnb-prototype` has the project code for the prototype we'll now be building. Change into that folder and list the contents:

```
$ cd vuebnb-prototype
$ ls -la
```

The folder contents should look like this:

```
Anthonys-MBP:vuebnb-prototype anthonygore$ ls -la
total 144
drwxr-xr-x  12 anthonygore  staff    408 10 Nov 13:12 .
drwxr-xr-x   5 anthonygore  staff    170 19 Sep 13:01 ..
drwxr-xr-x  16 anthonygore  staff    544  9 Nov 20:08 .git
-rw-r--r--   1 anthonygore  staff     21  8 Nov 21:02 .gitignore
-rw-r--r--   1 anthonygore  staff    714  8 Nov 21:02 README.md
-rw-r--r--   1 anthonygore  staff      0  8 Nov 21:02 app.js
-rw-r--r--@  1 anthonygore  staff  15086  8 Nov 21:02 favicon.ico
-rw-r--r--   1 anthonygore  staff    547  8 Nov 21:02 index.html
-rw-r--r--   1 anthonygore  staff  32812  8 Nov 21:02 logo.png
-rw-r--r--   1 anthonygore  staff    464  8 Nov 21:02 package.json
drwxr-xr-x   5 anthonygore  staff    170  8 Nov 20:36 sample
-rw-r--r--   1 anthonygore  staff    526  8 Nov 21:02 style.css
Anthonys-MBP:vuebnb-prototype anthonygore$
```

Figure 2.2. vuebnb-prototype project files

Unless otherwise specified, all further Terminal commands in this chapter will assume you're in the `vuebnb-prototype` folder.

NPM install

You'll now need to install the third-party scripts used in this project, including Vue.js itself. The NPM install method will read the included package.json file and download the required modules:

```
$ npm install
```

You'll now see a new node_modules directory has appeared in your project folder.

Main files

Open the vuebnb-prototype directory in your IDE. Note that the following index.html file is included. It's mostly comprised of boilerplate code, but also has some structural markup included in the body tag.

Also note that this file links to style.css, where our CSS rules will be added, and app.js, where our JavaScript will be added.

index.html:

```html
<!DOCTYPE html>
<html>
<head>
  <meta charset="UTF-8">
  <meta http-equiv="X-UA-Compatible" content="IE=edge,chrome=1">
  <meta name="viewport" content="width=device-width,initial-scale=1">
  <title>Vuebnb</title>
  <link href="node_modules/open-sans-all/css/open-sans.css"
rel="stylesheet">
  <link rel="stylesheet" href="style.css" type="text/css">
</head>
<body>
<div id="toolbar">
  <img class="icon" src="logo.png">
  <h1>vuebnb</h1>
</div>
<div id="app">
  <div class="container"></div>
</div>
<script src="app.js"></script>
</body>
</html>
```

Currently `app.js` is an empty file, but I have included some CSS rules in `style.css` to get us started.

`style.css`:

```css
body {
  font-family: 'Open Sans', sans-serif;
  color: #484848;
  font-size: 17px;
  margin: 0;
}

.container {
  margin: 0 auto;
  padding: 0 12px;
}

@media (min-width: 744px) {
  .container {
      width: 696px;
  }
}

#toolbar {
  display: flex;
  align-items: center;
  border-bottom: 1px solid #e4e4e4;
  box-shadow: 0 1px 5px rgba(0, 0, 0, 0.1);
}

#toolbar .icon {
  height: 34px;
  padding: 16px 12px 16px 24px;
  display: inline-block;
}

#toolbar h1 {
  color: #4fc08d;
  display: inline-block;
  font-size: 28px;
  margin: 0;
}
```

Opening in the browser

To view the project, locate the index.html file in your web browser. In Chrome, it's as simple as **File | Open File**. When it loads, you'll see a page that is mostly empty, other than the toolbar at the top.

Installing Vue.js

Now it's time to add the Vue.js library to our project. Vue was downloaded as part of our NPM install, so now we can simply link to the browser-build of Vue.js with a script tag.

index.html:

```
<body>
<div id="toolbar">...</div>
<div id="app">...</div>
<script src="node_modules/vue/dist/vue.js"></script>
<script src="app.js"></script>
</body>
```

 It's important that we include the Vue library *before* our own custom app.js script, as scripts run sequentially.

Vue will now be registered as a global object. We can test this by going to our browser and typing the following in the JavaScript console:

```
console.log(Vue);
```

Here is the result:

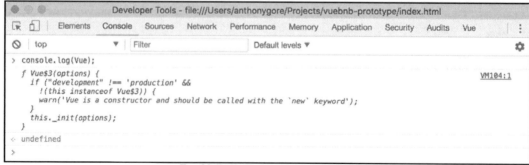

Figure 2.3. Checking Vue is registered as a global object

Page content

With our environment set up and starter code installed, we're now ready to take the first steps in building the Vuebnb prototype.

Let's add some content to the page, including the header image, the title, and the **About** section. We'll be adding structure to our HTML file and using Vue.js to insert the correct content where we need it.

The Vue instance

Looking at our app.js file, let's now create our root instance of Vue.js by using the new operator with the Vue object.

app.js:

```
var app = new Vue();
```

When you create a Vue instance, you will usually want to pass in a configuration object as an argument. This object is where your project's custom data and functions are defined.

app.js:

```
var app = new Vue({
  el: '#app'
});
```

As our project progresses, we'll be adding much more to this configuration object, but for now we've just added the el property that tells Vue where to mount itself in the page.

You can assign to it a string (a CSS selector) or an HTML node object. In our case, we've used the #app string, which is a CSS selector referring to the element with the app ID.

index.html:

```
<div id="app">
  <!--Mount element-->
</div>
```

Vue has dominion over the element it mounts on and any child node. For our project so far, Vue could manipulate the `div` with the `header` class, but it could not manipulate the `div` with the `toolbar` ID. Anything placed within this latter `div` will be invisible to Vue.

`index.html`:

```
<body>
<div id="toolbar">...</div>
<div id="app">
  <!--Vue only has dominion here-->
  <div class="header">...</header>
  ...
</div>
<script src="node_modules/vue/dist/vue.js"></script>
<script src="app.js"></script>
</body>
```

From now on, we'll refer to our mount node and its children as our template.

Data binding

A simple task for Vue is to bind some JavaScript data to the template. Let's create a `data` property in our configuration object and assign to it an object including a `title` property with a `'My apartment'` string value.

`app.js`:

```
var app = new Vue({
  el: '#app',
  data: {
    title: 'My apartment'
  }
});
```

Any property of this `data` object will be available within our template. To tell Vue where to bind this data, we can use *mustache* syntax, that is, double curly brackets, for example, `{{ myProperty }}`. When Vue instantiates, it compiles the template, replaces the mustache syntax with the appropriate text, and updates the DOM to reflect this. This process is called *text interpolation* and is demonstrated in the following code block.

`index.html`:

```
<div id="app">
  <div class="container">
    <div class="heading">
      <h1>{{ title }}</h1>
    </div>
  </div>
</div>
```

Will render as this:

```
<div id="app">
  <div class="container">
    <div class="heading">
      <h1>My apartment</h1>
    </div>
  </div>
</div>
```

Let's add a few more data properties now and enhance our template to include more of the page structure.

`app.js`:

```
var app = new Vue({
  el: '#app',
  data: {
    title: 'My apartment',
    address: '12 My Street, My City, My Country',
    about: 'This is a description of my apartment.'
  }
});
```

`index.html`:

```
<div class="container">
  <div class="heading">
    <h1>{{ title }}</h1>
    <p>{{ address }}</p>
  </div>
```

```
<hr>
<div class="about">
  <h3>About this listing</h3>
  <p>{{ about }}</p>
</div>
</div>
```

Let's also add some new CSS rules.

style.css:

```
.heading {
  margin-bottom: 2em;
}

.heading h1 {
  font-size: 32px;
  font-weight: 700;
}

.heading p {
  font-size: 15px;
  color: #767676;
}

hr {
  border: 0;
  border-top: 1px solid #dce0e0;
}

.about {
  margin-top: 2em;
}

.about h3 {
  font-size: 22px;
}

.about p {
  white-space: pre-wrap;
}
```

If you now save and refresh your page, it should look like this:

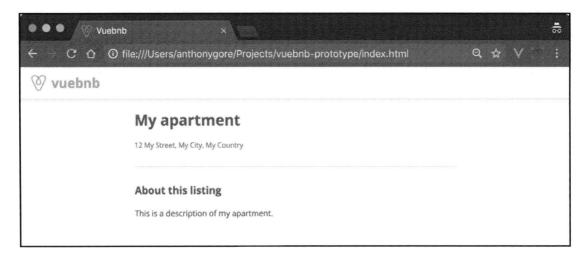

Figure 2.4. Listing page with basic data binding

Mock listing

While we're developing, it'd be nice to work with some mock data so that we can see how our completed page will look. I've included `sample/data.js` in the project for this very reason. Let's load it in our document, making sure it goes above our `app.js` file.

`index.html`:

```
<body>
<div id="toolbar">...</div>
<div id="app">...</div>
<script src="node_modules/vue/dist/vue.js"></script>
<script src="sample/data.js"></script>
<script src="app.js"></script>
</body>
```

Have a look at the file and you'll see that it declares a `sample` object. We will now utilize it in our data configuration.

`app.js`:

```
data: {
  title: sample.title,
  address: sample.address,
  about: sample.about
}
```

Once you save and refresh, you'll see more realistic data on the page:

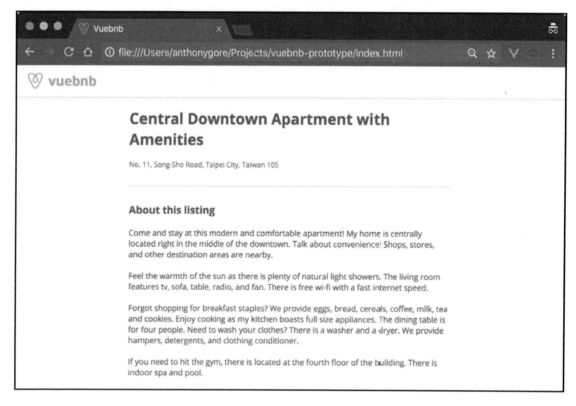

Figure 2.5. Page including mock-listing sample

Using global variables split over different script files in this way is not an ideal practice. We'll only be doing this in the prototype, though, and later we'll get this mock-listing sample from the server.

Header image

No room listing would be complete without a big, glossy image to show it off. We've got a header image in our mock listing that we'll now include. Add this markup to the page.

index.html:

```
<div id="app">
  <div class="header">
    <div class="header-img"></div>
  </div>
  <div class="container">...</div>
</div>
```

And this to the CSS file.

style.css:

```
.header {
  height: 320px;
}

.header .header-img {
  background-repeat: no-repeat;
  background-size: cover;
  background-position: 50% 50%;
  background-color: #f5f5f5;
  height: 100%;
}
```

You may be wondering why we're using a div rather than an img tag. To help with positioning, we're going to set our image as the background of the div with the header-img class.

Style binding

To set a background image, we must provide the URL as a property in a CSS rule like this:

```
.header .header-img {
  background-image: url(...);
}
```

Obviously, our header image should be specific to each individual listing, so we don't want to hard code this CSS rule. Instead, we can have Vue bind the URL from data to our template.

Vue can't access our CSS style sheet, but it can bind to an inline `style` attribute:

```
<div class="header-img" style="background-image: url(...);"></div>
```

You may think using a text interpolation is the solution here, for example:

```
<div class="header-img" style="background-image: {{ headerUrl }}"></div>
```

But this is not valid Vue.js syntax. This is, instead, a job for another Vue.js feature called a `directive`. Let's explore directives first and then come back to solving this problem.

Directives

Vue's directives are special HTML attributes with the *v-* prefix, for example, `v-if`, which provide a simple way to add functionality to our templates. Some examples of directives you can add to an element are:

- `v-if`: Conditionally render the element
- `v-for`: Render the element multiple times based on an array or object
- `v-bind`: Dynamically bind an attribute of the element to a JavaScript expression
- `v-on`: Attach an event listener to the element

There are more that we will explore throughout the book.

Usage

Just like normal HTML attributes, directives are usually name/value pairs in the form `name="value"`. To use a directive, simply add it to an HTML tag as you would an attribute, for example:

```
<p v-directive="value">
```

Expressions

If a directive requires a value, it will be an *expression*.

In the JavaScript language, expressions are small, evaluable statements that produce a single value. Expressions can be used wherever a value is expected, for example in the parenthesis of an `if` statement:

```
if (expression) {
   ...
}
```

The expression here could be any of the following:

- A mathematical expression, for example `x + 7`
- A comparison, for example `v <= 7`
- A Vue `data` property, for example `this.myval`

Directives and text interpolations both accept expression values:

```
<div v-dir="someExpression">{{ firstName + " " + lastName }}</div>
```

Example: v-if

`v-if` will conditionally render an element if its value is a *truthy* expression. In the following case, `v-if` will remove/insert the p element depending on the `myval` value:

```
<div id="app">
  <p v-if="myval">Hello Vue</p>
</div>
<script>
  var app = new Vue({
    el: '#app',
    data: {
      myval: true
```

```
      }
   });
</script>
```

Will renders as:

```
<div id="app">
   <p>Hello Vue</p>
</div>
```

If we add a consecutive element with the `v-else` directive (a special directive that requires no value), it will be symmetrically removed/inserted as `myval` changes:

```
<p v-if="myval">Hello Vue</p>
<p v-else>Goodbye Vue</p>
```

Arguments

Some directives take an *argument*, denoted by a colon after the directive name. For example, the `v-on` directive, which listens to DOM events, requires an argument to specify which event should be listened to:

```
<a v-on:click="doSomething">
```

Instead of `click`, the argument could be `mouseenter`, `keypress`, `scroll`, or any other event (including custom events).

Style binding (continued)

Coming back to our header image, we can use the `v-bind` directive with the `style` argument to bind a value to the `style` attribute.

`index.html`:

```
<div class="header-img" v-bind:style="headerImageStyle"></div>
```

`headerImageStyle` is an expression that evaluates to a CSS rule that sets the background image to the correct URL. It sounds very confusing, but when you see it working, it will be quite clear.

Let's now create `headerImageStyle` as a data property. When binding to a style attribute, you can use an object where the properties and values are equivalent to the CSS properties and values.

`app.js`:

```
data: {
  ...
  headerImageStyle: {
    'background-image': 'url(sample/header.jpg)'
  }
},
```

Save the code, refresh the page, and the header image will be shown:

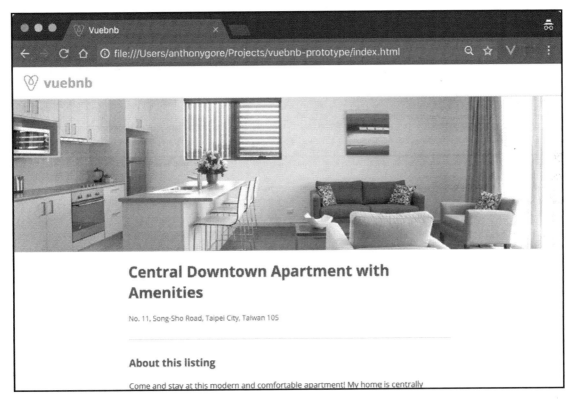

Figure 2.6. Page including header image

Inspect the page with your browser Dev Tools and notice how the `v-bind` directive has evaluated:

```
<div class="header-img" style="background-image:
url('sample/header.jpg');"></div>
```

Lists section

The next bit of content we'll add to our page is the **Amenities** and **Prices** lists:

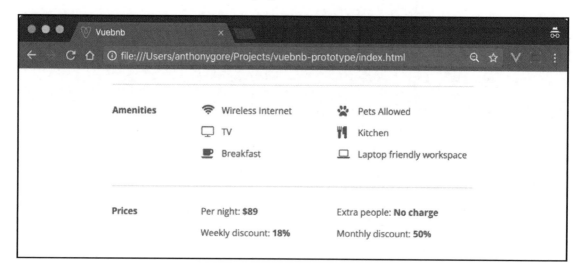

Figure 2.7. Lists section

If you look at the mock-listing sample, you'll see that the `amenities` and `prices` properties on the object are both arrays.

`sample/data.js`:

```
var sample = {
  title: '...',
  address: '...',
  about: '...',
  amenities: [
    {
      title: 'Wireless Internet',
      icon: 'fa-wifi'
    },
    {
```

```
        title: 'Pets Allowed',
        icon: 'fa-paw'
      },
      ...
    ],
    prices: [
      {
        title: 'Per night',
        value: '$89'
      },
      {
        title: 'Extra people',
        value: 'No charge'
      },
      ...
    ]
  }
```

Wouldn't it be easy if we could just loop over these arrays and print each item to the page? We can! This is what the v-for directive does.

First, let's add these as data properties on our root instance.

app.js:

```
data: {
  ...
  amenities: sample.amenities,
  prices: sample.prices
}
```

List rendering

The v-for directive requires a special type of expression in the form of item in items, where items is the source array, and item is an alias for the current array element being looped over.

Let's work on the amenities array first. Each member of this array is an object with a title and icon property, that is:

```
{ title: 'something', icon: 'something' }
```

We'll add the `v-for` directive into the template and the expression we assign to it will be `amenity in amenities`. The alias part of the expression, that is `amenity`, will refer, throughout the loop sequence, to each object in the array, starting with the first.

`index.html`:

```
<div class="container">
  <div class="heading">...</div>
  <hr>
  <div class="about">...</div>
  <div class="lists">
    <div v-for="amenity in amenities">{{ amenity.title }}</div>
  </div>
</div>
```

It will render as:

```
<div class="container">
  <div class="heading">...</div>
  <hr>
  <div class="about">...</div>
  <div class="lists">
    <div>Wireless Internet</div>
    <div>Pets Allowed</div>
    <div>TV</div>
    <div>Kitchen</div>
    <div>Breakfast</div>
    <div>Laptop friendly workspace</div>
  </div>
</div>
```

Icons

The second property of our amenity objects is `icon`. This is actually a class relating to an icon in the Font Awesome icon font. We've installed Font Awesome as an NPM module already, so add this to the head of the page to now use it.

`index.html`:

```
<head>
  ...
  <link rel="stylesheet" href="node_modules/open-sans-all/css/open-sans.css">
  <link rel="stylesheet" href="node_modules/font-awesome/css/font-awesome.css">
```

```
    <link rel="stylesheet" href="style.css" type="text/css">
  </head>
```

Now we can complete the structure of our amenities section in the template.

index.html:

```
<div class="lists">
  <hr>
  <div class="amenities list">
    <div class="title"><strong>Amenities</strong></div>
    <div class="content">
      <div class="list-item" v-for="amenity in amenities">
        <i class="fa fa-lg" v-bind:class="amenity.icon"></i>
        <span>{{ amenity.title }}</span>
      </div>
    </div>
  </div>
</div>
```

style.css:

```
.list {
  display: flex;
  flex-wrap: nowrap;
  margin: 2em 0;
}

.list .title {
  flex: 1 1 25%;
}

.list .content {
  flex: 1 1 75%;
  display: flex;
  flex-wrap: wrap;
}

.list .list-item {
  flex: 0 0 50%;
  margin-bottom: 16px;
}

.list .list-item > i {
  width: 35px;
}

@media (max-width: 743px) {
```

```
  .list .title {
    flex: 1 1 33%;
  }

  .list .content {
    flex: 1 1 67%;
  }

  .list .list-item {
    flex: 0 0 100%;
  }
}
```

Key

As you might expect, the DOM nodes generated by `v-for="amenity in amenities"` are reactively bound to the `amenities` array. If the content of `amenities` changes, Vue will automatically re-render the nodes to reflect the change.

When using `v-for`, it's recommended you provide a unique `key` property to each item in the list. This allows Vue to target the exact DOM nodes that need to be changed, making DOM updates more efficient.

Usually, the key would be a numeric ID, for example:

```
<div v-for="item in items" v-bind:key="item.id">
  {{ item.title }}
</div>
```

For the amenities and prices lists, the content is not going to change over the life of the app, so there's no need for us to provide a key. Some linters may warn you about this, but in this case, the warning can be safely ignored.

Prices

Let's now add the price list to our template as well.

index.html:

```
<div class="lists">
  <hr>
  <div class="amenities list">...</div>
  <hr>
  <div class="prices list">
    <div class="title">
      <strong>Prices</strong>
    </div>
    <div class="content">
      <div class="list-item" v-for="price in prices">
        {{ price.title }}: <strong>{{ price.value }}</strong>
      </div>
    </div>
  </div>
</div>
```

I'm sure you'll agree that looping a template is far easier than writing out every item. However, you may notice that there is still some common markup between these two lists. Later in the book we'll utilize components to make this part of the template even more modular.

Show more feature

We've run into a problem now that the **lists** section is after the **About** section.
The **About** section has an arbitrary length, and in some of the mock listings that we'll add you'll see that this section is quite long.

We don't want it to dominate the page and force the user to do a lot of unwelcome scrolling to see the **lists** section, so we need a way to hide some of the text if it's too long, yet allow the user to view the full text if they choose.

Let's add a **show more** UI feature that will crop the **About** text after a certain length and give the user a button to reveal the hidden text:

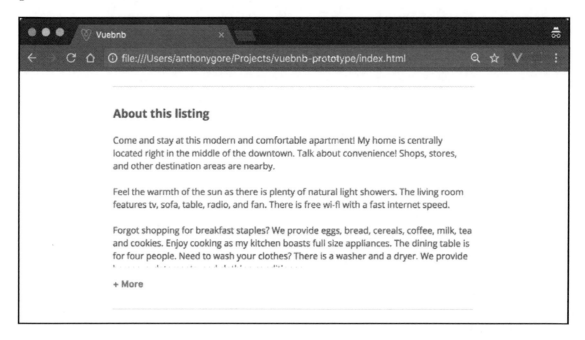

Figure 2.8. Show more feature

We'll start by adding a `contracted` class to the `p` tag that contains the `about` text interpolation. The CSS rule for this class will restrict its height to 250 pixels and hide any text overflowing the element.

`index.html`:

```
<div class="about">
  <h3>About this listing</h3>
  <p class="contracted">{{ about }}</p>
</div>
```

`style.css`:

```
.about p.contracted {
  height: 250px;
  overflow: hidden;
}
```

We'll also put a button after the p tag that the user can click to expand the section to full height.

index.html:

```
<div class="about">
  <h3>About this listing</h3>
  <p class="contracted">{{ about }}</p>
  <button class="more">+ More</button>
</div>
```

Here's the CSS that's needed, including a generic button rule that will provide base styling for all buttons that we'll add throughout the project.

style.css:

```
button {
  text-align: center;
  vertical-align: middle;
  user-select: none;
  white-space: nowrap;
  cursor: pointer;
  display: inline-block;
  margin-bottom: 0;
}

.about button.more {
  background: transparent;
  border: 0;
  color: #008489;
  padding: 0;
  font-size: 17px;
  font-weight: bold;
}

.about button.more:hover,
.about button.more:focus,
.about button.more:active {
  text-decoration: underline;
  outline: none;
}
```

To make this work, we need a way to remove the contracted class when the user clicks the **More** button. Seems like a good job for directives!

Class binding

How we'll approach this is to dynamically bind the `contracted` class. Let's create a `contracted` data property and set its initial value to `true`.

`app.js`:

```
data: {
  ...
  contracted: true
}
```

Like our style binding, we can bind this class to an object. In the expression, the `contracted` property is the name of the class to be bound, the `contracted` value is a reference to the data property of that same name, which is a Boolean. So if the `contracted` data property evaluates to `true`, that class will be bound to the element, and if it evaluates to `false`, it will not.

`index.html`:

```
<p v-bind:class="{ contracted: contracted }">{{ about }}</p>
```

It follows that when the page loads the `contracted` class is bound:

```
<p class="contracted">...</p>
```

Event listener

We now want to remove the `contracted` class automatically when the user clicks the **More** button. To do this job, we'll use the `v-on` directive, which listens to DOM events with a `click` argument.

The value of the `v-on` directive can be an expression that assigns `contracted` to `false`.

`index.html`:

```
<div class="about">
  <h3>About this listing</h3>
  <p v-bind:class="{ contracted: contracted }">{{ about }}</p>
  <button class="more" v-on:click="contracted = false">+ More</button>
</div>
```

Reactivity

When we click the **More** button, the `contracted` value changes and Vue will instantly update the page to reflect this change.

How does Vue know to do this? To answer this question we must first understand the concept of getters and setters.

Getters and setters

To assign a value to a property of a JavaScript object is as simple as:

```
var myObj = {
  prop: 'Hello'
}
```

To retrieve it is just as simple:

```
myObj.prop
```

There's no trick here. The point I want to make though, is that we can replace this normal assignment/retrieval mechanism of an object through use of getters and setters. These are special functions that allow custom logic for getting or setting the property's value.

Getters and setters are especially useful when one property's value is determined by another. Here's an example:

```
var person = {
  firstName: 'Abraham',
  lastName: 'Lincoln',
  get fullName() {
    return this.firstName + ' ' + this.lastName;
  },
  set fullName(name) {
    var words = name.toString().split(' ');
    this.firstName = words[0] || '';
    this.lastName = words[1] || '';
  }
}
```

The `get` and `set` functions of the `fullName` property are invoked whenever we attempt a normal assignment/retrieval of its value:

```
console.log(person.fullName); // Abraham Lincoln
person.fullName = 'George Washington';
console.log(person.firstName); // George
console.log(person.lastName) // Washington
```

Reactive data properties

Another one of Vue's initialization steps is to walk through all of the data properties and assign them getters and setters. If you look in the following screenshot, you can see how each property in our current app has a `get` and `set` function added to it:

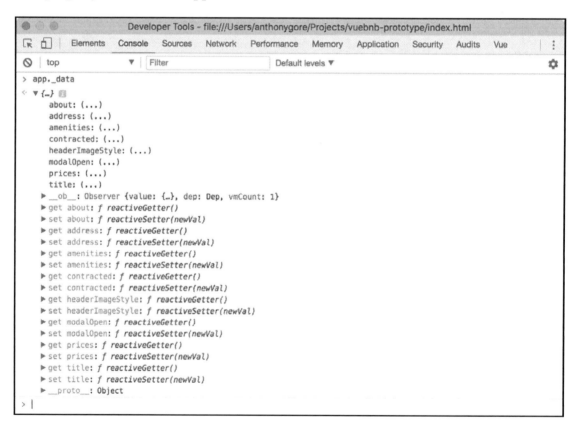

Figure 2.9. Getters and setters

Vue added these getters and setters to enable it to perform dependency tracking and change notification when the properties are accessed or modified. So, when the `contracted` value is changed by the `click` event, its `set` method is triggered. The `set` method will set the new value, but will also carry out a secondary task of informing Vue that a value has changed and any part of the page relying on it may need to be re-rendered.

> If you'd like to know more about Vue's reactivity system, check out the article *Reactivity In Vue.js (And Its Pitfalls)* at `https://vuejsdevelopers.com/2017/03/05/vue-js-reactivity/`.

Hiding the More button

Once the **About** section has been expanded, we want to hide the **More** button as it's no longer needed. We can use the `v-if` directive to achieve this in conjunction with the `contracted` property.

index.html:

```
<button v-if="contracted" class="more" v-on:click="contracted = false">
  + More
</button>
```

Image modal window

To prevent our header image from dominating the page, we've cropped it and limited its height. But what if the user wants to see the image in its full glory? A great UI design pattern to allow the user to focus on a single item of content is a *modal window*.

Here's what our modal will look like when opened:

Figure 2.10. Header image modal

Our modal will give a properly scaled view of the header image so the user can focus on the appearance of the lodgings without the distraction of the rest of the page.

Later in the book, we will insert an image carousel into the modal so the user can browse through a whole collection of room images!

For now, though, here are the required features for our modal:

1. Open the modal by clicking the header image
2. Freeze the main window
3. Show the image
4. Close the modal window with a close button or the *Escape* key

Opening

First, let's add a Boolean data property that will represent the opened or closed state of our modal. We'll initialize it to `false`.

`app.js`:

```
data: {
  ...
  modalOpen: false
}
```

We'll make it so that clicking our header image will set the modal to open. We'll also overlay a button labelled **View Photos** in the bottom-left corner of the header image to give a stronger signal to the user that they should click to show the image.

`index.html`:

```
<div
  class="header-img"
  v-bind:style="headerImageStyle"
  v-on:click="modalOpen = true"
>
  <button class="view-photos">View Photos</button>
</div>
```

Note that, by putting the click listener on the wrapping `div`, the click event will be captured regardless of whether the user clicks the `button` or the `div` due to DOM event propagation.

We'll add some more CSS to our header image to make the cursor a *pointer*, letting the user know the header can be clicked, and giving the header a relative position so the button can be positioned within it. We'll also add rules to style the button.

`style.css`:

```
.header .header-img {
  ...
  cursor: pointer;
  position: relative;
}

button {
  border-radius: 4px;
  border: 1px solid #c4c4c4;
  text-align: center;
  vertical-align: middle;
```

```
    font-weight: bold;
    line-height: 1.43;
    user-select: none;
    white-space: nowrap;
    cursor: pointer;
    background: white;
    color: #484848;
    padding: 7px 18px;
    font-size: 14px;
    display: inline-block;
    margin-bottom: 0;
}

.header .header-img .view-photos {
    position: absolute;
    bottom: 20px;
    left: 20px;
}
```

Let's now add the markup for our modal. I've put it after the other elements in the page, though it doesn't really matter as the modal will be out of the regular flow of the document. We remove it from the flow by giving it a `fixed` position in the following CSS.

`index.html`:

```
<div id="app">
  <div class="header">...</div>
  <div class="container">...</div>
  <div id="modal" v-bind:class="{ show : modalOpen }"></div>
</div>
```

The main modal `div` will act as a container for the rest of the modal content, but also as a background panel that will cover up the main window content. To achieve this, we use CSS rules to stretch it to completely cover the viewport by giving
it `top`, `right`, `bottom`, and `left` values of 0. We'll set the `z-index` to a high number to ensure the modal is stacked in front of any other element in the page.

Note also that the `display` is initially set to `none`, but we're dynamically binding a class to the modal called `show` that gives it block display. The addition/removal of this class will, of course, be bound to the value of `modalOpen`.

`style.css`:

```
#modal {
    display: none;
    position: fixed;
```

```
  top: 0;
  right: 0;
  bottom: 0;
  left: 0;
  z-index: 2000;
}

#modal.show {
  display: block;
}
```

Window

Let's now add markup for the window that will be overlaid on our background panel. The window will have a width constraint and will be centered in the viewport.

index.html:

```
<div id="modal" v-bind:class="{ show : modalOpen }">
  <div class="modal-content">
    <img src="sample/header.jpg"/>
  </div>
</div>
```

style.css:

```
.modal-content {
  height: 100%;
  max-width: 105vh;
  padding-top: 12vh;
  margin: 0 auto;
  position: relative;
}

.modal-content img {
  max-width: 100%;
}
```

Disabling the main window

When the modal is open, we want to prevent any interaction with the main window and also make a clear distinction between the main window and the child window. We can do this by:

- Dimming the main window
- Preventing body scroll

Dimming the main window

We could simply hide our main window when the modal is open, but it's better if the user can still be aware of where they are in flow of the app. To achieve this, we will *dim* the main window under a semi-transparent panel.

We can do this by giving our modal panel an opaque black background.

style.css:

```
#modal {
  ...
  background-color: rgba(0,0,0,0.85);
}
```

Preventing body scroll

We have a problem, though. Our modal panel, despite being full screen, is still a child of the body tag. This means we can still *scroll* the main window! We don't want users to interact with the main window in any way while the modal is open, so we must disable scrolling on the body.

The trick is to add the CSS overflow property to the body tag and set it to hidden. This has the effect of clipping any *overflow* (that is, part of the page not currently in view), and the rest of the content will be made invisible.

We'll need to dynamically add and remove this CSS rule, as we obviously want to be able to scroll through the page when the modal is closed. So, let's create a class called `modal-open` that we can apply to the `body` tag when the modal is open.

`style.css`:

```css
body.modal-open {
  overflow: hidden;
  position: fixed;
}
```

We can use `v-bind:class` to add/remove this class, right? Unfortunately, no. Remember that Vue only has dominion over the element where it is mounted:

```html
<body>
  <div id="app">
    <!--This is where Vue has dominion and can modify the page freely-->
  </div>
  <!--Vue is unable to change this part of the page or any ancestors-->
</body>
```

If we add a directive to the `body` tag, it will *not* be seen by Vue.

Vue's mount element

What if we just mounted Vue on the `body` tag, wouldn't that solve our problems? For example:

```js
new Vue({
  el: 'body'
});
```

This is not permitted by Vue and if you attempt it you will get this error: **Do not mount Vue to <html> or <body> - mount to normal elements instead**.

Remember that Vue has to compile the template and replaces the mount node. If you have script tags as children of the mount node, as you often do with `body`, or if your user has browser plugins that modify the document (many do) then all sorts of hell might break loose on the page when it replaces that node.

If you define your own root element with a unique ID, there should be no such conflict.

Watchers

So, how can we add/remove classes from the `body` if it's out of Vue's dominion? We'll have to do it the old-fashioned way with the browser's Web API. We need to run the following statements when the modal is opened or closed:

```
// Modal opens
document.body.classList.add('modal-open');

// Modal closes
document.body.classList.remove('modal-closed');
```

As discussed, Vue adds reactive getters and setters to each data property so that when data changes it knows to update the DOM appropriately. Vue also allows you to write custom logic that hooks into reactive data changes via a feature called *watchers*.

To add a watcher, first add the `watch` property to your Vue instance. Assign an object to this where each property has the name of a declared data property, and each value is a function. The function has two arguments: the old value and new value.

Whenever a data property changes, Vue will trigger any declared watcher methods:

```
var app = new Vue({
  el: '#app'
  data: {
    message: 'Hello world'
  },
  watch: {
    message: function(newVal, oldVal) {
      console.log(oldVal, ', ', newVal);
    }
  }
});

setTimeout(function() {
  app.message = 'Goodbye world';
  // Output: "Hello world, Goodbye world";
}, 2000);
```

Vue can't update the body tag for us, but it can trigger custom logic that will. Let's use a watcher to update the body tag when our modal is opened and closed.

app.js:

```
var app = new Vue({
  data: { ... },
  watch: {
    modalOpen: function() {
      var className = 'modal-open';
      if (this.modalOpen) {
        document.body.classList.add(className);
      } else {
        document.body.classList.remove(className);
      }
    }
  }
});
```

Now when you try to scroll the page you'll see it won't budge!

Closing

Users will need a way to close their modal and return to the main window. We'll overlay a button in the top-right corner that, when clicked, evaluates an expression to set modalOpen to false. The show class on our wrapper div will consequentially be removed, which means the display CSS property will return to none, thus removing the modal from the page.

index.html:

```
<div id="modal" v-bind:class="{ show : modalOpen }">
  <button v-on:click="modalOpen = false" class="modal-close">
    &times;
  </button>
  <div class="modal-content">
    <img src="sample/header.jpg"/>
  </div>
</div>
```

style.css:

```
.modal-close {
  position: absolute;
  right: 0;
```

```
    top: 0;
    padding: 0px 28px 8px;
    font-size: 4em;
    width: auto;
    height: auto;
    background: transparent;
    border: 0;
    outline: none;
    color: #ffffff;
    z-index: 1000;
    font-weight: 100;
    line-height: 1;
}
```

Escape key

Having a close button for our modal is handy, but most people's instinctual action for closing a window is the *Escape* key.

v-on is Vue's mechanism for listening to events and seems like a good candidate for this job. Adding the keyup argument will trigger a handler callback after *any* key is pressed while this input is focused:

```
<input v-on:keyup="handler">
```

Event modifiers

Vue makes it easy to listen for *specific* keys by offering *modifiers* to the v-on directive. Modifiers are postfixes denoted by a dot (.), for example:

```
<input v-on:keyup.enter="handler">
```

As you'd probably guess, the `.enter` modifier tells Vue to only call the handler when the event is triggered by the *Enter* key. Modifiers save you from having to remember the specific key code, and also make your template logic more obvious. Vue offers a variety of other key modifiers, including:

- `tab`
- `delete`
- `space`
- `esc`

With that in mind, it seems like we could close our modal with this directive:

```
v-on:keyup.esc="modalOpen = false"
```

But then what tag do we attach this directive to? Unfortunately, unless an input is focused on, key events are dispatched from the `body` element, which, as we know, is out of Vue's jurisdiction!

To handle this event we'll, once again, resort to the Web API.

`app.js`:

```
var app = new Vue({
    ...
});

document.addEventListener(</span>'keyup', function(evt) {
    if (evt.keyCode === 27 && app.modalOpen) {
        app.modalOpen = false;
    }
});
```

This works, with one caveat (discussed in the next section). But Vue can help us make it perfect.

Lifecycle hooks

When your main script is run and your instance of Vue is set up, it goes through a series of initialization steps. As we said earlier, Vue will walk through your data objects and make them reactive, as well as compile the template and mount to the DOM. Later in the lifecycle, Vue will also go through updating steps, and later still, tear-down steps.

Here is a diagram of the lifecycle instance taken from `http://vuejs.org`. Many of these steps concern concepts that we haven't yet covered, but you should get the gist:

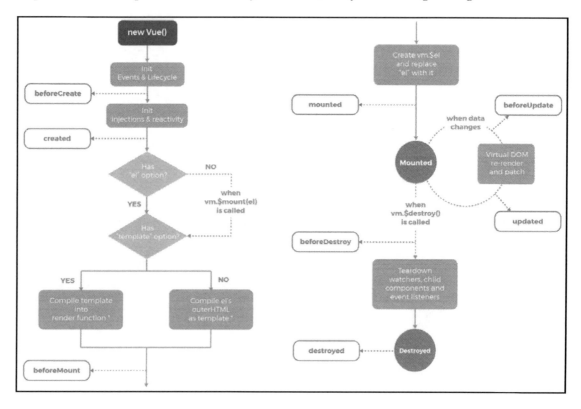

Figure 2.11. Vue.js lifecycle diagram

Vue allows you to execute custom logic at these different steps via *lifecycle hooks,* which are callbacks defined in the configuration object.

For example, here we utilize the `beforeCreate` and `created` hooks:

```
new Vue({
  data: {
    message: 'Hello'
  },
  beforeCreate: function() {
    console.log('beforeCreate message: ' + this.message);
    // "beforeCreate message: undefined"
  },
  created: function() {
```

```
        console.log('created: '+ this.message);
        // "created message: Hello"
    },
});
```

Vue will alias data properties to the context object *after* the `beforeCreate` hook is called but *before* the `created` hook is called, hence why `this.message` is `undefined` in the former.

The caveat I mentioned earlier about the *Escape* key listener is this: although unlikely, if the *Escape* key was pressed and our callback was called *before* Vue has proxied the data properties, `app.modalOpen` would be `undefined` rather than `true` and so our `if` statement would not control flow like we expect.

To overcome this we can set up the listener in the `created` lifecycle hook that will be called *after* Vue has proxied the data properties. This gives us a guarantee that `modalOpen` will be defined when the callback is run.

`app.js`:

```
function escapeKeyListener(evt) {
    if (evt.keyCode === 27 && app.modalOpen) {
        app.modalOpen = false;
    }
}

var app = new Vue({
    data: { ... },
    watch: { ... },
    created: function() {
        document.addEventListener('keyup', escapeKeyListener);
    }
});
```

Methods

The Vue configuration object also has a section for *methods*. Methods are not reactive, so you could define them outside of the Vue configuration without any difference in functionality, but the advantage to Vue methods is that they are passed the Vue instance as context and therefore have easy access to your other properties and methods.

Let's refactor our `escapeKeyListener` to be a `Vue` instance method.

app.js:

```
var app = new Vue({
  data: { ... },
  methods: {
    escapeKeyListener: function(evt) {
      if (evt.keyCode === 27 && this.modalOpen) {
        this.modalOpen = false;
      }
    }
  },
  watch: { ... },
  created: function() {
    document.addEventListener('keyup', this.escapeKeyListener);
  }
});
```

Proxied properties

You may have noticed that our `escapeKeyListener` method can refer to `this.modalOpen`. Shouldn't it be `this.methods.modalOpen`?

When a Vue instance is constructed, it proxies any data properties, methods, and computed properties to the instance object. This means that from within any method you can refer to `this.myDataProperty`, `this.myMethod`, and so on, rather than `this.data.myDataProperty` or `this.methods.myMethod`, as you might assume:

```
var app = new Vue({
  data: {
    myDataProperty: 'Hello'
  },
  methods: {
    myMethod: function() {
      return this.myDataProperty + ' World';
    }
  }
});

console.log(app.myMethod());
// Output: 'Hello World'
```

You can see these proxied properties by printing the Vue object in the browser console:

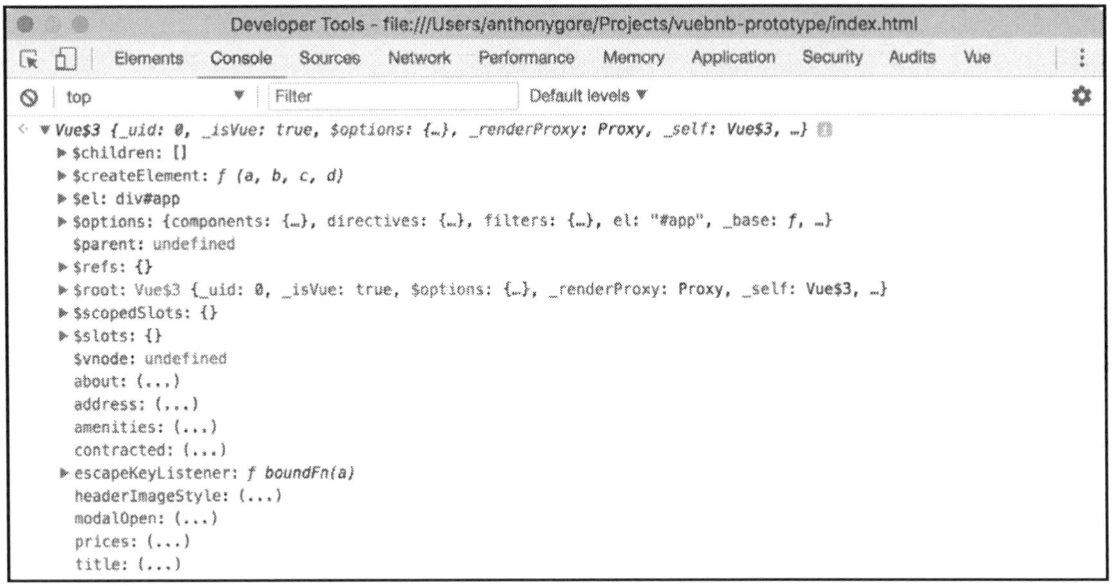

Figure 2.12. Our app's Vue instance

Now the simplicity of text interpolations might make more sense, they have the context of the Vue instance, and thanks to proxied properties, can be referenced like {{ myDataProperty }}.

However, while proxying to the root makes syntax terser, a consequence is that you can't name your data properties, methods, or computed properties with the same name!

Removing listener

To avoid any memory leaks, we should also use `removeEventListener` to get rid of the listener when the Vue instance is torn down. We can use the `destroy` hook and call our `escapeKeyListener` method for this purpose.

`app.js`:

```
new Vue({
  data: { ... },
  methods: { ... },
  watch: { ... },
  created: function() { ... },
  destroyed: function () {
```

```
        document.removeEventListener('keyup', this.escapeKeyListener);
    }
});
```

Summary

In this chapter, we got familiar with the essential features of Vue including installation and basic configuration, data binding, text interpolation, directives, methods, watchers and lifecycle hooks. We also learned about Vue's inner workings, including the reactivity system.

We then used this knowledge to set up a basic Vue project and create page content for the Vuebnb prototype with text, lists of information, a header image, and UI widgets like the **show more** button and the modal window.

In the next chapter, we'll take a brief break from Vue while we set up a backend for Vuebnb using Laravel.

3

Setting Up a Laravel Development Environment

In the first two chapters of the book, we introduced Vue.js. You should now be pretty comfortable with its basic features. In this chapter, we'll get a Laravel development environment up and running as we prepare to build the Vuebnb backend.

Topics covered in this chapter:

- A brief introduction to Laravel
- Setting up the Homestead virtual development environment
- Configuring Homestead to host Vuebnb

Laravel

Laravel is an open source MVC framework for PHP that is used to build robust web applications. Laravel is currently at version 5.5 and is among the most popular PHP frameworks, beloved for its elegant syntax and powerful features.

Laravel is suitable for creating a variety of web-based projects, such as the following:

- Websites with user authentication, such as a customer portal or a social network
- Web applications, such as an image cropper or a monitoring dashboard
- Web services, such as RESTful APIs

In this book, I'm assuming a basic knowledge of Laravel. You should be comfortable with installing and setting up Laravel and be familiar with its core features, such as routing, views, and middleware.

If you're new to Laravel or think you might need to brush up a bit, you should take an hour or two to read through Laravel's excellent documentation before continuing with this book: `https://laravel.com/docs/5.5/`.

Laravel and Vue

Laravel may seem like a monolithic framework because it includes features for building almost any kind of web application. Under the hood, though, Laravel is a collection of many separate modules, some developed as part of the Laravel project and some from third-party authors. Part of what makes Laravel great is its careful curation and seamless connection of these constituent modules.

Since Laravel version 5.3, Vue.js has been the default frontend framework included in a Laravel installation. There's no official reason why Vue was chosen over other worthy options, such as React, but my guess is that it's because Vue and Laravel share the same philosophy: simplicity and an emphasis on the developer experience.

Whatever the reason, Vue and Laravel offer an immensely powerful and flexible full-stack framework for developing web applications.

Environment

We'll be using Laravel 5.5 for the backend of Vuebnb. This version of Laravel requires PHP 7, several PHP extensions, and the following software:

- Composer
- A web server, such as Apache or Nginx
- A database, such as MySQL or MariaDB

 A complete list of requirements for Laravel can be found in the installation guide: `https://laravel.com/docs/5.5#installation`.

Rather than manually installing the Laravel requirements on your computer, I strongly recommend you use the *Homestead* development environment, which has everything you need pre-installed.

Homestead

Laravel Homestead is a virtual web application environment which runs on Vagrant and VirtualBox and can be run on any Windows, Mac, or Linux system.

Using Homestead will save you the headache of setting up an development environment from scratch. It will also ensure you have an identical environment to the one I'm using, which will make it easier for you to follow along with this book.

If you don't have Homestead installed on your computer, follow the directions in the Laravel documentation: `https://laravel.com/docs/5.5/homestead`. Use the default configuration options.

Once you've installed Homestead and launched the Vagrant box with the `vagrant up` command, you're ready to continue.

Vuebnb

In `Chapter 2`, *Prototyping Vuebnb, Your First Vue.js Project*, we made a prototype of the frontend of Vuebnb. The prototype was created from a single HTML file that we loaded directly from the browser.

Now we'll start working on the full-stack Vuebnb project, of which the prototype will soon be a critical part. This main project will be a full Laravel installation with a web server and database.

Project code

If you haven't already, you'll need to download the code base to your computer by cloning it from GitHub. Instructions are given in the *Code base* section in Chapter 1, *Hello Vue - An Introduction to Vue.js*.

The vuebnb folder within the code base has the project code that we now want to work with. Change into this folder and list the content:

```
$ cd vuebnb
$ ls -la
```

The folder contents should look like this:

```
● ● ●                          vuebnb — -bash — 87×7
[Anthonys-MacBook-Pro:vuebnb anthonygore$ ls
CHANGELOG.md      composer.json     phpunit.xml      scripts          yarn.lock
LICENSE           composer.lock     public           server.php
app               config            readme.md        storage
artisan           database          resources        tests
bootstrap         package.json      routes           webpack.mix.js
Anthonys-MacBook-Pro:vuebnb anthonygore$ ▐
```

Figure 3.1. vuebnb project files

Shared folders

The folders property of the Homestead.yaml file lists all of the folders you want to share between your computer and the Homestead environment.

Ensure the code base is shared with Homestead so that we can serve Vuebnb from Homestead's web server later in the chapter.

~/Homestead/Homestead.yaml:

```
    folders:
      - map: /Users/anthonygore/Projects/Full-Stack-Vue.js-2-and-Laravel-5
        to: /home/vagrant/projects
```

Terminal commands

All further Terminal commands in the book will be given relative to the project directory, that is, *vuebnb*, unless otherwise specified.

However, as the project directory is shared between your host computer and Homestead, Terminal commands can be run from either of these environments.

Homestead saves you from having to install any software on your host computer. But if you don't, many Terminal commands may not work, or may not work correctly, in the host environment. For example, if you don't have PHP installed on your host computer, you can't run Artisan commands from it:

```
$ php artisan --version
-bash: php: command not found
```

If this is the case for you, you'll need to run these commands from within Homestead environment by connecting first via SSH:

```
$ cd ~/Homestead
$ vagrant ssh
```

Change, then, to the project directory within the OS and the same Terminal command will now work:

```
$ cd ~/projects/vuebnb
$ php artisan --version
Laravel Framework 5.5.20
```

The only downside to running commands from Homestead is that they're slower due to the SSH connection. I'll leave it up to you to decide which you'd rather use.

Environment variables

A Laravel project requires certain environment variables to be set in a .env file. Create one now by copying the environment file sample:

```
$ cp .env.example .env
```

Generate an app key by running this command:

```
$ php artisan key:generate
```

I've preset most other relevant environment variables so you shouldn't have to change anything unless you've configured Homestead differently to me.

Composer install

To complete the installation process, we must run `composer install` to download all the required packages:

```
$ composer install
```

Database

We'll be using a relational database to persist data in our backend application. Homestead has MySQL running out of the box; you just have to provide configuration in the `.env` file to use it with Laravel. The default configuration will work without any further changes.

`.env`:

```
DB_CONNECTION=mysql
DB_HOST=192.168.10.10
DB_PORT=3306
DB_DATABASE=vuebnb
DB_USERNAME=homestead
DB_PASSWORD=secret
```

Whatever name you choose for your database (that is, the value of `DB_DATABASE`), make sure it's added to the `databases` array in your `Homestead.yaml` file.

`~/Homestead/Homestead.yaml`:

```
databases:
    ...
    - vuebnb
```

Serving the project

The main Vuebnb project is now installed. Let's get the web server to serve it at the local development domain `vuebnb.test`.

In the Homestead configuration file, map `vuebnb.test` to the project's `public` folder.

`~/Homestead/Homestead.yaml`:

```
sites:
  ...
  - map: vuebnb.test
    to: /home/vagrant/vuebnb/public
```

Local DNS entry

We also need to update our computer's host file so it understands the mapping between `vuebnb.test`, and the IP of the web server. The web server is in the Homestead box, which has the IP `192.168.10.10` by default.

To configure this on a Mac, open your host file, `/etc/hosts`, in a text editor and add this entry:

```
192.168.10.10 vuebnb.test
```

> The hosts file can normally be found
> at `C:\Windows\System32\Drivers\etc\hosts` on a Windows system.

Accessing the project

With all the configuration complete, we can now run `vagrant provision` from within the `Homestead` directory to complete the setup:

```
$ cd ~/Homestead
$ vagrant provision
# The next command will return you to the project directory
$ cd -
```

When the provisioning process completes, we should be able to see our site running when we navigate our browser to `http://vuebnb.test`:

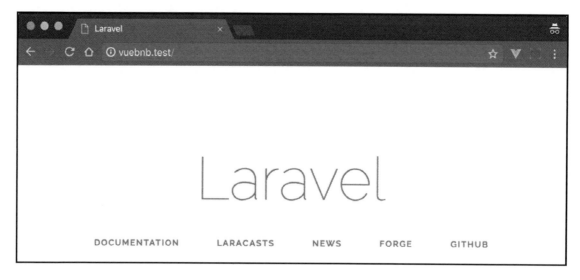

Figure 3.2. Laravel welcome view

Now we're ready to start developing Vuebnb!

Summary

In this brief chapter, we discussed the requirements for developing a Laravel project. We then installed and configured the Homestead virtual development environment to host our main project, Vuebnb.

In the next chapter, we will begin work on our main project by building a web service to supply data to the frontend of Vuebnb.

4
Building a Web Service with Laravel

In the last chapter, we got the Homestead development environment up and running, and began serving the main Vuebnb project. In this chapter, we will create a simple web service that will make Vuebnb's room listing data ready for display in the frontend.

Topics covered in this chapter:

- Using Laravel to create a web service
- Writing database migrations and seed files
- Creating API endpoints to make data publicly accessible
- Serving images from Laravel

Vuebnb room listings

In `Chapter 2`, *Prototyping Vuebnb, Your First Vue.js Project*, we built a prototype of the listing page of the frontend app. Soon we'll be removing the hardcoded data on this page and turning it into a template that can display any room listing.

We won't be adding functionality for a user to create their own room listing in this book. Instead, we'll use a package of mock data comprising 30 different listings, each with their own unique titles, descriptions, and images. We will seed the database with these listings and configure Laravel to serve them to the frontend as required.

Web service

A **web service** is an application that runs on a server and allows a client (such as a browser) to remotely write/retrieve data to/from the server over HTTP.

The interface of a web service will be one or more API endpoints, sometimes protected with authentication, that will return data in an XML or JSON payload:

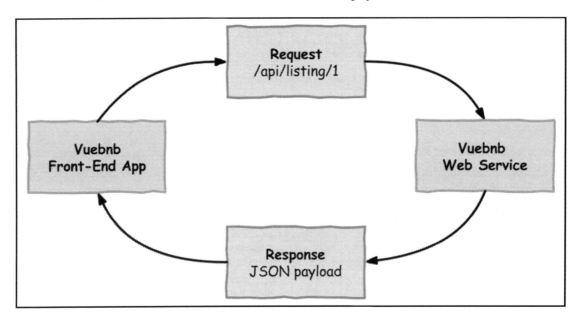

Figure 4.1. Vuebnb web service

Web services are a speciality of Laravel, so it won't be hard to create one for Vuebnb. We'll use routes for our API endpoints and represent the listings with Eloquent models that Laravel will seamlessly synchronize with the database:

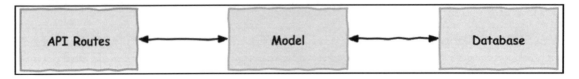

Figure 4.2. Web service architecture

Laravel also has inbuilt features to add API architectures such as REST, though we won't need this for our simple use case.

Mock data

The mock listing data is in the file `database/data.json`. This file includes a JSON-encoded array of 30 objects, with each object representing a different listing. Having built the listing page prototype, you'll no doubt recognize a lot of the same properties on these objects, including the title, address, and description.

`database/data.json`:

```
[
  {
    "id": 1,
    "title": "Central Downtown Apartment with Amenities",
    "address": "...",
    "about": "...",
    "amenity_wifi": true,
    "amenity_pets_allowed": true,
    "amenity_tv": true,
    "amenity_kitchen": true,
    "amenity_breakfast": true,
    "amenity_laptop": true,
    "price_per_night": "$89"
    "price_extra_people": "No charge",
    "price_weekly_discount": "18%",
    "price_monthly_discount": "50%",
  },
  {
    "id": 2,
    ...
  },
  ...
]
```

Each mock listing includes several images of the room as well. Images aren't really part of a web service, but they will be stored in a public folder in our app to be served as needed.

The image files are not in the project code, but are in the code base we downloaded from GitHub. We'll copy them into our project folder later in the chapter.

Database

Our web service will require a database table for storing the mock listing data. To set this up we'll need to create a schema and migration. We'll then create a seeder that will load and parse our mock data file and insert it into the database, ready for use in the app.

Migration

A `migration` is a special class that contains a set of actions to run against the database, such as creating or modifying a database table. Migrations ensure your database gets set up identically every time you create a new instance of your app, for example, installing in production or on a teammate's machine.

To create a new migration, use the `make:migration` Artisan CLI command. The argument of the command should be a snake-cased description of what the migration will do:

```
$ php artisan make:migration create_listings_table
```

You'll now see your new migration in the `database/migrations` directory. You'll notice the filename has a prefixed timestamp, such as `2017_06_20_133317_create_listings_table.php`. The timestamp allows Laravel to determine the proper order of the migrations, in case it needs to run more than one at a time.

Your new migration declares a class that extends `Migration`. It overrides two methods: `up`, which is used to add new tables, columns, or indexes to your database; and `down`, which is used to delete them. We'll implement these methods shortly.

`2017_06_20_133317_create_listings_table.php`:

```php
<?php

use Illuminate\Support\Facades\Schema;
use Illuminate\Database\Schema\Blueprint;
use Illuminate\Database\Migrations\Migration;

class CreateListingsTable extends Migration
{
  public function up()
  {
    //
  }
```

```
public function down()
{
  //
}
}
```

Schema

A **schema** is a blueprint for the structure of a database. For a relational database such as MySQL, the schema will organize data into tables and columns. In Laravel, schemas are declared by using the Schema facade's create method.

We'll now make a schema for a table to hold Vuebnb listings. The columns of the table will match the structure of our mock listing data. Note that we set a default false value for the amenities and allow the prices to have a NULL value. All other columns require a value.

The schema will go inside our migration's up method. We'll also fill out the down with a call to Schema::drop.

2017_06_20_133317_create_listings_table.php:

```
public function up()
{
  Schema::create('listings', function (Blueprint $table) {
    $table->primary('id');
    $table->unsignedInteger('id');
    $table->string('title');
    $table->string('address');
    $table->longText('about');

    // Amenities
    $table->boolean('amenity_wifi')->default(false);
    $table->boolean('amenity_pets_allowed')->default(false);
    $table->boolean('amenity_tv')->default(false);
    $table->boolean('amenity_kitchen')->default(false);
    $table->boolean('amenity_breakfast')->default(false);
    $table->boolean('amenity_laptop')->default(false);

    // Prices
    $table->string('price_per_night')->nullable();
    $table->string('price_extra_people')->nullable();
    $table->string('price_weekly_discount')->nullable();
    $table->string('price_monthly_discount')->nullable();
  });
}
```

```
public function down()
{
    Schema::drop('listings');
}
```

 A **facade** is an object-oriented design pattern for creating a static proxy to an underlying class in the service container. The facade is not meant to provide any new functionality; its only purpose is to provide a more memorable and easily readable way of performing a common action. Think of it as an object-oriented helper function.

Execution

Now that we've set up our new migration, let's run it with this Artisan command:

```
$ php artisan migrate
```

You should see an output like this in the Terminal:

```
Migrating: 2017_06_20_133317_create_listings_table
Migrated:  2017_06_20_133317_create_listings_table
```

To confirm the migration worked, let's use Tinker to show the new table structure. If you've never used Tinker, it's a REPL tool that allows you to interact with a Laravel app on the command line. When you enter a command into Tinker it will be evaluated as if it were a line in your app code.

Firstly, open the Tinker shell:

```
$ php artisan tinker
```

Now enter a PHP statement for evaluation. Let's use the DB facade's `select` method to run an SQL DESCRIBE query to show the table structure:

```
>>>> DB::select('DESCRIBE listings;');
```

The output is quite verbose so I won't reproduce it here, but you should see an object with all your table details, confirming the migration worked.

Seeding mock listings

Now that we have a database table for our listings, let's seed it with the mock data. To do so we're going to have to do the following:

1. Load the `database/data.json` file
2. Parse the file
3. Insert the data into the listings table

Creating a seeder

Laravel includes a seeder class that we can extend called `Seeder`. Use this Artisan command to implement it:

```
$ php artisan make:seeder ListingsTableSeeder
```

When we run the seeder, any code in the `run` method is executed.

`database/ListingsTableSeeder.php`:

```php
<?php

use Illuminate\Database\Seeder;

class ListingsTableSeeder extends Seeder
{
  public function run()
  {
    //
  }
}
```

Loading the mock data

Laravel provides a `File` facade that allows us to open files from disk as simply as `File::get($path)`. To get the full path to our mock data file we can use the `base_path()` helper function, which returns the path to the root of our application directory as a string.

It's then trivial to convert this JSON file to a PHP array using the built-in json_decode method. Once the data is an array, it can be directly inserted into the database given that the column names of the table are the same as the array keys.

database/ListingsTableSeeder.php:

```
public function run()
{
  $path = base_path() . '/database/data.json';
  $file = File::get($path);
  $data = json_decode($file, true);
}
```

Inserting the data

In order to insert the data, we'll use the DB facade again. This time we'll call the table method, which returns an instance of Builder. The Builder class is a fluent query builder that allows us to query the database by chaining constraints, for example, DB::table(...)->where(...)->join(...) and so on. Let's use the insert method of the builder, which accepts an array of column names and values.

database/seeds/ListingsTableSeeder.php:

```
public function run()
{
  $path = base_path() . '/database/data.json';
  $file = File::get($path);
  $data = json_decode($file, true);
  DB::table('listings')->insert($data);
}
```

Executing the seeder

To execute the seeder we must call it from the DatabaseSeeder.php file, which is in the same directory.

database/seeds/DatabaseSeeder.php:

```
<?php

use Illuminate\Database\Seeder;

class DatabaseSeeder extends Seeder
```

```
{
  public function run()
  {
    $this->call(ListingsTableSeeder::class);
  }
}
```

With that done, we can use the Artisan CLI to execute the seeder:

```
$ php artisan db:seed
```

You should see the following output in your Terminal:

```
Seeding: ListingsTableSeeder
```

We'll again use Tinker to check our work. There are 30 listings in the mock data, so to confirm the seed was successful, let's check for 30 rows in the database:

```
$ php artisan tinker
>>>> DB::table('listings')->count();
# Output: 30
```

Finally, let's inspect the first row of the table just to be sure its content is what we expect:

```
>>>> DB::table('listings')->get()->first();
```

Here is the output:

```
=> {#732
  +"id": 1,
  +"title": "Central Downtown Apartment with Amenities",
  +"address": "No. 11, Song-Sho Road, Taipei City, Taiwan 105",
  +"about": "...",
  +"amenity_wifi": 1,
  +"amenity_pets_allowed": 1,
  +"amenity_tv": 1,
  +"amenity_kitchen": 1,
  +"amenity_breakfast": 1,
  +"amenity_laptop": 1,
  +"price_per_night": "$89",
  +"price_extra_people": "No charge",
  +"price_weekly_discount": "18%",
  +"price_monthly_discount": "50%"
}
```

If yours looks like that you're ready to move on!

Listing model

We've now successfully created a database table for our listings and seeded it with mock listing data. How do we access this data now from the Laravel app?

We saw how the DB facade lets us execute queries on our database directly. But Laravel provides a more powerful way to access data via the **Eloquent ORM**.

Eloquent ORM

Object-Relational Mapping (ORM) is a technique for converting data between incompatible systems in object-oriented programming languages. Relational databases such as MySQL can only store scalar values such as integers and strings, organized within tables. We want to make use of rich objects in our app, though, so we need a means of robust conversion.

Eloquent is the ORM implementation used in Laravel. It uses the **active record** design pattern, where a model is tied to a single database table, and an instance of the model is tied to a single row.

To create a model in Laravel using Eloquent ORM, simply extend the Illuminate\Database\Eloquent\Model class using Artisan:

```
$ php artisan make:model Listing
```

This generates a new file.

app/Listing.php:

```php
<?php

namespace App;

use Illuminate\Database\Eloquent\Model;

class Listing extends Model
{
    //
}
```

How do we tell the ORM what table to map to, and what columns to include? By default, the `Model` class uses the class name (`Listing`) in lowercase (`listing`) as the table name to use. And, by default, it uses all the fields from the table.

Now, any time we want to load our listings we can use code such as this, anywhere in our app:

```php
<?php

// Load all listings
$listings = \App\Listing::all();

// Iterate listings, echo the address
foreach ($listings as $listing) {
  echo $listing->address . '\n' ;
}

/*
 * Output:
 *
 * No. 11, Song-Sho Road, Taipei City, Taiwan 105
 * 110, Taiwan, Taipei City, Xinyi District, Section 5, Xinyi Road, 7
 * No. 51, Hanzhong Street, Wanhua District, Taipei City, Taiwan 108
 * ...
 */
```

Casting

The data types in a MySQL database don't completely match up to those in PHP. For example, how does an ORM know if a database value of 0 is meant to be the number 0, or the Boolean value of `false`?

An Eloquent model can be given a `$casts` property to declare the data type of any specific attribute. `$casts` is an array of key/values where the key is the name of the attribute being cast, and the value is the data type we want to cast to.

For the listings table, we will cast the amenities attributes as Booleans.

app/Listing.php:

```php
<?php

namespace App;

use Illuminate\Database\Eloquent\Model;

class Listing extends Model
{
  protected $casts = [
    'amenity_wifi' => 'boolean',
    'amenity_pets_allowed' => 'boolean',
    'amenity_tv' => 'boolean',
    'amenity_kitchen' => 'boolean',
    'amenity_breakfast' => 'boolean',
    'amenity_laptop' => 'boolean'
  ];
}
```

Now these attributes will have the correct type, making our model more robust:

```php
echo gettype($listing->amenity_wifi());

// boolean
```

Public interface

The final piece of our web service is the public interface that will allow a client app to request the listing data. Since the Vuebnb listing page is designed to display one listing at a time, we'll at least need an endpoint to retrieve a single listing.

Let's now create a route that will match any incoming GET requests to the URI /api/listing/{listing} where {listing} is an ID. We'll put this in the routes/api.php file, where routes are automatically given the /api/ prefix and have middleware optimized for use in a web service by default.

We'll use a closure function to handle the route. The function will have a $listing argument, which we'll type hint as an instance of the Listing class, that is, our model. Laravel's service container will resolve this as an instance with the ID matching {listing}.

We can then encode the model as JSON and return it as a response.

`routes/api.php`:

```php
<?php

use App\Listing;

Route::get('listing/{listing}', function(Listing $listing) {
  return $listing->toJson();
});
```

We can test this works by using the `curl` command from the Terminal:

```
$ curl http://vuebnb.test/api/listing/1
```

The response will be the listing with ID 1:

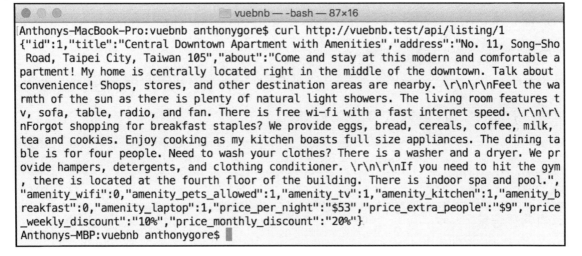

Figure 4.3. JSON response from Vuebnb web service

Controller

We'll be adding more routes to retrieve the listing data as the project progresses. It's a best practice to use a `controller` class for this functionality to keep a separation of concerns. Let's create one with Artisan CLI:

```
$ php artisan make:controller ListingController
```

We'll then move the functionality from the route into a new method, `get_listing_api`.

app/Http/Controllers/ListingController.php:

```php
<?php

namespace App\Http\Controllers;

use Illuminate\Http\Request;
use App\Listing;

class ListingController extends Controller
{
  public function get_listing_api(Listing $listing)
  {
    return $listing->toJson();
  }
}
```

For the `Route::get` method we can pass a string as the second argument instead of a `closure` function. The string should be in the form `[controller]@[method]`, for example, `ListingController@get_listing_web`. Laravel will correctly resolve this at runtime.

routes/api.php:

```php
<?php

Route::get('/listing/{listing}', 'ListingController@get_listing_api');
```

Images

As stated at the beginning of the chapter, each mock listing comes with several images of the room. These images are not in the project code and must be copied from a parallel directory in the code base called `images`.

Copy the contents of this directory into the `public/images` folder:

```
$ cp -a ../images/. ./public/images
```

Once you've copied these files, `public/images` will have 30 sub-folders, one for each mock listing. Each of these folders will contain exactly four main images and a thumbnail image:

```
● ● ●                    vuebnb — -bash — 87×12
Anthonys-MBP:vuebnb anthonygore$ ls public/images/
1               16          22          29          8
10              17          23          3           9
11              18          24          30          header.jpg
12              19          25          4           logo.png
13              2           26          5           logo_grey.png
14              20          27          6
15              21          28          7
Anthonys-MBP:vuebnb anthonygore$ ls public/images/1
Image_1.jpg             Image_2.jpg             Image_4.jpg
Image_1_thumb.jpg       Image_3.jpg
Anthonys-MBP:vuebnb anthonygore$ 
```

Figure 4.4. Image files in the public folder

Accessing images

Files in the `public` directory can be directly requested by appending their relative path to the site URL. For example, the default CSS file, `public/css/app.css`, can be requested at `http://vuebnb.test/css/app.css`.

The advantage of using the `public` folder, and the reason we've put our images there, is to avoid having to create any logic for accessing them. A frontend app can then directly call the images in an `img` tag.

 You may think it's inefficient for our web server to serve images like this, and you'd be right. Later in the book, we'll serve the images from a CDN when in production mode.

Let's try to open one of the mock listing images in our browser to test this thesis: `http://vuebnb.test/images/1/Image_1.jpg`:

Figure 4.5. Mock listing image displayed in browser

Image links

The payload for each listing in the web service should include links to these new images so a client app knows where to find them. Let's add the image paths to our listing API payload so it looks like this:

```
{
  "id": 1,
  "title": "...",
  "description": "...",
  ...
  "image_1": "http://vuebnb.test/app/image/1/Image_1.jpg",
  "image_2": "http://vuebnb.test/app/image/1/Image_2.jpg",
  "image_3": "http://vuebnb.test/app/image/1/Image_3.jpg",
  "image_4": "http://vuebnb.test/app/image/1/Image_4.jpg"
}
```

 The thumbnail image won't be used until later in the project.

To implement this, we'll use our model's toArray method to make an array representation of the model. We'll then easily be able to add new fields. Each mock listing has exactly four images, numbered 1 to 4, so we can use a for loop and the asset helper to generate fully-qualified URLs to files in the public folder.

We finish by creating an instance of the Response class by calling the response helper. We use the json; method and pass in our array of fields, returning the result.

app/Http/Controllers/ListingController.php:

```php
public function get_listing_api(Listing $listing)
{
  $model = $listing->toArray();
  for($i = 1; $i <=4; $i++) {
    $model['image_' . $i] = asset(
      'images/' . $listing->id . '/Image_' . $i . '.jpg'
    );
  }
  return response()->json($model);
}
```

The /api/listing/{listing} endpoint is now ready for consumption by a client app.

Summary

In this chapter, we built a web service with Laravel to make the Vuebnb listing data publicly accessible.

This involved setting up a database table using a migration and schema, then seeding the database with mock listing data. We then created a public interface for the web service using routes. This returned the mock data as a JSON payload, including links to our mock images.

In the next chapter, we'll introduce Webpack and the Laravel Mix build tool to set up a full-stack development environment. We'll migrate the Vuebnb prototype into the project, and refactor it to fit the new workflow.

5
Integrating Laravel and Vue.js with Webpack

In this chapter, we'll migrate the Vuebnb frontend prototype into our main Laravel project, achieving the first full-stack iteration of Vuebnb. This fully-integrated environment will include a Webpack build step, allowing us to incorporate more sophisticated tools and techniques as we continue to build the frontend.

Topics covered in this chapter:

- An introduction to Laravel's out-of-the-box frontend app
- A high-level overview of Webpack
- How to configure Laravel Mix to compile frontend assets
- Migrating the Vuebnb prototype into the full-stack Laravel environment
- Using ES2015 with Vue.js, including syntax and polyfills for older browsers
- Switching hard-coded data in the frontend app to backend data

Laravel frontend

We think of Laravel as being a backend framework, but a fresh Laravel project includes boilerplate code and configuration for a frontend app as well.

The out-of-the-box frontend includes JavaScript and Sass asset files, as a well as a `package.json` file that specifies dependencies such as Vue.js, jQuery, and Bootstrap.

Let's take a look at this boilerplate code and configuration so we get an idea of how the Vuebnb frontend app will fit into our Laravel project when we begin the migration.

JavaScript

JavaScript assets are kept in the `resources/assets/js` folder. There are several `.js` files in this directory, as well as a sub-directory component, with a `.vue` file. This latter file will be explained in another chapter so we'll ignore it for now.

The main JavaScript file is `app.js`. You'll see the familiar Vue constructor in this file, but also some syntax that may not be as familiar. On the first line is a `require` function that is intended to import an adjacent file, `bootstrap.js`, which in turn loads other libraries including jQuery and Lodash.

`require` is not a standard JavaScript function and must be resolved somehow before this code can be used in a browser.

`resources/assets/js/app.js`:

```
require('./bootstrap');

window.Vue = require('vue');

Vue.component('example', require('./components/Example.vue'));

const app = new Vue({
  el: '#app'
});
```

CSS

If you haven't heard of *Sass* before, it's a CSS extension that makes it easier to develop CSS. A default Laravel installation includes the `resources/assets/sass` directory, which includes two boilerplate Sass files.

The main Sass file is `app.scss`. Its job is to import other Sass files including the Bootstrap CSS framework.

`resources/assets/sass/app.scss`:

```
// Fonts
@import url("https://fonts.googleapis.com/css?family=Raleway:300,400,600");

// Variables
@import "variables";

// Bootstrap
@import "~bootstrap-sass/assets/stylesheets/bootstrap";
```

Node modules

Another key aspect of the Laravel frontend is the `package.json` file in the root of the project directory. Similar to `composer.json`, this file is used for configuration and dependency management, only for Node modules rather than PHP.

One of the properties of `package.json` is devDependencies, which specifies the modules required in the development environment, including jQuery, Vue, and Lodash.

`package.json`:

```
{
  ...
  "devDependencies": {
    "axios": "^0.17",
    "bootstrap-sass": "^3.3.7",
    "cross-env": "^5.1",
    "jquery": "^3.2",
    "laravel-mix": "^1.4",
    "lodash": "^4.17.4",
    "vue": "^2.5.3"
  }
}
```

Views

To serve the frontend app with Laravel, it needs to be included in a view. The only out-of-the-box view provided is the **welcome** view, located at `resources/views/welcome.blade.php`, which is used as a boilerplate home page.

The **welcome** view does not actually include the frontend app and it's left to the user to install it themselves. We'll look at how to do this later in the chapter.

Asset compilation

The files in `resources/assets` include functions and syntax that can't be used directly in a browser. For example, the `require` method used in `app.js`, which is designed to import a JavaScript module, is not a native JavaScript method and is not part of the standard Web API:

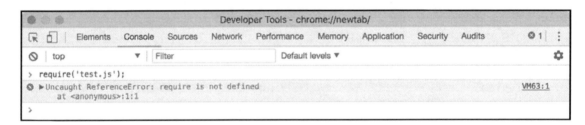

Figure 5.1. require is not defined in the browser

A build tool is needed to take these asset files, resolve any non-standard functions and syntax, and output code that the browser can use. There are a number of popular build tools for frontend assets including Grunt, Gulp, and Webpack:

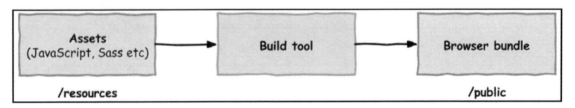

Figure 5.2. Asset compilation process

The reason we go to the effort of using this asset compilation process is so we can author our frontend app without the constraints of what a browser allows. We can introduce a variety of handy development tools and features that'll allow us to write our code and fix problems more easily.

Webpack

Webpack is the default build tool supplied with Laravel 5.5 and we'll be making use of it in the development of Vuebnb.

What makes Webpack different to other popular build tools, such as Gulp and Grunt, is that it's first and foremost a *module bundler*. Let's begin our overview of Webpack by getting an understanding of how the module bundling process works.

Dependencies

In a frontend application, we are likely to have dependencies for third-party JavaScript libraries or even other files in our own code base. For example, the Vuebnb prototype is dependent on Vue.js and the mock-listing data file:

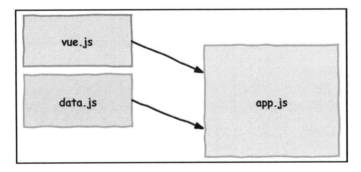

Figure 5.3. Vuebnb prototype dependencies

There's no real way of managing these dependencies in a browser, other than to ensure any shared functions and variables have global scope and that scripts are loaded in the right order.

For example, since `node_modules/vue/dist/vue.js` defines a global `Vue` object and is loaded first, we're able to use the `Vue` object in our `app.js` script. If either of those conditions was not met, `Vue` would not be defined when `app.js` ran, resulting in an error:

```
<script src="node_modules/vue/dist/vue.js"></script>
<script src="sample/data.js"></script>
<script src="app.js"></script>
```

This system has a number of downsides:

- Global variables introduce possibilities of naming collisions and accidental mutations
- Script loading order is fragile and can be easily broken as the app grows
- We can't utilize performance optimizations, such as loading scripts asynchronously

Modules

A solution to the dependency management problem is to use a module system, such as CommonJS or native ES modules. These systems allow JavaScript code to be modularized and imported into other files.

Here is a CommonJS example:

```
// moduleA.js
module.exports = function(value) {
  return value * 2;
}

// moduleB.js
var multiplyByTwo = require('./moduleA');
console.log(multiplyByTwo(2));

// Output: 4
```

And here is a Native ES modules example:

```
// moduleA.js
export default function(value) {
  return value * 2;
}

// moduleB.js
import multiplyByTwo from './moduleA';
```

```
console.log(multiplyByTwo(2));

// Output:  4
```

The problem is that CommonJS cannot be used in a browser (it was designed for server-side JavaScript) and native ES modules are only now getting browser support. If we want to use a module system in a project, we'll need a build tool: Webpack.

Bundling

The process of resolving modules into browser-friendly code is called **bundling**. Webpack begins the bundling process with the **entry file** as a starting point. In the Laravel frontend app, resources/assets/js/app.js is the entry file.

Webpack analyzes the entry file to find any dependencies. In the case of app.js, it will find three: bootstrap, vue, and Example.vue.

resources/assets/js/app.js:

```
require('./bootstrap');

window.Vue = require('vue');

Vue.component('example', require('./components/Example.vue'));

...
```

Webpack will resolve these dependencies and then analyze them to find any dependencies that they might have. This process continues until all dependencies of the project are found. The result is a graph of dependencies that, in a large project, might include hundreds of different modules.

Webpack uses this graph of dependencies as a blueprint for bundling all the code into a single browser-friendly file:

```
<script src="bundle.js"></script>
```

Loaders

Part of what makes Webpack so powerful is that during the bundling process it can *transform* a module with one or more Webpack loaders.

For example, *Babel* is a compiler that transforms next-generation JavaScript syntax such as ES2015 into standard ES5. The Webpack Babel loader is one of the most popular as it allows developers to write their code using modern features, but still provide support in older browsers.

For example, in the entry file, we see the ES2015 `const` declaration that isn't supported by IE10.

`resources/assets/js/app.js`:

```
const app = new Vue({
  el: '#app'
});
```

If the Babel loader is used, `const` will be transformed to `var` before it's added to the bundle.

`public/js/app.js`:

```
var app = new Vue({
  el: '#app'
});
```

Laravel Mix

One of the downsides of Webpack is that configuring it is arduous. To make thing easier, Laravel includes a module called *Mix* that takes the most commonly-used Webpack options and puts them behind a simple API.

The Mix configuration file can be found in the root of the project directory. Mix configuration involves chaining methods to the `mix` object that declare the basic build steps of your app. For example, the `js` method takes two arguments, the entry file and the output directory, and the Babel loader is applied by default. The `sass` method works in an equivalent way.

webpack.mix.js:

```
let mix = require('laravel-mix');
mix.js('resources/assets/js/app.js', 'public/js')
  .sass('resources/assets/sass/app.scss', 'public/css');
```

Running Webpack

Now that we have a high-level understanding of Webpack, let's run it and see how it bundles the default frontend asset files.

First, ensure you have all the development dependencies installed:

```
$ npm install
```

CLI

Webpack is typically runs from the command line, for example:

```
$ webpack [options]
```

Rather than figuring out the correct CLI option ourselves, we can use one of the Weback scripts predefined in `package.json`. For example, the `development` script will run Webpack with options suitable for creating a development build.

package.json:

```
"scripts": {
  ...
  "development": "cross-env NODE_ENV=development
node_modules/webpack/bin/webpack.js --progress --hide-modules --
config=node_modules/laravel-mix/setup/webpack.config.js",
  ...
}
```

First build

Let's now run the `dev` script (a shortcut for the `development` script):

```
$ npm run dev
```

After this runs, you should see an output in the Terminal similar to the following:

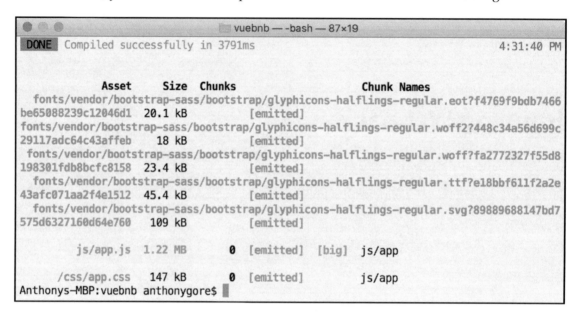

Figure 5.4. Webpack Terminal output

This output tells us a number of things, but most importantly that the build was successful and what files were created in the output including fonts, JavaScript, and CSS. Note that the output file path is relative not to the project root but to the `public` directory, so the `js/apps.js` file will be found at `public/js/app.js`.

JavaScript

Inspecting the output JavaScript file, `public/js/app.js`, we see a whole lot of code in there - around 42,000 lines! That's because jQuery, Lodash, Vue, and the other JavaScript dependencies have all been bundled into this one file. It's also because we've used a development build that does not include minification or uglification.

If you search through the file, you'll see that the code from our entry file, app.js, has been transpiled to ES5 as expected:

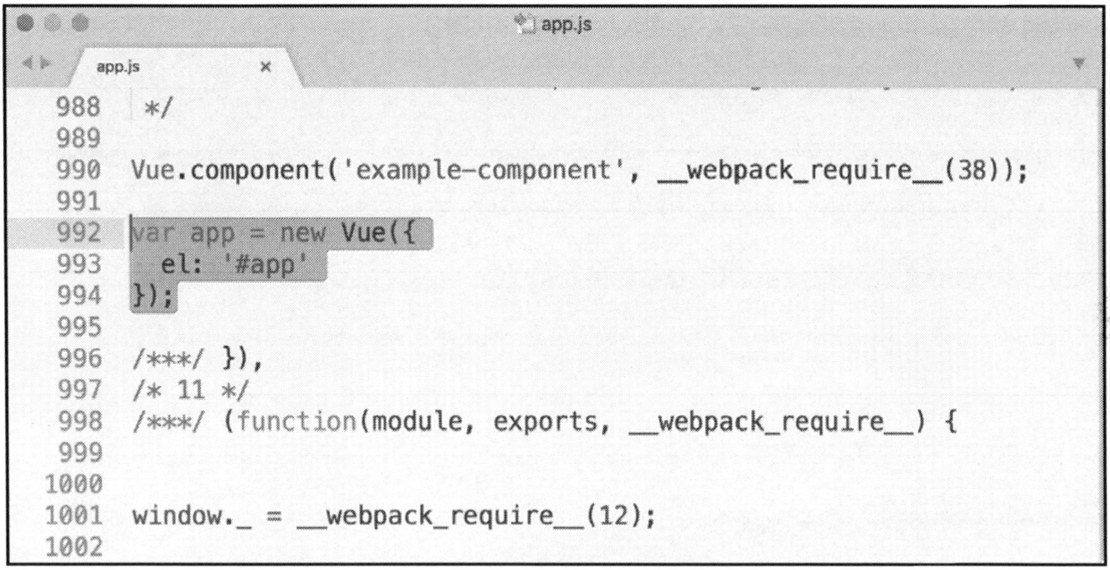

```
●  ● ●                              app.js
◄ ►    app.js               ×
 988    */
 989
 990    Vue.component('example-component', __webpack_require__(38));
 991
 992    var app = new Vue({
 993      el: '#app'
 994    });
 995
 996    /***/ }),
 997    /* 11 */
 998    /***/ (function(module, exports, __webpack_require__) {
 999
1000
1001    window._ = __webpack_require__(12);
1002
```

Figure 5.5. Bundle file public/js/app.js

CSS

We also have a CSS bundle file, public/css/app.css. If you inspect this file you will find the imported Bootstrap CSS framework has been included and the Sass syntax has been compiled to plain CSS.

Fonts

You might think it's strange that there are fonts in the output, since Mix did not include any explicit font configuration. These fonts are dependencies of the Bootstrap CSS framework and Mix, by default, will output them individually rather than in a font bundle.

Migrating Vuebnb

Now that we're familiar with the default Laravel frontend app code and configuration, we're ready to migrate the Vuebnb prototype into the main project. This migration will allow us to have all our source code in one place, plus we can utilize this more sophisticated development environment for building the remainder of Vuebnb.

The migration will involve:

1. Removing any unnecessary modules and files
2. Moving the prototype files into the Laravel project structure
3. Modifications to the prototype files to adapt them to the new environment

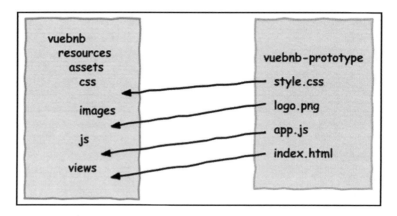

Figure 5.6. Vuebnb prototype migration

Removing unnecessary dependencies and files

Let's begin by removing the Node dependencies we no longer need. We'll keep `axis` as it'll be used in a later chapter, and `cross-env` because it ensures our NPM scripts can be run in a variety of environments. We'll get rid of the rest:

```
$ npm uninstall bootstrap-sass jquery lodash --save-dev
```

This command will leave your dev dependencies looking like this.

`package.json`:

```
"devDependencies": {
  "axios": "^0.17",
  "cross-env": "^5.1",
  "laravel-mix": "^1.4",
  "vue": "^2.5.3"
}
```

Next, we'll remove the files we don't need. This includes several of the JavaScript assets, all of the Sass plus the **welcome** view:

```
$ rm -rf \
resources/assets/js/app.js \
resources/assets/js/bootstrap.js \
resources/assets/js/components/* \
resources/assets/sass \
resources/views/welcome.blade.php
```

Since we're removing all the Sass files, we'll also need to remove the `sass` method in the Mix configuration.

`webpack.mix.js`:

```
let mix = require('laravel-mix');
mix
  .js('resources/assets/js/app.js', 'public/js')
;
```

Now our frontend app is free from clutter and we can move the prototype files into their new home.

HTML

Let's now copy the contents of `index.html` from the prototype project we completed in Chapter 2, *Prototyping Vuebnb, Your First Vue.js Project*, into a new file, `app.blade.php`. This will allow the template to be used as a Laravel view:

```
$ cp ../vuebnb-prototype/index.html ./resources/views/app.blade.php
```

We'll also update the home web route to point to this new view instead of **welcome**.

routes/web.php:

```php
<?php

Route::get('/', function () {
  return view('app');
});
```

Syntax clash

Using the prototype template file as a view will cause a small issue as Vue and Blade share a common syntax. For example, look at the heading section where Vue.js interpolates the title and address of a listing.

resources/views/app.blade.php:

```
<div class="heading">
  <h1>{{ title }}</h1>
  <p>{{ address }}</p>
</div>
```

When Blade processes this, it will think the double curly brackets are its own syntax and will generate a PHP error as neither title nor address are defined functions.

There is a simple solution: escape these double curly brackets to let Blade know to ignore them. This can be done by placing an @ symbol as a prefix.

resources/views/app.blade.php:

```
<div class="heading">
  <h1>@{{ title }}</h1>
  <p>@{{ address }}</p>
</div>
```

Once you've done that for each set of double curly brackets in the file, load the home route in the browser to test the new view. Without the JavaScript or CSS it doesn't look great, but at least we can confirm it works:

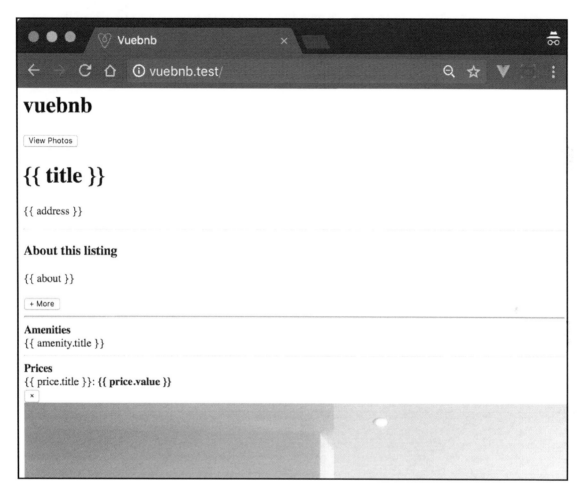

Figure 5.7. Home route

JavaScript

Let's now move the prototype's main script file, app.js, into the Laravel project:

```
$ cp ../vuebnb-prototype/app.js ./resources/assets/js/
```

Given the current Mix settings, this will now be the entry file of the JavaScript bundle. This means JavaScript dependencies at the bottom of the view can be replaced with the bundle, that is.

resources/views/app.blade.php:

```
<script src="node_modules/vue/dist/vue.js"></script>
<script src="sample/data.js"></script>
<script src="app.js"></script>
```

Can be replaced with,

resources/views/app.blade.php:

```
<script src="{{ asset('js/app.js') }}"></script>
```

Mock data dependency

Let's copy the mock data dependency into the project as well:

```
$ cp ../vuebnb-prototype/sample/data.js ./resources/assets/js/
```

Currently, this file declares a global variable sample that is then picked up in the entry file. Let's make this file a module by replacing the variable declaration with an ES2015 export default.

resources/assets/js/data.js:

```
export default {
  ...
}
```

We can now import this module at the top of our entry file. Note that Webpack can guess the file extension in an import statement so you can omit the `.js` from `data.js`.

resources/assets/js/app.js:

```
import sample from './data';

var app = new Vue({
  ...
});
```

 While Laravel has opted to use CommonJS syntax for including modules, that is `require`, we will use native ES module syntax, that is `import`. This is because ES modules are making their way into the JavaScript standard, and it's more consistent with the syntax used by Vue.

Displaying modules with Webpack

Let's run a Webpack build to make sure the JavaScript migration is working so far:

```
$ npm run dev
```

If all is well, you'll see the JavaScript bundle file being output:

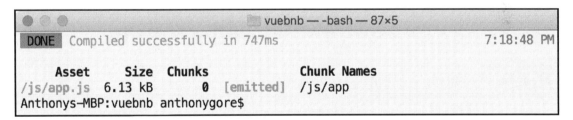

Figure 5.8. Webpack Terminal output

It'd be nice to know that the mock data dependency was added without having to manually inspect the bundle to find the code. We can do this by telling Webpack to print the modules it has processed in the Terminal output.

In the `development` script in our `package.json`, a `--hide-modules` flag has been set, as some developers prefer a succinct output message. Let's remove it for now and instead add the `--display-modules` flag, so the script looks like this:

```
"scripts": {
  ...
  "development": "cross-env NODE_ENV=development
node_modules/webpack/bin/webpack.js --progress --display-modules --
config=node_modules/laravel-mix/setup/webpack.config.js",
  ...
}
```

Now run the build again, and we get this more verbose terminal output:

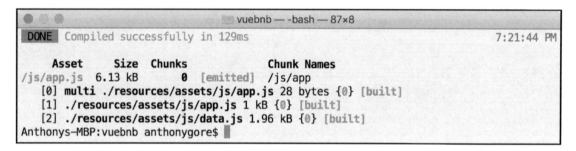

Figure 5.9. Webpack Terminal output with the display-modules flag

This assures us that both our `app.js` and `data.js` files are included in the bundle.

Vue.js dependency

Let's now import Vue.js as a dependency of our entry file.

`resources/assets/js/app.js`:

```
import Vue from 'vue';
import sample from './data';

var app = new Vue({
  ...
});
```

Running the build again, we'll now see Vue.js in the list of modules in the Terminal output, plus some dependencies that it has introduced:

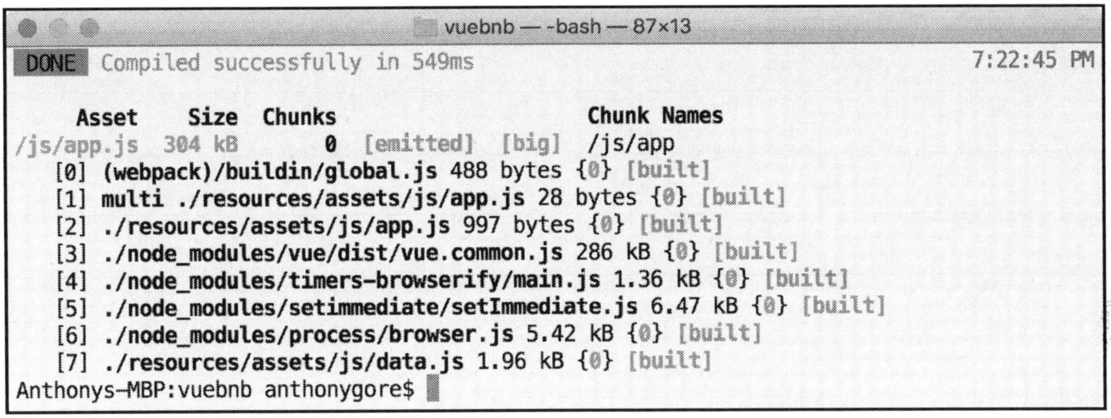

```
● ● ●                    🗎 vuebnb — -bash — 87×13
DONE  Compiled successfully in 549ms                              7:22:45 PM

      Asset    Size  Chunks                  Chunk Names
/js/app.js   304 kB       0  [emitted]  [big]  /js/app
    [0] (webpack)/buildin/global.js 488 bytes {0} [built]
    [1] multi ./resources/assets/js/app.js 28 bytes {0} [built]
    [2] ./resources/assets/js/app.js 997 bytes {0} [built]
    [3] ./node_modules/vue/dist/vue.common.js 286 kB {0} [built]
    [4] ./node_modules/timers-browserify/main.js 1.36 kB {0} [built]
    [5] ./node_modules/setimmediate/setImmediate.js 6.47 kB {0} [built]
    [6] ./node_modules/process/browser.js 5.42 kB {0} [built]
    [7] ./resources/assets/js/data.js 1.96 kB {0} [built]
Anthonys-MBP:vuebnb anthonygore$ ▊
```

Figure 5.10. Webpack Terminal output showing Vue.js

You may be wondering how `import Vue from 'vue'` resolves, as it doesn't seem to be a proper file reference. Webpack will, by default, check the `node_modules` folder in the project for any dependencies, saving you from having to put `import Vue from 'node_modules/vue';`.

But how, then, does it know the entry file of this package? Looking at the Webpack Terminal output in the preceding screenshot, you can see that it has included `node_modules/vue/dist/vue.common.js`. It knows to use this file because, when Webpack is adding node modules as dependencies, it checks their `package.json` file and looks for the `main` property, which in the case of Vue is.

`node_modules/vue/package.json`:

```
{
  ...
  "main": "dist/vue.runtime.common.js",
  ...
}
```

However, Laravel Mix overrides this to force a different Vue build.

`node_modules/laravel-mix/setup/webpack.config.js`:

```
alias: {
  'vue$': 'vue/dist/vue.common.js'
}
```

In short, `import Vue from 'vue'` is effectively the same as `import Vue from 'node_modules/vue/dist/vue.common.js'`.

> We'll explain the different Vue builds in `Chapter 6`, *Composing Widgets with Vue.js Components.*

With that done, our JavaScript has been successfully migrated. Loading the home route again, we can better make out the listing page of Vuebnb with the JavaScript now included:

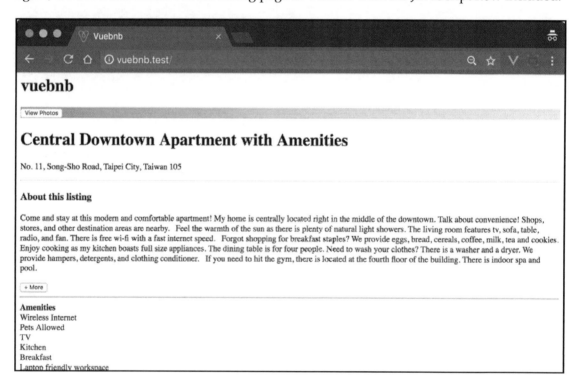

Figure 5.11. Home route with JavaScript migrated

CSS

To migrate CSS, we'll copy `style.css` from the prototype into the Laravel project. The default Laravel frontend app used Sass rather than CSS, so we'll need to make a directory for CSS assets first:

```
$ mkdir ./resources/assets/css
$ cp ../vuebnb-prototype/style.css ./resources/assets/css/
```

Let's then make a new declaration in our Mix config to get a CSS bundle using the `styles` method.

webpack.mix.js:

```
mix
  .js('resources/assets/js/app.js', 'public/js')
  .styles('resources/assets/css/style.css', 'public/css/style.css')
;
```

We'll now link to the CSS bundle in our view by updating the link's `href`.

resources/views/app.blade.php:

```
<link rel="stylesheet" href="{{ asset('css/style.css') }}" type="text/css">
```

Font styles

We also have the Open Sans and Font Awesome style sheets to include. First, install the font packages with NPM:

```
$ npm i --save-dev font-awesome open-sans-all
```

We'll modify our Mix configuration to bundle our app CSS, Open Sans, and Font Awesome CSS together. We can do this by passing an array to the first argument of the `styles` method.

webpack.mix.js:

```
mix
  .js('resources/assets/js/app.js', 'public/js')
  .styles([
    'node_modules/open-sans-all/css/open-sans.css',
    'node_modules/font-awesome/css/font-awesome.css',
    'resources/assets/css/style.css'
```

```
    ], 'public/css/style.css')
  ;
```

Mix will append statistics about the CSS bundle into the Terminal output:

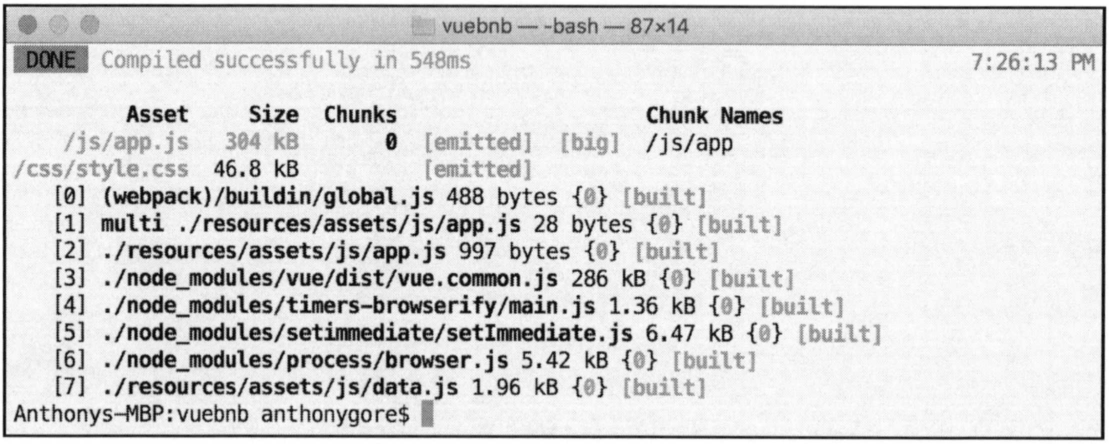

```
● ● ●                    vuebnb — -bash — 87×14
DONE  Compiled successfully in 548ms                                    7:26:13 PM

         Asset      Size  Chunks                    Chunk Names
     /js/app.js    304 kB       0  [emitted]  [big]  /js/app
 /css/style.css   46.8 kB          [emitted]
     [0] (webpack)/buildin/global.js 488 bytes {0} [built]
     [1] multi ./resources/assets/js/app.js 28 bytes {0} [built]
     [2] ./resources/assets/js/app.js 997 bytes {0} [built]
     [3] ./node_modules/vue/dist/vue.common.js 286 kB {0} [built]
     [4] ./node_modules/timers-browserify/main.js 1.36 kB {0} [built]
     [5] ./node_modules/setimmediate/setImmediate.js 6.47 kB {0} [built]
     [6] ./node_modules/process/browser.js 5.42 kB {0} [built]
     [7] ./resources/assets/js/data.js 1.96 kB {0} [built]
Anthonys-MBP:vuebnb anthonygore$ █
```

Figure 5.12. Webpack Terminal output with CSS

Remember to remove the links to the font style sheets from the view as these will now be in the CSS bundle.

Fonts

Open Sans and Font Awesome need both a CSS style sheet, and the relevant font files. Like CSS, Webpack can bundle fonts as modules, but we currently don't need to take advantage of this. Instead, we'll use the `copy` method, which tells Mix to copy the fonts from their home directory into the `public` folder where they can be accessed by the frontend app.

`webpack.mix.js`:

```
mix
  .js('resources/assets/js/app.js', 'public/js')
  .styles([
    'node_modules/open-sans-all/css/open-sans.css',
    'node_modules/font-awesome/css/font-awesome.css',
    'resources/assets/css/style.css'
  ], 'public/css/style.css')
  .copy('node_modules/open-sans-all/fonts',  'public/fonts')
  .copy('node_modules/font-awesome/fonts',  'public/fonts')
  ;
```

After building again, you'll now see a `public/fonts` folder in the project structure.

Images

We'll now migrate the images, including the logo for the toolbar, and the mock data header image:

```
$ cp ../vuebnb-prototype/logo.png ./resources/assets/images/
$ cp ../vuebnb-prototype/sample/header.jpg ./resources/assets/images/
```

Let's chain on another `copy` method to include these in the `public/images` directory.

`webpack.mix.js`:

```
mix
  .js('resources/assets/js/app.js', 'public/js')
  .styles([
    'node_modules/open-sans-all/css/open-sans.css',
    'node_modules/font-awesome/css/font-awesome.css',
    'resources/assets/css/style.css'
  ], 'public/css/style.css')
  .copy('node_modules/open-sans-all/fonts', 'public/fonts')
  .copy('node_modules/font-awesome/fonts', 'public/fonts')
  .copy('resources/assets/images', 'public/images')
;
```

We also need to ensure the view is pointing to the correct file location for the images. In the toolbar.

`resources/views/app.blade.php`:

```
<div id="toolbar">
  <img class="icon" src="{{ asset('images/logo.png') }}">
  <h1>vuebnb</h1>
</div>
```

And in the modal.

`resources/views/app.blade.php`:

```
<div class="modal-content">
  <img src="{{ asset('images/header.jpg') }}"/>
</div>
```

Don't forget that the `headerImageStyle` data property in the entry file also needs to be updated.

resources/assets/js/app.js:

```
headerImageStyle: {
  'background-image': 'url(/images/header.jpg)'
},
```

While not exactly an image, we'll also migrate the `favicon`. This can be put straight into the `public` folder:

$ cp ../vuebnb-prototype/favicon.ico ./public

After building again, we'll now have the Vuebnb client app prototype fully migrated:

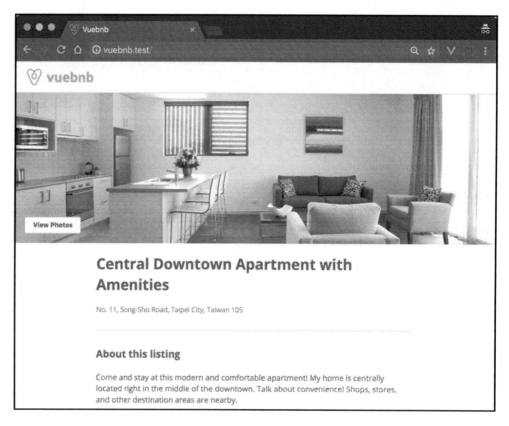

Figure 5.13. Vuebnb client app prototype served from Laravel

Development tools

We can utilize some handy development tools to improve our frontend workflow, including:

- Watch mode
- BrowserSync

Watch mode

So far, we've been running builds of our app manually using `npm run dev` every time we make a change. Webpack also has a watch mode where it automatically runs a build when a dependency changes. Thanks to the design of Webpack, it is able to efficiently complete these automatic builds by only rebuilding modules that have changed.

To use watch mode, run the `watch` script included in `package.json`:

```
$ npm run watch
```

To test that it works, add this at the bottom of `resources/assets/js/app.js`:

```
console.log("Testing watch");
```

If watch mode is running correctly, saving this file will trigger a build, and you'll see updated build statistics in the Terminal. If you then refresh the page you'll see the **Testing watch** message in the console.

To turn off watch mode, press *Ctrl* + *C* in the Terminal. It can then be restarted at any time. Don't forget to remove the `console.log` once you're satisfied watch mode is working.

 I'll assume you're using *watch* for the rest of the book, so I won't remind you to build your project after changes anymore!

BrowserSync

Another useful development tool is BrowserSync. Similar to watch mode, BrowserSync monitors your files for changes, and when one occurs inserts the change into the browser. This saves you from having to do a manual browser refresh after every build.

To use BrowserSync, you'll need to have the Yarn package manager installed. If you're running terminal commands from within the Vagrant Box, you're all set, as Yarn is pre-installed with Homestead. Otherwise, follow the installation instructions for Yarn here: `https://yarnpkg.com/en/docs/install`.

BrowserSync has been integrated with Mix and can be used by chaining a call to the `browserSync` method in your Mix configuration. Pass an options object with the app's URL as a `proxy` property, for example, `browserSync({ proxy: http://vuebnb.test })`.

We have the app's URL stored as an environment variable in the `.env` file, so let's get it from there rather than hard-coding into our Mix file. First, install the NPM `dotenv` module, which reads a `.env` file into a Node project:

```
$ npm i dotenv --save-devpm
```

Require the `dotenv` module at the top of the Mix configuration file and use the `config` method to load `.env`. Any environment variables will then be available as properties of the `process.env` object.

We can now pass an options object to the `browserSync` method with `process.env.APP_URL` assigned to `proxy`. I also like to use the `open: false` option as well, which prevents BrowserSync from automatically opening a tab.

`webpack.mix.js`:

```
require('dotenv').config();
let mix = require('laravel-mix');
mix
  ...
  .browserSync({
    proxy: process.env.APP_URL,
    open: false
  })
;
```

BrowserSync runs on its own port, 3000 by default. When you run `npm run watch` again, open a new tab at `localhost:3000`. After you make changes to your code you'll find they are automatically reflected in this BrowserSync tab!

Note that if you run BrowserSync inside your Homestead box you can access it at `vuebnb.test:3000`.

Even though the BrowserSync server runs on a different port to the web server, I will continue to refer to URLs in the app without specifying the port to avoid any confusion, for example, `vuebnb.test` rather than `localhost:3000` or `vuebnb.test:3000`.

ES2015

The `js` Mix method applies the Babel plugin to Webpack, ensuring that any ES2015 code is transpiled down to browser-friendly ES5 before it's added to the bundle file.

We wrote the Vuebnb frontend app prototype using only ES5 syntax, as we ran it directly in the browser without any build step. But now we can take advantage of ES2015 syntax, which includes a lot of handy features.

For example, we can use a shorthand for assigning a function to an object property.

`resources/assets/js/app.js:`

```
escapeKeyListener: function(evt) {
  ...
}
```

Can be changed to this:

```
escapeKeyListener(evt) {
  ...
}
```

There are several instances of this in `app.js` that we can change. There aren't any other opportunities for using ES2015 syntax in our code yet, though in the coming chapters we'll see more.

Polyfills

The ES2015 proposal includes new syntax, but also new APIs, such as `Promise`, and additions to existing APIs, such as `Array` and `Object`.

The Webpack Babel plugin can transpile ES2015 syntax, but new API methods require polyfilling. A **polyfill** is a script that is run in the browser to cover an API or API method that may be missing.

For example, `Object.assign` is a new API method that is not supported in Internet Explorer 11. If we want to use it in our frontend app, we have to check at the top of our script whether the API method exists, and if not, we define it manually with a polyfill:

```
if (typeof Object.assign != 'function') {
  // Polyfill to define Object.assign
}
```

Speaking of which, `Object.assign` is a handy way of merging objects and would be useful in our frontend app. Let's use it in our code, then add a polyfill to ensure the code will run in older browsers.

Look at the `data` object in our entry file, `resources/assets/js/app.js`. We are manually assigning each property of the `sample` object to the `data` object, giving it the same property name. To save having to repeat ourselves, we can instead use `Object.assign` and simply merge the two objects. In practice, this doesn't do anything different, it's just more succinct code.

`resources/assets/js/app.js`:

```
data: Object.assign(sample, {
  headerImageStyle: {
    'background-image': 'url(/images/header.jpg)'
  },
  contracted: true,
  modalOpen: false
}),
```

To polyfill `Object.assign` we must install a new `core-js` dependency, which is a library of polyfills for most new JavaScript APIs. We'll use some other `core-js` polyfills later in the project:

```
$ npm i --save-dev core-js
```

At the top of `app.js`, add this line to include the `Object.assign` polyfill:

```
import "core-js/fn/object/assign";
```

After this builds, refresh your page to see whether it works. Most likely you will not notice any difference unless you can test this on an older browser, such as Internet Explorer, but now you have the assurance that this code will run almost anywhere.

Mock data

We've now completely migrated the Vuebnb prototype into our Laravel project, plus we've added a build step. Everything in the frontend app is working as it was in Chapter 2, *Prototyping Vuebnb, Your First Vue.js Project*.

However, we still have mock data hard-coded into the frontend app. In this last part of the chapter, we're going to remove that hard-coded data and replace it with data from the backend.

Routes

Currently, the home route, that is, /, loads our frontend app. But what we've built for our frontend app so far is not meant to be a home page! We'll be building that in future chapters.

What we've built is the *listing* page, which should be at a route like /listing/5, where 5 is the ID of the mock data listing being used.

Page	Route
Home page	/
Listing page	/listing/{listing}

Let's modify the route to reflect this.

routes/web.php:

```php
<?php

use App\Listing;

Route::get('/listing/{listing}', function ($id) {
  return view('app');
});
```

Just like in our api/listing/{listing} route, the dynamic segment is meant to match the ID for one of our mock data listings. If you recall from the previous chapter, we created 30 mock data listings with an ID range of 1 to 30.

If we now type hint the `Listing` model in the `closure` function's profile, Laravel's service container will pass in a model with an ID that matches that dynamic route segment.

`routes/web.php`:

```
Route::get('/listing/{listing}', function (Listing $listing) {
  // echo $listing->id // will equal 5 for route /listing/5
  return view('app');
});
```

One cool in-built feature is, if the dynamic segment does not match a model, for example `/listing/50` or `/listing/somestring`, Laravel will abort the route and return a 404.

Architecture

Given that we can retrieve the correct listing model in the route handler, and that, thanks to the Blade templating system, we can dynamically insert content into our *app* view, an obvious architecture emerges: we can inject the model into the head of the page. That way, when the Vue app loads, it will have immediate access to the model:

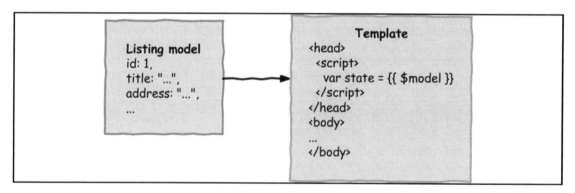

Figure 5.14. Inline listing model into the head of the page

Injecting data

Getting the mock-listing data into the client app will take several steps. We'll begin by converting the model to an array. The `view` helper can then be used to make the model available within the template at runtime.

```
routes/web.php:

   Route::get('/listing/{listing}', function (Listing $listing) {
     $model = $listing->toArray();
     return view('app', [ 'model' => $model ]);
   });
```

Now, in the Blade template, we'll create a script in the head of the document. By using double curly brackets, we can interpolate the model directly into the script.

```
resources/views/app.blade.php:

   <head>
     ...
     <script type="text/javascript">
       console.log({{ $model[ 'id' ] }});
     </script>
   </head>
```

If we now go to the /listing/5 route, we will see the following in our page source:

```
   <script type="text/javascript">
     console.log(5);
   </script>
```

And you will see the following in our console:

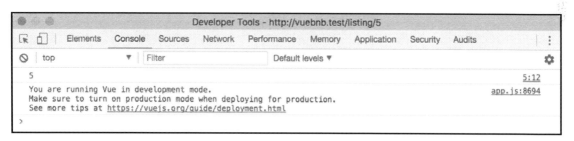

Figure 5.15. Console output after injecting model ID

JSON

We'll now encode the entire model as JSON within the view. The JSON format is good because it can be stored as a string and can be parsed by both PHP and JavaScript.

In our inline script, let's format the model as a JSON string and assign to a `model` variable.

`resources/views/app.blade.php`:

```
<script type="text/javascript">
  var model = "{!! addslashes(json_encode($model)) !!}";
  console.log(model);
</script>
```

Notice we also had to wrap `json_encode` in another global function, `addslashes`. This function will add backslashes before any character that needs to be escaped. It's necessary to do this because the JavaScript JSON parser doesn't know which quotes in the string are part of the JavaScript syntax, and which are part of the JSON object.

We also had to use a different kind of Blade syntax for interpolation. A feature of Blade is that statements within double curly brackets `{{ }}` are automatically sent through PHP's `htmlspecialchars` function to prevent XSS attacks. This will, unfortunately, invalidate our JSON object. The solution is to use the alternative `{!! !!}` syntax, which does not validate the contents. This is safe to do in this scenario because we're sure we're not using any user-supplied content.

Now if we refresh the page, we'll see the JSON object as a string in the console:

Figure 5.16. Model as a JSON string in the console

If we change the log command to `console.log(JSON.parse(model));`, we see our model not as a string, but as a JavaScript object:

Figure 5.17. Model as an object in the console

We've now successfully gotten our model from the backend into the frontend app!

Sharing data between scripts

We have another issue to overcome now. The inline script in the head of the document, which is where our model object is, is a different script to the one where we have our client application, which is where it's needed.

As we've discussed in the previous section, multiple scripts and global variables are generally not preferred as they make the app fragile. But in this scenario, they're a necessity. The safest way to share an object or function between two scripts is to make it a property of the global `window` object. That way, it's very obvious from your code that you're intentionally using a global variable:

```
// scriptA.js
window.myvar = 'Hello World';

// scriptB.js
console.log(window.myvar); // Hello World
```

If you add additional scripts to your project, particularly third-party ones, they might also add to the `window` object, and there's a possibility of a naming collision. To avoid this the best we can, we'll make sure we use a very specific property name.

`resources/views/app.blade.php`:

```
<script type="text/javascript">
  window.vuebnb_listing_model = "{!! addslashes(json_encode($model)) !!}"
</script>
```

Now, over in the entry file of the frontend app, we can work with this `window` property in our script.

`resources/assets/js/app.js`:

```
let model = JSON.parse(window.vuebnb_listing_model);

var app = new Vue({
  ...
});
```

Replacing the hard-coded model

We now have access to our listing model in the entry file, so let's switch it with our hard-coded model in the `data` property assignment.

`resources/assets/js/app.js`:

```
let model = JSON.parse(window.vuebnb_listing_model);

var app = new Vue({
  el: '#app'
  data: Object.assign(model, {
    ...
  })
  ...
});
```

With that done, we can now remove the `import sample from './data';` statement from the top of `app.js`. We can also delete the sample data files as they won't be used any further in the project:

```
$ rm resources/assets/js/data.js resources/assets/images/header.jpg
```

Amenities and prices

If you refresh the page now, it will load, but the script will have some errors. The problem is that the amenities and prices data are structured differently in the frontend app to how they are in the backend. This is because the model initially came from our database, which stores scalar values. In JavaScript, we can use richer objects which allow us to nest data, making it much easier to work with and manipulate.

Here is how the model object currently looks. Notice that the amenities and prices are scalar values:

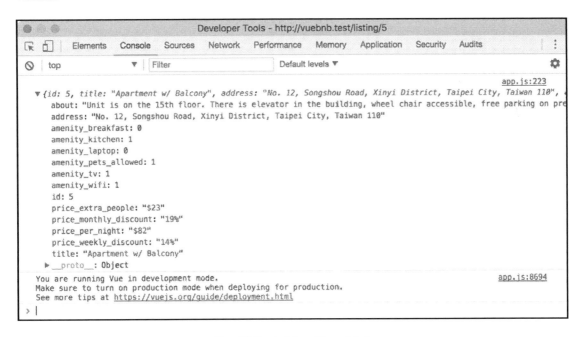

Figure 5.18. How the listing model currently looks

This is how we need it to look, with the amenities and prices as arrays:

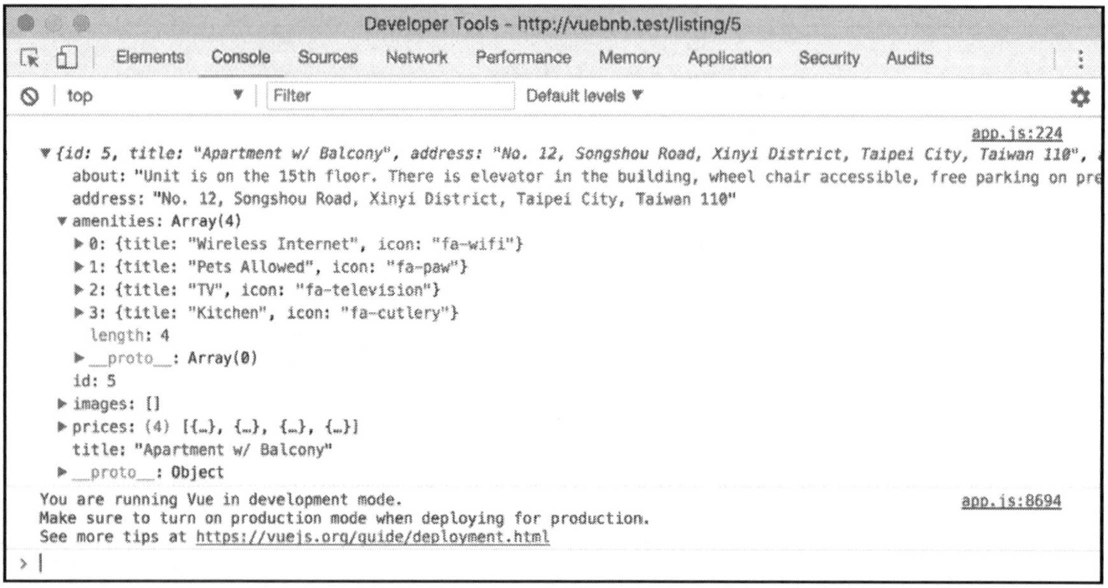

Figure 5.19. How the listing model should look

To fix this problem, we'll need to transform the model before we pass it to Vue. To save you having to think too much about this, I've put the transformation function into a file, `resources/assets/js/helpers.js`. This file is a JavaScript module that we can import into our entry file and use by simply passing the model object into the function.

`resources/assets/js/app.js`:

```
import Vue from 'vue';
import { populateAmenitiesAndPrices } from './helpers';

let model = JSON.parse(window.vuebnb_listing_model);
model = populateAmenitiesAndPrices(model)</span>;
```

Once we've added this and refreshed the page, we should see the new model data in the text parts of the page (although still with the hard-coded images):

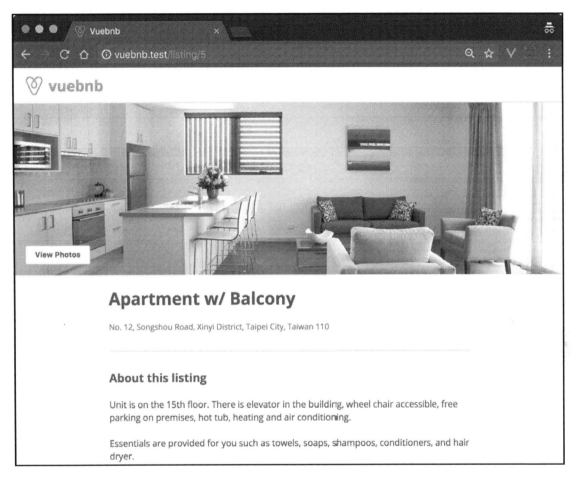

Figure 5.20. New model data in page with hard-coded images

Image URLs

The last thing to do is replace the hard-coded images' URLs in the frontend app. These URLs are not currently a part of the model, so need to be manually added to the model before we inject it into the template.

We've already done a very similar job back in Chapter 4, *Building a Web Service With Laravel*, for the API listing route.

app/Http/Controllers/ListingController.php:

```php
public function get_listing_api(Listing $listing)
{
  $model = $listing->toArray();
  for($i = 1; $i <=4; $i++) {
    $model['image_' . $i] = asset(
      'images/' . $listing->id . '/Image_' . $i . '.jpg'
    );
  }
  return response()->json($model);
}
```

In fact, our web route will end up with identical code to this API route, only instead of returning JSON, it will return a view.

Let's share the common logic. Begin by moving the route closure function into a new get_listing_web method in the listing controller.

app/Http/Controllers/ListingController.php:

```php
<?php

namespace App\Http\Controllers;

use Illuminate\Http\Request;
use App\Listing;

class ListingController extends Controller
{
  public function get_listing_api(Listing $listing)
  {
    ...
  }

  public function get_listing_web(Listing $listing)
  {
    $model = $listing->toArray();
    return view('app', ['model' => $model]);
  }
}
```

Then adjust the route to call this new controller method.

routes/web.php:

```php
<?php

Route::get('/listing/{listing}', 'ListingController@get_listing_web');
```

Let's now update the controller so *both* the web and API routes get the images' URLs added to their model. We'll first create a new `add_image_urls` method, which abstracts the logic that was used in `get_listing_api`. Now both of the route-handling methods will call this new method.

app/Http/Controllers/ListingController.php:

```php
<?php

namespace App\Http\Controllers;

use Illuminate\Http\Request;
use App\Listing;

class ListingController extends Controller
{
    private function add_image_urls($model, $id)
    {
        for($i = 1; $i <=4; $i++) {
            $model['image_' . $i] = asset(
                'images/' . $id . '/Image_' . $i . '.jpg'
            );
        }
        return $model;
    }

    public function get_listing_api(Listing $listing)
    {
        $model = $listing->toArray();
        $model = $this->add_image_urls($model, $listing->id);
        return response()->json($model);
    }

    public function get_listing_web(Listing $listing)
    {
        $model = $listing->toArray();
        $model = $this->add_image_urls($model, $listing->id);
```

```
        return view('app', ['model' => $model]);
    }
}
```

With that done, if we refresh the app and open **Vue Devtools**, we should see that we have the image URLs as an `images` data property:

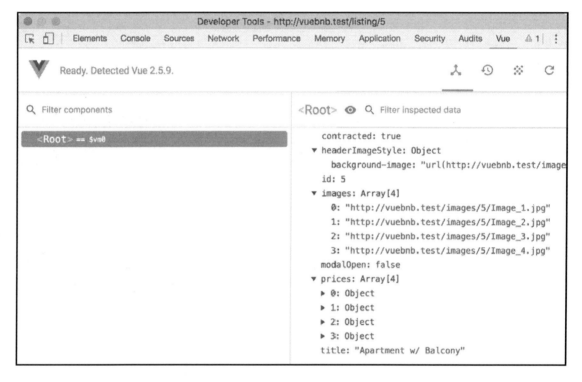

Figure 5.21. Images are now a data property as shown in Vue Devtools

Replacing the hard-coded image URLs

The final step is to use these image URLs from the backend instead of the hard-coded URL. Remembering that `images` is an array of URLs, we'll use the first image as a default, that is, `images[0]`.

First, we'll update the entry file,

`resources/assets/js/app.js:`

```
    headerImageStyle: {
```

```
    'background-image': `url(${model.images[0]})`
  }
```

Then the view for the modal image.

`resources/views/app.blade.php`:

```
  <div class="modal-content">
    <img v-bind:src="images[0]"/>
  </div>
```

With that done, after a rebuild and page refresh, you'll see the content of mock data listing #5 in the page:

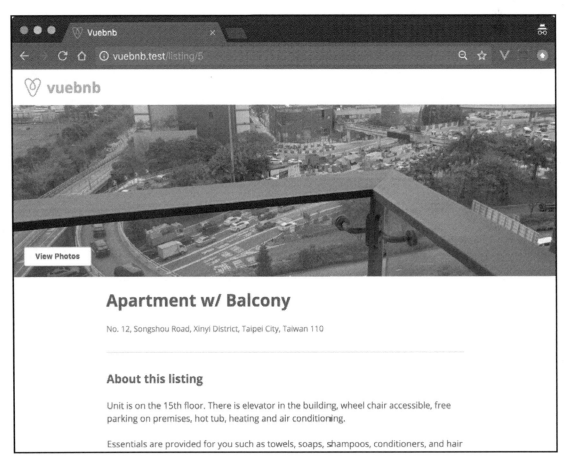

Figure 5.22. Listing page with mock data

To verify, and to admire our work, let's try another route, for example, /listing/10:

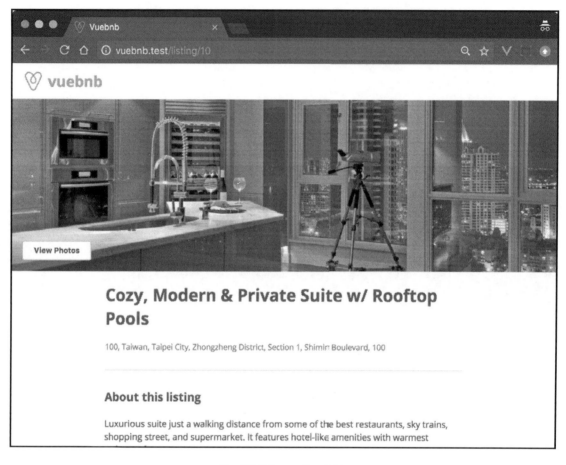

Figure 5.23. Listing page with mock data

Summary

In this chapter, we got familiar with the files and configuration of Laravel's default frontend app. We then migrated the Vuebnb client app prototype into our Laravel project, achieving the first full-stack iteration of Vuebnb.

We also learned about Webpack, seeing how it addresses the JavaScript dependency management problem by bundling modules into a browser-friendly build file. We set up Webpack in our project via Laravel Mix, which offers a simple API for common build scenarios.

We then investigated tools for making our frontend development process easier, including Webpack watch mode and BrowserSync.

Finally, we saw how to get data from the backend into the frontend app by injecting it into the document head.

In Chapter 6, *Composing Widgets with Vue.js Components*, we will be introduced to one of the most important and powerful tools for building user interfaces with Vue.js: components. We will build an image carousel for Vuebnb, and use knowledge of components to refactor the Vuebnb client app into a flexible component-based architecture.

6

Composing Widgets with Vue.js Components

Components are becoming an essential aspect of frontend development, and are a feature in most modern frontend frameworks, including Vue, React, Angular, Polymer, and so on. Components are even becoming native to the web through a new standard called **Web Components**.

In this chapter, we will use components to create an image carousel for Vuebnb, which allows users to peruse the different photos of a room listing. We'll also refactor Vuebnb to conform to a component-based architecture.

Topics covered in this chapter:

- What components are and how to create them with Vue.js
- Component communication through props and events
- Single-file components-one of Vue's most useful features
- Adding custom content to a component with slots
- The benefit of architecting apps entirely from components
- How render functions can be used to skip the template compiler
- Using the runtime-only build of Vue to lighten the bundle size

Components

When we're constructing a template for a web app, we can use HTML elements such as `div`, `table`, and `span`. This variety of elements makes it easy to create whatever structures we need for organizing content on the page.

What if we could create our own custom elements, through, for example, `my-element`? This would allow us to create reusable structures specifically designed for our app.

Components are a tool for creating custom elements in Vue.js. When we register a component, we define a template which renders as one or more standard HTML elements:

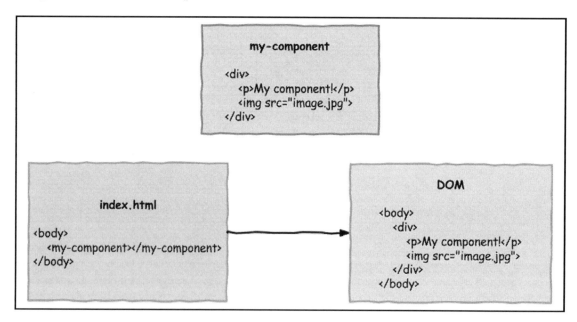

Figure 6.1. Components facilitate reusable markup and render as standard HTML

Registration

There are many ways to register a component, but the easiest is to use the `component` API method. The first argument is the name you want to give the component, the second is the configuration object. The configuration object will often include a `template` property to declare the component's markup using a string:

```
Vue.component('my-component', {
  template: '<div>My component!</div>'
});

new Vue({
  el: '#app'
});
```

Once we've registered a component like this, we can use it within our project:

```
<div id="app">
  <my-component></my-component>
  <!-- Renders as <div>My component!</div> -->
</div>
```

Data

In addition to reusable markup, components allow us to reuse JavaScript functionality. The configuration object can not only include a template but can also include its own state, just like the Vue instance. In fact, each component can be thought of as a mini-instance of Vue with its own data, methods, lifecycle hooks, and so on.

We treat component data slightly differently to the Vue instance though, as components are meant to be reusable. For example, we might create a bank of check-box components like this:

```
<div id="app">
  <check-box></check-box>
  <check-box></check-box>
  <check-box></check-box>
</div>
<script>
  Vue.component('check-box', {
    template: '<div v-on:click="checked = !checked"></div>'
    data: {
      checked: false
    }
  });
</script>
```

As it is, if a user clicks a checkbox div, the checked state toggles from true to false for every checkbox simultaneously! This is not what we want, but it is what will happen, as all instances of the component refer to the same data object and therefore have the same state.

To give each instance its own unique state, the `data` property shouldn't be an object, but a factory function that returns an object. That way, every time the component is instantiated, it links to a fresh data object. Implementing this is as simple as:

```
data() {
  return {
    checked: false
  }
}
```

Image carousel

Let's build a new feature for the Vuebnb frontend app using components. As you'll recall from previous chapters, each of our mock data listings has four different images, and we're passing the URLs to the frontend app.

To allow the user to peruse these images, we're going to create an image carousel. This carousel will replace the static image that currently occupies the modal window that pops up when you click the header of a listing.

Begin by opening the app view. Remove the static image and replace it with a custom HTML element `image-carousel`.

`resources/views/app.blade.php`:

```
<div class="modal-content">
  <image-carousel></image-carousel>
</div>
```

 A component can be referred to in your code by a kebab-case name such as `my-component`, a PascalCase name such as `MyComponent`, or a camelCase name such as `myComponent`. Vue sees these all as the same component. However, in a DOM or string template, the component should always be kebab-cased. Vue doesn't enforce this, but markup in the page gets parsed by the browser before Vue gets to work with it, so it should conform to W3C naming conventions or the parser may strip it out.

Let's now register the component in our entry file. The template of this new component will simply be the image tag we removed from the view, wrapped in a `div`. We add this wrapping element, as component templates must have a single root element, and we'll soon be adding more elements inside it.

As a proof of concept, the component data will include an array of hard-coded image URLs. Once we learn how to pass data into a component, we will remove these hard-coded URLs and replace them with dynamic ones from our model.

resources/assets/js/app.js:

```
Vue.component('image-carousel', {
  template: `<div class="image-carousel">
                <img v-bind:src="images[0]"/>
            </div>`,
  data() {
    return {
      images: [
        '/images/1/Image_1.jpg',
        '/images/1/Image_2.jpg',
        '/images/1/Image_3.jpg',
        '/images/1/Image_4.jpg'
      ]
    }
  }
});

var app = new Vue({
  ...
});
```

Before we test this component, let's make an adjustment to our CSS. We previously had a rule to ensure the image inside the modal window stretched to full width by using the `.modal-content img` selector. Let's instead use the `.image-carousel` selector for this rule, as we're decoupling the image from the modal window.

resources/assets/css/style.css:

```
.image-carousel img {
  width: 100%;
}
```

After your code has rebuilt, navigate the browser to /listing/1 and you should see no difference, as the component should render in almost exactly the same way as the previous markup did.

If we check Vue Devtools, however, and open up to the **Components** tab, you'll see that we now have the `ImageCarousel` component nested below the `Root` instance. Selecting `ImageCarousel`, we can even inspect its state:

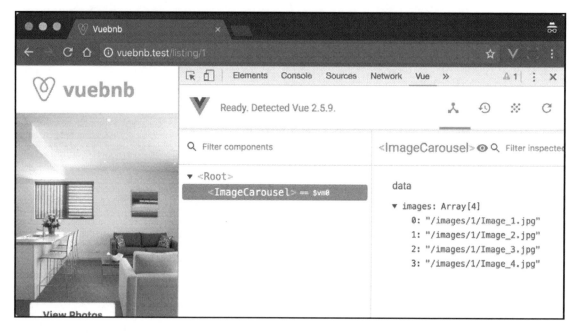

Figure 6.2. Vue Devtools showing ImageCarousel component

Changing images

The point of a carousel is to allow the user to peruse a collection of images without having to scroll the page. To permit this functionality, we'll need to create some UI controls.

But first, let's add a new data property, `index`, to our component, which will dictate the current image being displayed. It will be initialized at 0 and the UI controls will later be able to increment or decrement the value.

We will bind the image source to the array item at position `index`.

resources/assets/js/app.js:

```
Vue.component('image-carousel', {
  template: `<div class="image-carousel">
            <img v-bind:src="images[index]"/>
```

```
      </div>`,
  data() {
    return {
      images: [
        '/images/1/Image_1.jpg',
        '/images/1/Image_2.jpg',
        '/images/1/Image_3.jpg',
        '/images/1/Image_4.jpg'
      ],
      index: 0
    }
  }
});
```

A page refresh should, again, reveal no change to what you see on screen. However, if you initialize the value of index to 1, 2, or 3, you will find a different image is shown when you re-open the modal window:

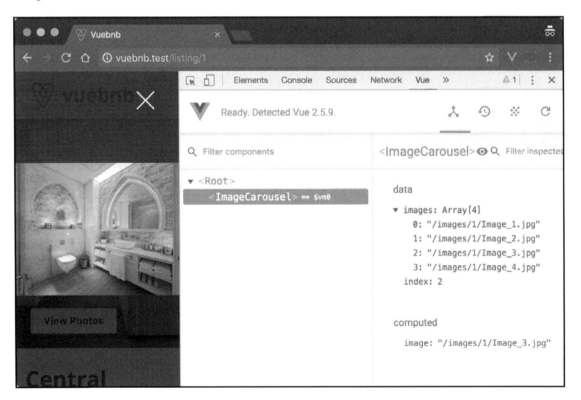

Figure 6.3. Setting index to 2 selects a different URL and a different image is shown

Computed properties

It's convenient to write logic straight into our template as an expression, for example, v-if="myExpression". But what about more complex logic that can't be defined as an expression, or simply becomes too verbose for the template?

For this scenario, we use **computed properties**. These are properties we add to our Vue configuration that can be thought of as reactive methods which are rerun whenever a dependent value is changed.

In the following example, we've declared a computed property, message, under the computed configuration section. Note the function is dependent on val, that is, the returned value of of message will be different as val changes.

When this script runs, Vue will note any dependencies of message and will set up reactive binding so that, unlike a regular method, the function will be rerun whenever the dependencies change:

```
<script>
  var app = new Vue({
    el: '#app',
    data: {
      val: 1
    },
    computed: {
      message() {
        return `The value is ${this.val}`
      }
    }
  });

  setTimeout(function() {
    app.val = 2;
  }, 2000);
</script>
<div id="app">
  <!--Renders as "The value is 1"-->
  <!--After 2 seconds, re-renders as "The value is 2"-->
  {{ message }}
</div>
```

Going back to the image carousel, let's make the template terser by abstracting the expression bound to the image `src` into a computed property.

`resources/assets/js/app.js`:

```
Vue.component('image-carousel', {
  template: `<div class="image-carousel">
               <img v-bind:src="image"/>
             </div>`,
  data() { ... },
  computed: {
    image() {
      return this.images[this.index];
    }
  }
});
```

Composing with components

Components can be nested in other components in the same way that standard HTML elements can be nested. For example, component B can be a child of component A, if component A declares component B in its template:

```
<div id="app">
  <component-a></component-a>
</div>
<script>
  Vue.component('component-a', {
    template: `
      <div>
        <p>Hi I'm component A</p>
        <component-b></component-b>
      </div>`
  });

  Vue.component('component-b', {
    template: `<p>And I'm component B</p>`
  });

  new Vue({
    el: '#app'
  });
</script>
```

This renders as:

```
<div id="app">
  <div>
    <p>Hi I'm component A</p>
    <p>And I'm component B</p>
  </div>
</div>
```

Registration scope

While some components are designed for use anywhere in an app, other components may be designed with a more specific purpose. When we register a component using the API, that is, Vue.component, that component is *globally* registered and can be used within any other component or instance.

We can also *locally* register a component by declaring it in the components option in the root instance, or in another component:

```
Vue.component('component-a', {
  template: `
    <div>
      <p>Hi I'm component A</p>
      <component-b></component-b>
    </div>`,
  components: {
    'component-b': {
      template: `<p>And I'm component B</p>`

    }
  }
});
```

Carousel controls

To allow a user to change the currently shown image in the carousel, let's create a new component, CarouselControl. This component will be presented as an arrowhead that floats over the carousel and will respond to a user's click. We'll use two instances, as there will be a left and right arrow for either decrementing or incrementing the image index.

We'll register `CarouselControl` locally for the `ImageCarousel` component. The `CarouselControl` template will render as an `i` tag, which is often used for displaying icons. A good icon for carousels is the Font Awesome *chevron* icon, which is an elegantly shaped arrowhead. Currently, we don't have a way to distinguish between the left and right, so for now, both instances will have a left-facing icon.

resources/assets/js/app.js:

```
Vue.component('image-carousel', {
  template: `
    <div class="image-carousel">
      <img v-bind:src="image">
      <div class="controls">
        <carousel-control></carousel-control>
        <carousel-control></carousel-control>
      </div>
    </div>
  `,
  data() { ... },
  computed: { ... },
  components: {
    'carousel-control': {
      template: `<i class="carousel-control fa fa-2x fa-chevron-left"></i>`
    }
  }
});
```

To have these controls float nicely over our image carousel, we'll add some new rules to our CSS file as well.

resources/assets/css/style.css:

```
.image-carousel {
  height: 100%;
  margin-top: -12vh;
  position: relative;
  display: flex;
  align-items: center;
  justify-content: center;
}

.image-carousel .controls {
  position: absolute;
  width: 100%;
  display: flex;
  justify-content: space-between;
}
```

```
.carousel-control {
  padding: 1rem;
  color: #ffffff;
  opacity: 0.85
}

@media (min-width: 744px) {
  .carousel-control {
      font-size: 3rem;
  }
}
```

With that code added, open the modal window to see our handywork so far:

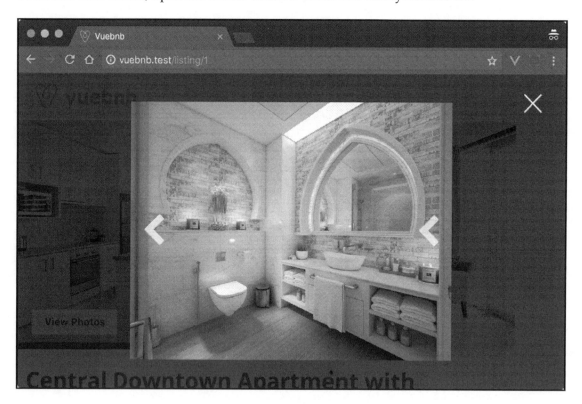

Figure 6.4. Carousel controls added to the image carousel

Communicating with components

A key aspect of components is that they are reusable, which is why we give them their own state to keep them independent from the rest of the app. However, we may still want to send in data, or send it out. Components have an interface for communicating with other parts of the app, which we will now explore.

Props

We can send data to a component through a custom HTML property know as a *prop*. We must also register this custom property in an array, `props`, in the component's configuration. In the following example, we've created a prop, `title`:

```
<div id="app">
  <my-component title="My component!"></my-component>
  <!-- Renders as <div>My component!</div> -->
</div>
<script>
  Vue.component('my-component', {
    template: '<div>{{ title }}</div>',
    props: ['title']
  });

  new Vue({
    el: '#app'
  });
</script>
```

A prop can be used just like any data property of the component: you can interpolate it in the template, use it in methods and computed properties, and so on. However, you should not mutate prop data. Think of prop data as being *borrowed* from another component or instance - only the owner should change it.

 Props are proxied to the instance just like data properties, meaning you can refer to a prop as `this.myprop` within that component's code. Be sure to name your props uniquely to your data properties to avoid a clash!

One-way data flow

Since props must be declared in the template where the component is used, prop data can only pass from a parent to a child. This is why you shouldn't mutate a prop - since data flows down, the change will not be reflected in the parent, and therefore you will have different versions of what is meant to be the same bit of state.

If you do need to tell the owner to change the data, there is a separate interface for passing data from a child to a parent, which we'll see later.

Dynamic props

We can reactively bind data to a component using the `v-bind` directive. When the data changes in the parent, it will automatically flow down to the child.

In the following example, the value of `title` in the root instance gets programmatically updated after two seconds. This change will automatically flow down to `MyComponent`, which will reactively re-render to display the new value:

```html
<div id="app">
  <my-component :title="title"></my-component>
  <!-- Renders initially as <div>Hello World</div> -->
  <!-- Re-renders after two seconds as <div>Goodbye World</div> -->
</div>
<script>
  Vue.component('my-component', {
    template: '<div>{{ title }}</div>',
    props: [ 'title' ]
  });

  var app = new Vue({
    el: '#app',
    data: {
      title: 'Hello World'
    }
  });

  setTimeout(() => {
    app.title = 'Goodbye World'
  }, 2000);
</script>
```

> Since the v-bind directive is used so commonly in templates, you can omit the directive name as a shorthand: `<div v-bind:title="title">` can be shortened to `<div :title="title">`.

Image URLs

When we created `ImageCarousel`, we hard-coded the image URLs. With props, we now have a mechanism for sending dynamic data from the root instance down to a component. Let's bind the root instance data property `images` to a prop, also called `images`, in our `ImageCarousel` declaration.

resources/views/app.blade.php:

```
<div class="modal-content">
  <image-carousel :images="images"></image-carousel>
</div>
```

Now, delete the data property `images` in the `ImageCarousel` component, and instead declare `images` as a prop.

resources/assets/js/app.js:

```
Vue.component('image-carousel', {
  props: ['images'],
  data() {
    return {
      index: 0
    }
  },
  ...
}
```

The root instance will now be responsible for the state of the image URLs, and the image carousel component will just be responsible for displaying them.

Using Vue Devtools, we can inspect the state of the image carousel component, which now includes `images` as a prop value instead of a data value:

Figure 6.5. Image URLs are props sent to the ImageCarousel component

Now that the image URLs are coming from the model, we can access other listing routes, such as `/listing/2`, and see the correct image displaying in the modal window again.

Distinguishing carousel controls

The `CarouselControl` component should have two possible states: either left-pointing or right-pointing. When clicked by the user, the former will ascend through the available images, the latter will descend.

This state should not be internally determined, but instead passed down from `ImageCarousel`. To do so, let's add a prop `dir` to `CarouselControl` that will take a string value, and should be either `left` or `right`.

With the `dir` prop, we can now bind the correct icon to the `i` element. This is done with a computed property which appends the prop's value to the string `fa-chevron-`, resulting in either `fa-chevron-left` or `fa-chevron-right`.

`resources/assets/js/app.js`:

```
Vue.component('image-carousel', {
  template: `
    <div class="image-carousel">
      <img :src="image">
      <div class="controls">
        <carousel-control dir="left"></carousel-control>
        <carousel-control dir="right"></carousel-control>
      </div>
    </div>
  `,
  ...
  components: {
    'carousel-control': {
      template: `<i :class="classes"></i>`,
      props: [ 'dir' ],
      computed: {
        classes() {
          return 'carousel-control fa fa-2x fa-chevron-' + this.dir;
        }
      }
    }
  }
}
```

Now we can see the carousel control icons correctly directed:

Figure 6.6. Carousel control icons are now correctly directed

Custom events

Our carousel controls are displaying nicely, but they still don't do anything! When they're clicked, we need them to tell `ImageCarousel` to either increment or decrement its `index` value, which will result in the image being changed.

Dynamic props won't work for this task, as props can only send data down from a parent to a child. What do we do when the child needs to send data up to the parent?

Custom events can be emitted from a child component and listened to by its parent. To implement this, we use the $emit instance method in the child, which takes the event name as the first argument and an arbitrary number of additional arguments for any data to be sent along with the event, such as this.$emit('my-event', 'My event payload');.

The parent can listen to this event using the v-on directive in the template where the component is declared. If you handle the event with a method, any arguments sent with the event will be passed to this method as parameters.

Consider this example, where a child component, MyComponent, emits an event called toggle to tell the parent, the root instance, to change the value of a data property, toggle:

```
<div id="app">
  <my-component @toggle="toggle = !toggle"></my-component>
  {{ message }}
</div>
<script>
  Vue.component('my-component', {
    template: '<div v-on:click="clicked">Click me</div>',
    methods: {
      clicked: function() {
        this.$emit('toggle');
      }
    }
  });

  new Vue({
    el: '#app',
    data: {
      toggle: false
    },
    computed: {
      message: function() {
        return this.toggle ? 'On' : 'Off';
      }
    }
  });
</script>
```

Changing carousel images

Returning to CarouselControl, let's respond to a user's click by using the v-on directive and triggering a method, clicked. This method will, in turn, emit a custom event, change-image, which will include a payload of either -1 or 1, depending on whether the state of the component is left or right.

> Just like with v-bind, there is a shorthand for v-on as well. Simply replace v-on: with @; for instance, <div @click="handler"></div> is the equivalent of <div v-on:click="handler"></div>.

resources/assets/js/app.js:

```
components: {
  'carousel-control': {
    template: `<i :class="classes" @click="clicked"></i>`,
    props: [ 'dir' ],
    computed: {
      classes() {
        return 'carousel-control fa fa-2x fa-chevron-' + this.dir;
      }
    },
    methods: {
      clicked() {
        this.$emit('change-image', this.dir === 'left' ? -1 : 1);
      }
    }
  }
}
```

Open Vue Devtools to the **Events** tab, and, at the same time, click on the carousel controls. Custom events are logged here, so we can verify `change-image` is being emitted:

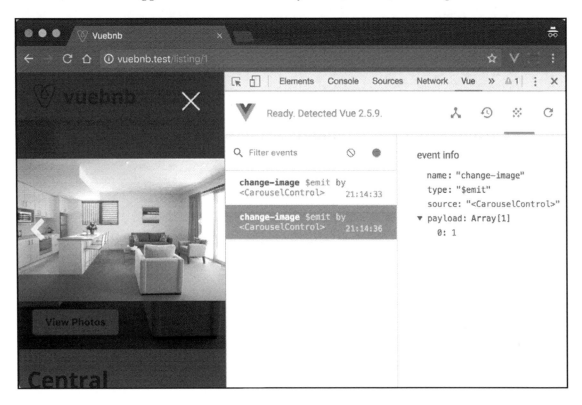

Figure 6.7. Screenshot showing a custom event and its payload

`ImageCarousel` will now need to listen for the `change-image` event via the v-on directive. The event will be handled by a method `changeImage` which will have a single parameter, `val`, reflecting the payload being sent in the event. The method will then use `val` to step the value of `index`, ensuring it loops to the start or end if it exceeds the bounds of the array it indexes.

resources/assets/js/app.js:

```
Vue.component('image-carousel', {
  template: `
    <div class="image-carousel">
      <img :src="image">
      <div class="controls">
        <carousel-control
```

```
                    dir="left"
                    @change-image="changeImage"
                  ></carousel-control>
                  <carousel-control
                    dir="right"
                    @change-image="changeImage"
                  ></carousel-control>
                </div>
              </div>
            `,
            ...
         methods: {
           changeImage(val) {
             let newVal = this.index + parseInt(val);
             if (newVal < 0) {
               this.index = this.images.length -1;
             } else if (newVal === this.images.length) {
               this.index = 0;
             } else {
               this.index = newVal;
             }
           }
         },
         ...
      }
```

With this done, the image carousel will now work perfectly:

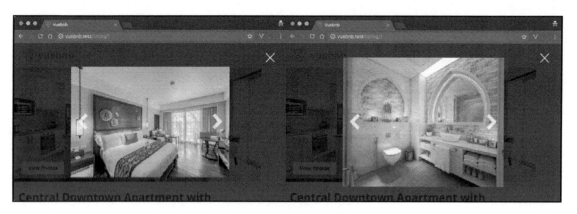

Figure 6.8. The state of the image carousel after the image has been changed

Single-file components

Single-File Components (SFCs) are files with a .vue extension that contain the complete definition of a single component and can be imported into your Vue.js app. SFCs make it simple to create and use components, and come with a variety of other benefits which we'll soon explore.

SFCs are similar to HTML files but have (at most) three root elements:

- template
- script
- style

The component definition goes inside the script tag and will be exactly like any other component definition except:

- It will export an ES module
- It will not need a template property (or a render function; more on that later)

The component's template will be declared as HTML markup inside the template tag. This should be a welcome relief from writing cumbersome template strings!

The style tag is a feature unique to SFCs and can contain any CSS rules you need for the component. This mostly just helps with the organization of your CSS.

Here's an example of the declaration and usage of a single-file component.

MyComponent.vue:

```
<template>
  <div id="my-component">{{ title }}</div>
</template>
<script>
  export default {
    data() {
      title: 'My Component'
    }
  };
</script>
<style>
  .my-component {
    color: red;
  }
</style>
```

app.js:

```
import 'MyComponent' from './MyComponent.vue';

new Vue({
  el: '#app',
  components: {
    MyComponent
  }
});
```

Transformation

To use a single-file component in your app, you simply `import` it like it were an ES module. The *.vue* file is not a valid JavaScript module file, however. Just like we use the Webpack Babel plugin to transpile our ES2015 code into ES5 code, we must use *Vue Loader* to transform *.vue* files into JavaScript modules.

Vue Loader is already configured by default with Laravel Mix, so there's nothing further we need to do in this project; any SFCs we import will just work!

 To learn more about Vue Loader, check out the documentation at `https:/ /vue-loader.vuejs.org/`.

Refactoring components to SFCs

Our `resource/assets/js/app.js` file is almost 100 lines long now. If we keep adding components, it will start to get unmanageable, so it's time to think about splitting it up.

Let's begin by refactoring our existing components to be SFCs. First, we'll create a new directory, then we will create the `.vue` files:

```
$ mkdir resources/assets/components
$ touch resources/assets/components/ImageCarousel.vue
$ touch resources/assets/components/CarouselControl.vue
```

Starting with `ImageCarousel.vue`, the first step is to create the three root elements.

`resources/assets/components/ImageCarousel.vue`:

```
<template></template>
<script></script>
<style></style>
```

Now, we move the `template` string into the `template` tag, and the component definition into the `script` tag. The component definition must be exported as a module.

`resources/assets/components/ImageCarousel.vue`:

```
<template>
  <div class="image-carousel">
    <img :src="image">
    <div class="controls">
      <carousel-control
        dir="left"
        @change-image="changeImage"
      ></carousel-control>
      <carousel-control
        dir="right"
        @change-image="changeImage"
      ></carousel-control>
    </div>
  </div>
</template>
<script>
  export default {
    props: [ 'images' ],
    data() {
      return {
        index: 0
      }
    },
    computed: {
      image() {
        return this.images[this.index];
      }
    },
    methods: {
      changeImage(val) {
        let newVal = this.index + parseInt(val);
        if (newVal < 0) {
          this.index = this.images.length -1;
        } else if (newVal === this.images.length) {
```

```
            this.index = 0;
          } else {
            this.index = newVal;
          }
        }
      },
      components: {
        'carousel-control': {
          template: `<i :class="classes" @click="clicked"></i>`,
          props: [ 'dir' ],
          computed: {
            classes() {
              return 'carousel-control fa fa-2x fa-chevron-' + this.dir;
            }
          },
          methods: {
            clicked() {
              this.$emit('change-image', this.dir === 'left' ? -1 : 1);
            }
          }
        }
      }
    }
  </script>
  <style></style>
```

Now we can import this file into our app and register it locally in the root instance. As mentioned, Vue is able to automatically switch between kebab-case component names and Pascal-case ones. This means we can use the object shorthand syntax inside the component configuration and Vue will correctly resolve it.

resources/assets/js/app.js:

```
  import ImageCarousel from '../components/ImageCarousel.vue';

  var app = new Vue({
    ...
    components: {
      ImageCarousel
    }
  });
```

Be sure to delete any remaining code from the original `ImageCarousel` component definition in `app.js` before moving on.

CSS

SFCs allow us to add style to a component, helping to better organize our CSS code. Let's move the CSS rules we created for the image carousel into this new SFC's `style` tag:

```
<template>...</template>
<script>...</script>
<style>
  .image-carousel {
    height: 100%;
    margin-top: -12vh;
    position: relative;
    display: flex;
    align-items: center;
    justify-content: center;
  }

  .image-carousel img {
    width: 100%;
  }

  .image-carousel .controls {
    position: absolute;
    width: 100%;
    display: flex;
    justify-content: space-between;
  }
</style>
```

When the project builds, you should find it still appears the same. The interesting thing, though, is where the CSS has ended up in the build. If you check `public/css/style.css`, you'll find it's not there.

It's actually included in the JavaScript bundle as a string:

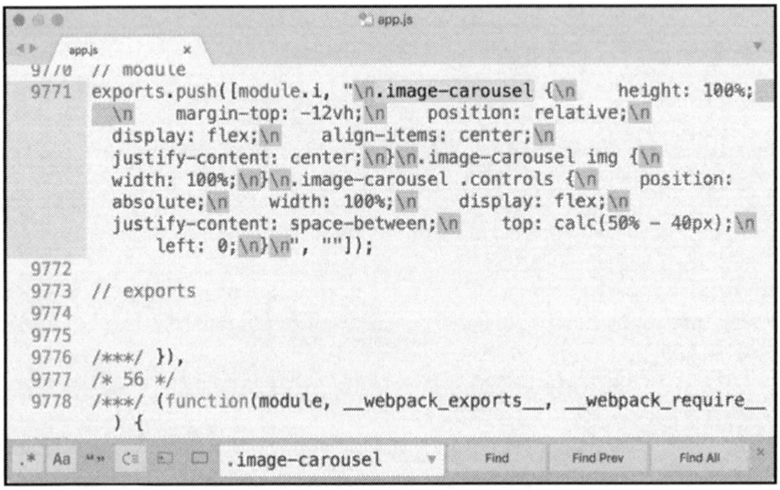

Figure 6.9. CSS stored as a string in the JavaScript bundle file

To use it, Webpack's bootstrapping code will inline this CSS string into the head of the document when the app runs:

Figure 6.10. Inlined CSS in document head

Inlining CSS is actually the default behavior of Vue Loader. However, we can override this and get Webpack to write SFC styles to their own file. Add the following to the bottom of the Mix configuration.

webpack.mix.js:

```
mix.options({
  extractVueStyles: 'public/css/vue-style.css'
});
```

Now an additional file, `public/css/vue-style.css`, will be outputted in the build:

```
●  ●  ●                          vuebnb — -bash — 87×6
DONE  Compiled successfully in 1100ms                              11:46:14 AM

           Asset     Size  Chunks                    Chunk Names
       /js/app.js   333 kB       0  [emitted]  [big]  /js/app
  css/vue-style.css  1.22 kB      0  [emitted]         /js/app
     /css/style.css  46.1 kB         [emitted]
```

Figure 6.11. Webpack output including single-file component styles

We'll need to load this new file in our view, after the main style sheet.

resources/views/app.blade.php:

```
<head>
  ...
  <link rel="stylesheet" href="{{ asset('css/style.css') }}"
type="text/css">
  <link rel="stylesheet" href="{{ asset('css/vue-style.css') }}"
type="text/css">
  ...
</head>
```

CarouselControl

Let's now abstract our `CarouselControl` component into an SFC, and move any relevant CSS rules from `resources/assets/css/style.css` as well.

resources/assets/components/CarouselControl.vue:

```
<template>
  <i :class="classes" @click="clicked"></i>
</template>
<script>
```

```
export default {
  props: [ 'dir' ],
  computed: {
    classes() {
      return 'carousel-control fa fa-2x fa-chevron-' + this.dir;
    }
  },
  methods: {
    clicked() {
      this.$emit('change-image', this.dir === 'left' ? -1 : 1);
    }
  }
}
</script>
<style>
  .carousel-control {
    padding: 1rem;
    color: #ffffff;
    opacity: 0.85
  }

  @media (min-width: 744px) {
    .carousel-control {
      font-size: 3rem;
    }
  }
</style>
```

This file can now be imported by the `ImageCarousel` component.

`resources/assets/components/ImageCarousel.vue:`

```
<template>...</style>
<script>
  import CarouselControl from '../components/CarouselControl.vue';

  export default {
    ...
    components: {
      CarouselControl
    }
  }
</script>
<style>...</style>
```

With that done, our existing components have been refactored to SFCs. This has not made any obvious difference to the functionality of our app (although it is slightly faster, as I'll explain later), but it will make development easier as we continue.

Content distribution

Imagine you're going to build a component-based Vue.js app that resembles the following structure:

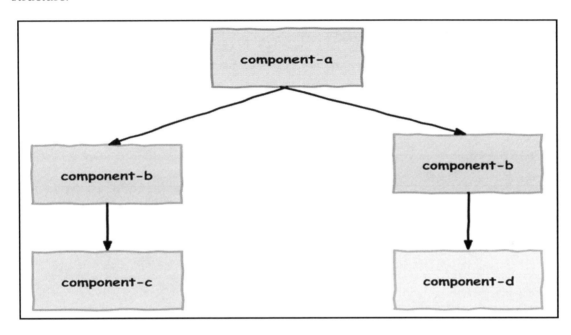

Figure 6.12. Component-based Vue.js app

Notice that in the left-branch of the above diagram, `ComponentC` is declared by `ComponentB`. However, in the right branch, `ComponentD` is declared by a different instance of `ComponentB`.

With what you know about components so far, how would you make the template for `ComponentB`, given that it has to declare two different components? Perhaps it would include a `v-if` directive to use either `ComponentC` or `ComponentD` depending on some variable passed down as a prop from `ComponentA`. This approach would work, however, it makes `ComponentB` very inflexible, limiting its reusability in other parts of the app.

Slots

We've learned so far that the content of a component is defined by its own template, not by its parent, so we wouldn't expect the following to work:

```
<div id="app">
  <my-component>
    <p>Parent content</p>
  </my-component>
</div>
```

But it will work if `MyComponent` has a *slot*. Slots are distribution outlets inside a component, defined with the special `slot` element:

```
Vue.component('my-component', {
  template: `
    <div>
      <slot></slot>
      <p>Child content</p>
    </div>`
});

new Vue({
  el: '#app'
});
```

This renders as:

```
<div id="app">
  <div>
    <p>Parent content</p>
    <p>Child content</p>
  </div>
</div>
```

If `ComponentB` has a slot in its template, like this:

```
Vue.component('component-b', {
  template: '<slot></slot>'
});
```

We can solve the problem just stated without having to use a cumbersome `v-for`:

```
<component-a>
  <component-b>
    <component-c></component-c>
  </component-b>
```

```
  <component-b>
    <component-d></component-d>
  </component-b>
</component-a>
```

It's important to note that content declared inside a component in the parent template is compiled in the scope of the parent. Although it is rendered inside the child, it cannot access any of the child's data. The following example should distinguish this:

```
<div id="app">
  <my-component>
    <!--This works-->
    <p>{{ parentProperty }}</p>

    <!--This does not work. childProperty is undefined, as this content-->
    <!--is compiled in the parent's scope-->
    <p>{{ childProperty }}
  </my-component>
</div>
<script>
  Vue.component('my-component', {
    template: `
      <div>
        <slot></slot>
        <p>Child content</p>
      </div>`,
    data() {
      return {
        childProperty: 'World'
      }
    }
  });

  new Vue({
    el: '#app',
    data: {
      parentProperty: 'Hello'
    }
  });
</script>
```

Modal window

A lot of the functionality left in our root Vue instance concerns the modal window. Let's abstract this into a separate component. First, we'll create the new component file:

```
$ touch resources/assets/components/ModalWindow.vue
```

Now, we'll transplant the markup from the view to the component. To ensure the carousel stays decoupled from the modal window, we'll replace the ImageCarousel declaration in the markup with a slot.

resources/assets/components/ModalWindow.vue:

```
<template>
  <div id="modal" :class="{ show : modalOpen }">
    <button @click="modalOpen = false" class="modal-close">&times;</button>
    <div class="modal-content">
      <slot></slot>
    </div>
  </div>
</template>
<script></script>
<style></style>
```

We can now declare a ModalWindow element in the hole we just created in the view, with an ImageCarousel as content for the slot.

resources/views/app.blade.php:

```
<div id="app">
  <div class="header">...</div>
  <div class="container">...</div>
  <modal-window>
    <image-carousel :images="images"></image-carousel>
  </modal-window>
</div>
```

We will now move the needed functionality from the root instance and place it inside the script tag.

resources/assets/components/ModalWindow.vue:

```
<template>...</template>
<script>
  export default {
    data() {
```

```
      return {
        modalOpen: false
      }
    },
    methods: {
      escapeKeyListener(evt) {
        if (evt.keyCode === 27 && this.modalOpen) {
          this.modalOpen = false;
        }
      }
    },
    watch: {
      modalOpen() {
        var className = 'modal-open';
        if (this.modalOpen) {
          document.body.classList.add(className);
        } else {
          document.body.classList.remove(className);
        }
      }
    },
    created() {
      document.addEventListener('keyup', this.escapeKeyListener);
    },
    destroyed() {
      document.removeEventListener('keyup', this.escapeKeyListener);
    },
  }
</script>
<style></style>
```

Next we import `ModalWindow` in the entry file.

`resources/assets/js/app.js`:

```
import ModalWindow from '../components/ModalWindow.vue';

var app = new Vue({
  el: '#app',
  data: Object.assign(model, {
    headerImageStyle: {
      'background-image': `url(${model.images[0]})`
    },
    contracted: true
  }),
  components: {
    ImageCarousel,
    ModalWindow
```

```
    }
  });
```

Finally, let's move any modal-related CSS rules into the SFC as well:

```
<template>...</template>
<script>...</script>
<style>
  #modal {
    display: none;
    position: fixed;
    top: 0;
    right: 0;
    bottom: 0;
    left: 0;
    z-index: 2000;
    background-color: rgba(0,0,0,0.85);
  }

  #modal.show {
    display: block;
  }

  body.modal-open {
    overflow: hidden;
    position: fixed;
  }

  .modal-close {
    cursor: pointer;
    position: absolute;
    right: 0;
    top: 0;
    padding: 0px 28px 8px;
    font-size: 4em;
    width: auto;
    height: auto;
    background: transparent;
    border: 0;
    outline: none;
    color: #ffffff;
    z-index: 1000;
    font-weight: 100;
    line-height: 1;
  }

  .modal-content {
    height: 100%;
```

```
    max-width: 105vh;
    padding-top: 12vh;
    margin: 0 auto;
    position: relative;
  }
</style>
```

After the project builds, you'll notice the modal window won't open. We'll fix that in the next section.

If you check Vue Devtools, you'll see a `ModalWindow` component in the hierarchy of components now:

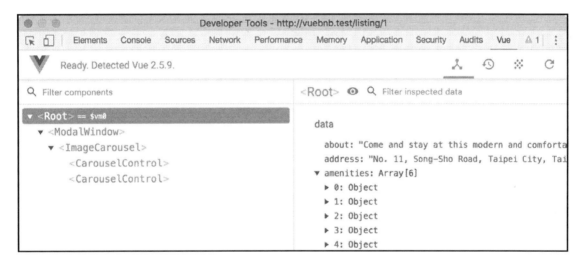

Figure 6.13. Vue Devtools showing hierarchy of components

 The representation of our app in Vue Devtools is slightly misleading. It makes it seem as though `ImageCarousel` is a child of `ModalWindow`. Even though `ImageCarousel` renders within `ModalWindow` due to the slot, these components are actually siblings!

Refs

In its initial state, the modal window is hidden with a `display: none` CSS rule. To open the modal, the user must click the header image. A click event listener will then set the root instance data property `modalOpen` to true, which will, in turn, add a class to the modal to overwrite the `display: none` to `display: block`.

After refactoring, however, `modalOpen` has been moved into the `ModalWindow` component along with the rest of the modal logic, and hence the modal opening functionality is currently broken. One possible way to fix this is to let the root instance manage the opened/closed state of the modal by moving the logic back into the root instance. We could then use a prop to inform the modal when it needs to open. When the modal is closed (this happens in the scope of the modal component, where the close button is) it would send an event to the root instance to update the state.

This approach would work, but it's not in the spirit of making our components decoupled and reusable; the modal component should manage its own state. How, then, can we allow the modal to keep its state, but let the root instance (the parent) change it? An event won't work, as events can only flow up, not down.

`ref` is a special property that allows you to directly reference a child component's data. To use it, declare the `ref` property and assign it a unique value, such as `imagemodal`.

`resources/views/app.blade.php`:

```
<modal-window ref="imagemodal">
  . . .
</modal-window>
```

Now the root instance has access to this specific `ModalWindow` component's data via the `$refs` object. This means we can change the value of `modalOpen` inside a root instance method, just like we could from within `ModalWindow`.

`resources/assets/js/app.js`:

```
var app = new Vue({
  . . .
  methods: {
    openModal() {
      this.$refs.imagemodal.modalOpen = true;
    },
  }
});
```

Now we can call the `openModal` method in the header image's click listener, thus restoring the modal opening functionality.

`resources/views/app.blade.php`:

```
<div id="app">
  <div class="header">
    <div class="header-img" :style="headerImageStyle" @click="openModal">
      <button class="view-photos">View Photos</button>
    </div>
  </div>
  ...
</div>
```

It is an anti-pattern to use `ref` when the normal methods of interacting with a component, props and events, are sufficient. `ref` is usually only required for communicating with elements that fall outside of the normal flow of a page, as a modal window does.

Header image

Let's now abstract the header image into a component. Firstly, create a new `.vue` file:

```
$ touch resources/assets/components/HeaderImage.vue
```

Now move in the markup, data, and CSS. Take note of the following modifications:

- An event `header-clicked` must be emitted. This will be used to open the modal
- The image URL is passed as a prop, `image-url`, then transformed to be an inline style rule via a computed property

`resource/assets/components/HeaderImage.vue`:

```
<template>
  <div class="header">
    <div
      class="header-img"
      :style="headerImageStyle"
      @click="$emit('header-clicked')"
    >
      <button class="view-photos">View Photos</button>
    </div>
  </div>
</template>
```

```
<script>
  export default {
    computed: {
      headerImageStyle() {
        return {
          'background-image': `url(${this.imageUrl})`
        };
      }
    },
    props: [ 'image-url' ]
  }
</script>
<style>
  .header {
    height: 320px;
  }

  .header .header-img {
    background-repeat: no-repeat;
    -moz-background-size: cover;
    -o-background-size: cover;
    background-size: cover;
    background-position: 50% 50%;
    background-color: #f5f5f5;
    height: 100%;
    cursor: pointer;
    position: relative;
  }

  .header .header-img button {
    font-size: 14px;
    padding: 7px 18px;
    color: #484848;
    line-height: 1.43;
    background: #ffffff;
    font-weight: bold;
    border-radius: 4px;
    border: 1px solid #c4c4c4;
  }

  .header .header-img button.view-photos {
    position: absolute;
    bottom: 20px;
    left: 20px;
  }
</style>
```

Once you've imported this component in `resources/assets/js/app.js`, declare it in the main template. Be sure to bind the `image-url` prop and handle the click event.

`resources/views/app.blade.php`:

```
<div id="app">
  <header-image
    :image-url="images[0]"
    @header-clicked="openModal"
  ></header-image>
  <div class="container">...</div>
  <modal-window>...</modal-window>
</div>
```

Feature lists

Let's continue our process of refactoring Vuebnb into components, and abstract the amenities and prices lists. These lists have a similar purpose and structure, so it makes sense that we create a single, versatile component for both.

Let's remind ourselves of how the markup for the lists currently looks.

`resources/views/app.blade.php`:

```
<div class="lists">
  <hr>
  <div class="amenities list">
    <div class="title"><strong>Amenities</strong></div>
    <div class="content">
      <div class="list-item" v-for="amenity in amenities">
        <i class="fa fa-lg" :class="amenity.icon"></i>
        <span>@{{ amenity.title }}</span>
      </div>
    </div>
  </div>
  <hr>
  <div class="prices list">
    <div class="title"><strong>Prices</strong></div>
    <div class="content">
      <div class="list-item" v-for="price in prices">
        @{{ price.title }}: <strong>@{{ price.value }}</strong>
      </div>
    </div>
  </div>
</div>
```

The main difference between the two lists is inside the `<div class="content">...</div>` section, as the data being displayed in each list has a slightly different structure. The amenities have an icon and a title whereas the prices have a title and a value. We'll use a slot in this section to allow the parent to customize the content for each.

But first, let's create the new `FeatureList` component file:

```
$ touch resources/assets/components/FeatureList.vue
```

We'll move the markup for one of the lists in, using a slot to replace the list content. We'll also add a prop for the title and move in any list-related CSS.

resources/assets/components/FeatureList.vue:

```
<template>
  <div>
    <hr>
    <div class="list">
      <div class="title"><strong>{{ title }}</strong></div>
      <div class="content">
        <slot></slot>
      </div>
    </div>
  </div>
</template>
<script>
  export default {
    props: ['title']
  }
</script>
<style>
  hr {
    border: 0;
    border-top: 1px solid #dce0e0;
  }
  .list {
    display: flex;
    flex-wrap: nowrap;
    margin: 2em 0;
  }

  .list .title {
    flex: 1 1 25%;
  }

  .list .content {
```

```
      flex: 1 1 75%;
      display: flex;
      flex-wrap: wrap;
    }

    .list .list-item {
      flex: 0 0 50%;
      margin-bottom: 16px;
    }

    .list .list-item > i {
      width: 35px;
    }

    @media (max-width: 743px) {
      .list .title {
        flex: 1 1 33%;
      }

      .list .content {
        flex: 1 1 67%;
      }

      .list .list-item {
        flex: 0 0 100%;
      }
    }
  </style>
```

Go ahead and import `FeatureList` into `resources/assets/js/app.js`, and add it to the locally registered components. Now we can use `FeatureList` in our main template, with a separate instance for each list.

`resources/views/app.blade.php`:

```
  <div id="app">
    ...
    <div class="container">
      ...
      <div class="lists">
        <feature-list title="Amenities">
          <div class="list-item" v-for="amenity in amenities">
            <i class="fa fa-lg" :class="amenity.icon"></i>
            <span>@{{ amenity.title }}</span>
          </div>
        </feature-list>
        <feature-list title="Prices">
```

```
        <div class="list-item" v-for="price in prices">
          @{{ price.title }}: <strong>@{{ price.value }}</strong>
        </div>
      </feature-list>
    </div>
  </div>
</div>
```

Scoped slots

The `FeatureList` component works but is quite weak. The majority of the content comes through the slot and so it seems like the parent is doing too much work, and the child too little. Given that there's repeated code in both declarations of the component (`<div class="list-item" v-for="...">`), it'd be good to delegate this to the child.

To allow our component template to be more versatile, we can use a *scoped slot* instead of a regular slot. Scoped slots allow you to pass a *template* to the slot instead of passing a rendered element. When this template is declared in the parent, it will have access to any props supplied in the child.

For example, a component `child` with a scoped slot might look like the following:

```
<div>
  <slot my-prop="Hello from child"></slot>
</div>
```

A parent that uses this component will declare a `template` element, which will have a property `slot-scope` that names an alias object. Any props added to the slot in the child template are available as properties of the alias object:

```
<child>
  <template slot-scope="props">
    <span>Hello from parent</span>
    <span>{{ props.my-prop }}</span>
  </template>
</child>
```

This renders as:

```
<div>
  <span>Hello from parent</span>
  <span>Hello from child</span>
</div>
```

Let's go through the steps of including a scoped slot with our `FeatureList` component. The goal is to be able to pass the list items array in as a prop and get the `FeatureList` component to iterate them. That way, `FeatureList` is taking ownership of any repeated functionality. The parent will then provide a template to define how each list item should display.

`resources/views/app.blade.php`:

```
<div class="lists">
  <feature-list title="Amenities" :items="amenities">
    <!--template will go here-->
  </feature-list>
  <feature-list title="Prices" :items="prices">
    <!--template will go here-->
  </feature-list>
</div>
```

Focusing now on the `FeatureList` component, follow these steps:

1. Add `items` to the props array in the configuration object
2. `items` will be array which we iterate inside the `<div class="content">` section
3. In the loop, `item` is an alias to any particular list item. We can create a slot and bind that list item to the slot using `v-bind="item"`. (We haven't used v-bind without an argument before, but this will bind the properties of an entire object to the element. This is useful as the amenities and prices objects have different properties and we now don't have to specify them.)

`resources/assets/components/FeatureList.vue`:

```
<template>
  <div>
    <hr>
    <div class="list">
      <div class="title"><strong>{{ title }}</strong></div>
      <div class="content">
        <div class="list-item" v-for="item in items">
          <slot v-bind="item"></slot>
        </div>
      </div>
    </div>
  </div>
</template>
<script>
  export default {
```

```
    props: ['title', 'items']
  }
</script>
<style>...</style>
```

Now we'll return to our view. Let's work on the amenities list first:

1. Declare a `template` element inside the `FeatureList` declaration.
2. The template must include the `slot-scope` property to which we assign an alias, `amenity`. This alias allows us to access the scoped props.
3. Inside the template, we can use exactly the same markup we had before to display our amenity list items.

`resources/views/app.blade.php`:

```
<feature-list title="Amenities" :items="amenities">
  <template slot-scope="amenity">
    <i class="fa fa-lg" :class="amenity.icon"></i>
    <span>@{{ amenity.title }}</span>
  </template>
</feature-list>
```

Here's the complete main template with prices as well.

`resources/views/app.blade.php`:

```
<div id="app">
  ...
  <div class="container">
    ...
    <div class="lists">
      <feature-list title="Amenities" :items="amenities">
        <template slot-scope="amenity">
          <i class="fa fa-lg" :class="amenity.icon"></i>
          <span>@{{ amenity.title }}</span>
        </template>
      </feature-list>
      <feature-list title="Prices" :items="prices">
        <template slot-scope="price">
          @{{ price.title }}: <strong>@{{ price.value }}</strong>
        </template>
      </feature-list>
    </div>
  </div>
</div>
```

Although this approach has just as much markup as before, it has delegated more common functionality to the component, which makes for a more robust design.

Expandable text

We created functionality back in Chapter 2, *Prototyping Vuebnb, Your First Vue.js Project*, to allow the **About** text to be partially contracted when the page loads and expanded to its full length by clicking a button. Let's abstract this functionality into a component as well:

```
$ touch resources/assets/components/ExpandableText.vue
```

Move all the markup, configuration, and CSS into the new component. Note that we use a slot for the text content.

resources/assets/components/ExpandableText.vue:

```
<template>
  <div>
    <p :class="{ contracted: contracted }">
      <slot></slot>
    </p>
    <button v-if="contracted" class="more" @click="contracted = false">
      + More
    </button>
  </div>
</template>
<script>
  export default {
    data() {
      return {
        contracted: true
      }
    }
  }
</script>
<style>
  p {
    white-space: pre-wrap;
  }

  .contracted {
    height: 250px;
    overflow: hidden;
  }
```

```
.about button.more {
  background: transparent;
  border: 0;
  color: #008489;
  padding: 0;
  font-size: 17px;
  font-weight: bold;
}

.about button.more:hover,
.about button.more:focus,
.about button.more:active {
  text-decoration: underline;
  outline: none;
}
</style>
```

Once you've imported this component in `resources/assets/js/app.js`, declare it in the main template, remembering to interpolate the `about` data property in the slot.

`resource/views/app.blade.php`:

```
<div id="app">
  <header-image>...</header-image>
  <div class="container">
    <div class="heading">...</div>
    <hr>
    <div class="about">
      <h3>About this listing</h3>
      <expandable-text>@{{ about }}</expandable-text>
    </div>
    ...
  </div>
</div>
```

With that done, most of the data and functionality of the Vuebnb client app has been abstracted into components. Let's take a look at `resources/assets/js/app.js` and see how bare it has become!

`resources/assets/js/app.js`:

```
...

import ImageCarousel from '../components/ImageCarousel.vue';
import ModalWindow from '../components/ModalWindow.vue';
import FeatureList from '../components/FeatureList.vue';
import HeaderImage from '../components/HeaderImage.vue';
import ExpandableText from '../components/ExpandableText.vue';

var app = new Vue({
  el: '#app',
  data: Object.assign(model, {}),
  components: {
    ImageCarousel,
    ModalWindow,
    FeatureList,
    HeaderImage,
    ExpandableText
  },
  methods: {
    openModal() {
      this.$refs.imagemodal.modalOpen = true;
    }
  }
});
```

Virtual DOM

Let's change tack now and discuss how Vue renders components. Take a look at this example:

```
Vue.component('my-component', {
  template: '<div id="my-component">My component</div>'
});
```

In order for Vue to be able to render this component to the page, it will first transform the template string into a JavaScript object using an internal template compiler library:

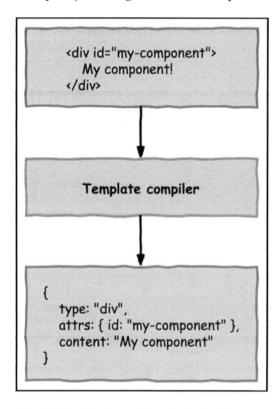

Figure 6.14. How the template compiler turns a template string into an object

Once the template has been compiled, any state or directives can easily be applied. For example, if the template includes a `v-for`, a simple for-loop can be used to multiply the nodes and interpolate the correct variables.

After that, Vue can interface with the DOM API to synchronize the page with the state of the component.

Render functions

Rather than supplying a string template for your component, you can instead supply a `render` function. Without understanding the syntax, you can probably tell from the following example that the `render` function is generating a semantically equivalent template to the string template in the previous example. Both define a `div` with an `id` attribute of `my-component` and with inner text of `My component`:

```
Vue.component ('my-component'</span>, {
  render(createElement) {
    createElement('div', {attrs:{id:'my-component'}}, 'My component');
    // Equivalent to <div id="my-component">My component</div>
  }
})
```

Render functions are more efficient because they don't require Vue to first compile the template string. The downside, though, is that writing a render function is not as easy or expressive as markup syntax, and, once you get a large template, will be difficult to work with.

Vue Loader

Wouldn't it be great if we could create HTML markup templates in development, then get Vue's template compiler to turn them into `render` functions as part of the build step? That would be the best of both worlds.

This is exactly what happens to single-file components when Webpack transforms them via *Vue Loader*. Take a look at the following snippet of the JavaScript bundle and you can see the `ImageCarousel` component after Webpack has transformed and bundled it:

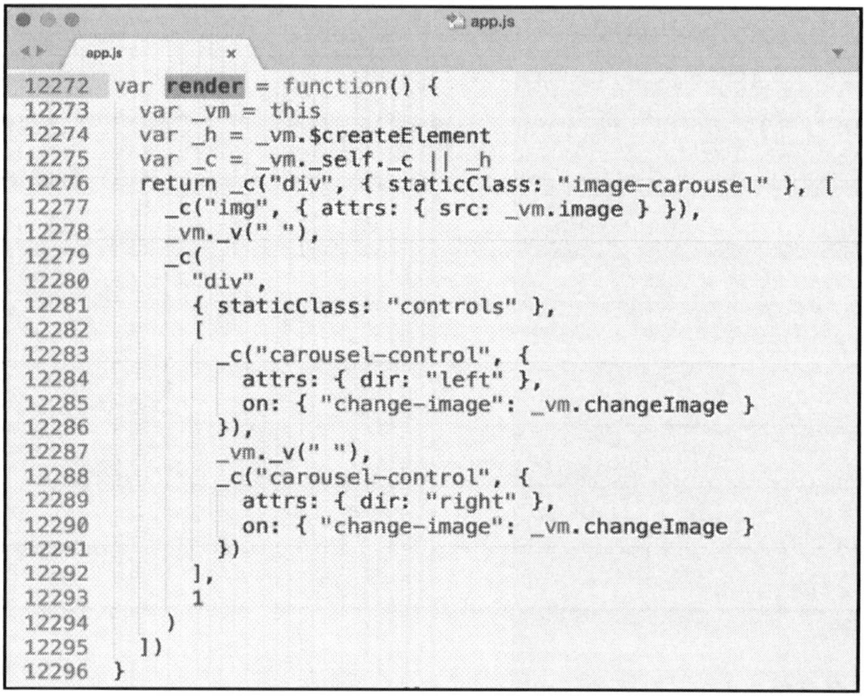

```
                                                    app.js
  ◀ ▶    app.js              ✕                                          ▼
12272  var render = function() {
12273    var _vm = this
12274    var _h = _vm.$createElement
12275    var _c = _vm._self._c || _h
12276    return _c("div", { staticClass: "image-carousel" }, [
12277      _c("img", { attrs: { src: _vm.image } }),
12278      _vm._v(" "),
12279      _c(
12280        "div",
12281        { staticClass: "controls" },
12282        [
12283          _c("carousel-control", {
12284            attrs: { dir: "left" },
12285            on: { "change-image": _vm.changeImage }
12286          }),
12287          _vm._v(" "),
12288          _c("carousel-control", {
12289            attrs: { dir: "right" },
12290            on: { "change-image": _vm.changeImage }
12291          })
12292        ],
12293        1
12294      )
12295    ])
12296  }
```

Figure 6.15. image-carousel component in the bundle file

Refactoring the main template as single-file component

The template for our app's root instance is the content within the `#app` element in the *app* view. A DOM template like this requires the Vue template compiler, just like any string template does.

If we were able to abstract this DOM template into an SFC as well, it would mean all our frontend app templates would be built as `render` functions and would not need to invoke the template compiler at runtime.

Let's create a new SFC for the main template and call it `ListingPage`, as this part of the app is our listing page:

```
$ touch resources/assets/components/ListingPage.vue
```

We'll move the main template, root configuration and any relevant CSS into this component. Take note of the following:

- We need to put the template inside a wrapping `div` as components must have a single root element
- We can now remove the @ escapes as this file won't be processed by Blade
- The component is now adjacent to the other components we created, so be sure to change the relative paths of the imports

`resource/assets/components/ListingPage.vue`:

```
<template>
  <div>
    <header-image
      :image-url="images[0]"
      @header-clicked="openModal"
    ></header-image>
    <div class="container">
      <div class="heading">
        <h1>{{ title }}</h1>
        <p>{{ address }}</p>
      </div>
      <hr>
      <div class="about">
        <h3>About this listing</h3>
        <expandable-text>{{ about }}</expandable-text>
      </div>
      <div class="lists">
        <feature-list title="Amenities" :items="amenities">
          <template slot-scope="amenity">
            <i class="fa fa-lg" :class="amenity.icon"></i>
            <span>{{ amenity.title }}</span>
          </template>
        </feature-list>
        <feature-list title="Prices" :items="prices">
          <template slot-scope="price">
            {{ price.title }}: <strong>{{ price.value }}</strong>
          </template>
        </feature-list>
      </div>
    </div>
  </div>
```

```
      <modal-window ref="imagemodal">
        <image-carousel :images="images"></image-carousel>
      </modal-window>
    </div>
  </template>
  <script>
    import { populateAmenitiesAndPrices } from '../js/helpers';

    let model = JSON.parse(window.vuebnb_listing_model);
    model = populateAmenitiesAndPrices(model);

    import ImageCarousel from './ImageCarousel.vue';
    import ModalWindow from './ModalWindow.vue';
    import FeatureList from './FeatureList.vue';
    import HeaderImage from './HeaderImage.vue';
    import ExpandableText from './ExpandableText.vue';

    export default {
      data() {
        return Object.assign(model, {});
      },
      components: {
        ImageCarousel,
        ModalWindow,
        FeatureList,
        HeaderImage,
        ExpandableText
      },
      methods: {
        openModal() {
          this.$refs.imagemodal.modalOpen = true;
        }
      }
    }
  </script>
  <style>
    .about {
      margin: 2em 0;
    }

    .about h3 {
      font-size: 22px;
    }
  </style>
```

Mounting the root-level component with a render function

Now the mount element in our main template will be empty. We need to declare the Listing component, but we don't want to do it in the view.

resources/views/app.blade.php:

```
<body>
<div id="toolbar">
  <img class="icon" src="{{ asset('images/logo.png') }}">
  <h1>vuebnb</h1>
</div>
<div id="app">
  <listing></listing>
</div>
<script src="{{ asset('js/app.js') }}"></script>
</body>
```

If we do it like that, we wouldn't fully eliminate all string and DOM templates from our app, so we'll keep the mount element empty.

resources/views/app.blade.php:

```
...

<div id="app"></div>

...
```

We can now declare Listing with a render function inside our root instance.

resources/assets/js/app.js:

```
import "core-js/fn/object/assign";
import Vue from 'vue';

import ListingPage from '../components/ListingPage.vue';

var app = new Vue({
  el: '#app',
  render: h => h(ListingPage)
});
```

To avoid getting side-tracked, I won't explain the syntax of `render` functions here, as this is the only one we'll write throughout the book. If you'd like to learn more about `render` functions, check out the Vue.js documentation at `https://vuejs.org/`.

Now that Vuebnb is no longer using string or DOM templates, we don't need the template compiler functionality anymore. There's a special build of Vue we can use which doesn't include it!

Vue.js builds

There are a number of different environments and use cases for running Vue.js. In one project, you might load Vue directly in the browser, in another you may load it on a Node.js server for the purpose of server rendering. As such, there are different *builds* of Vue provided so you can choose the most suitable one.

Looking in the *dist* folder of the Vue NPM package, we can see eight different Vue.js builds:

```
● ● ●                          📁 dist — -bash — 87×14
[Anthonys-MBP:vuebnb anthonygore$ cd node_modules/vue/dist/            ]
[Anthonys-MBP:dist anthonygore$ ls -l                                  ]
total 3784
-rw-r--r--  1 anthonygore  staff    4282 18 Aug 10:48 README.md
-rw-r--r--  1 anthonygore  staff  286869 28 Nov 04:43 vue.common.js
-rw-r--r--  1 anthonygore  staff  278610 23 Nov 06:13 vue.esm.browser.js
-rw-r--r--  1 anthonygore  staff  286852 28 Nov 04:43 vue.esm.js
-rw-r--r--  1 anthonygore  staff  284067 28 Nov 04:43 vue.js
-rw-r--r--  1 anthonygore  staff   86676 28 Nov 04:43 vue.min.js
-rw-r--r--  1 anthonygore  staff  208010 28 Nov 04:43 vue.runtime.common.js
-rw-r--r--  1 anthonygore  staff  207993 28 Nov 04:43 vue.runtime.esm.js
-rw-r--r--  1 anthonygore  staff  205957 28 Nov 04:43 vue.runtime.js
-rw-r--r--  1 anthonygore  staff   61382 28 Nov 04:43 vue.runtime.min.js
Anthonys-MBP:dist anthonygore$ ▊
```

Figure 6.16. The various builds in the node_modules/vue/dist folder

The Vue.js website provides a table to explain these eight different builds:

	UMD	CommonJS	ES Module
Full	**vue.js**	**vue.common.js**	**vue.esm.js**
Runtime-only	vue.runtime.js	vue.runtime.common.js	vue.runtime.esm.js
Full (production)	vue.min.js	-	-
Runtime-only (production)	vue.runtime.min.js	-	-

Module system

The columns of the table categorize the builds as either *UMD*, *CommonJS*, or *ES Module*. We discussed CommonJS and ES modules back in `Chapter 5`, *Integrating Laravel And Vue.js with Webpack*, but we didn't mention **UMD (Universal Module Definition)**. The main things you need to know about UMD is that it's yet another module pattern, and that it works well in a browser. UMD is the choice if you are directly linking to Vue in a `script` tag.

Production builds

The rows of the table are split into two types: full or runtime, and with or without production.

A *production* build is used in a deployed app, as opposed to one running in development. It has been minified, and any warnings, comments, or other development options are turned off or stripped out. The point is to make the build as small and secure as possible, which is what you'd want in production.

Note that there is only a UMD version of the production build as only UMD runs directly in a browser. CommonJS and ES Module are to be used in conjunction with a build tool, like Webpack, which provides its own production processing.

Full build vs runtime-only

As we've been discussing, Vue includes a template compiler for converting any string or DOM templates to render functions at runtime. The *full* build includes the template compiler and is what you would normally use. However, if you've already transformed your templates into render functions in development, you can use the *runtime-only* build, which drops the compiler and is about 30% smaller!

Selecting a build

A good build for Vuebnb is `vue.runtime.esm.js` since we're using Webpack and we don't need the template compiler. We could also use `vue.runtime.common.js`, but that wouldn't be consistent with our use of ES modules elsewhere in the project. In practice, though, there is no difference as Webpack will process them in the same way.

Remember that we include Vue at the top of our entry file with the statement `import Vue from 'vue'`. The last `'vue'` is an *alias* to the Vue build that Webpack resolves when it runs. Currently, this alias is defined within the default Mix configuration and is set to the build `vue.common.js`. We can override that configuration by adding the following to the bottom of our `webpack.mix.js` file.

`webpack.mix.js`:

```
...

mix.webpackConfig({
  resolve: {
    alias: {
      'vue$': 'vue/dist/vue.runtime.esm.js'
    }
  }
});
```

After a new build, we should expect to see a smaller bundle size due to the template compiler being removed. In the following screenshot, I've shown the bundle before and after I ran a `dev` build in a separate **Terminal** tab:

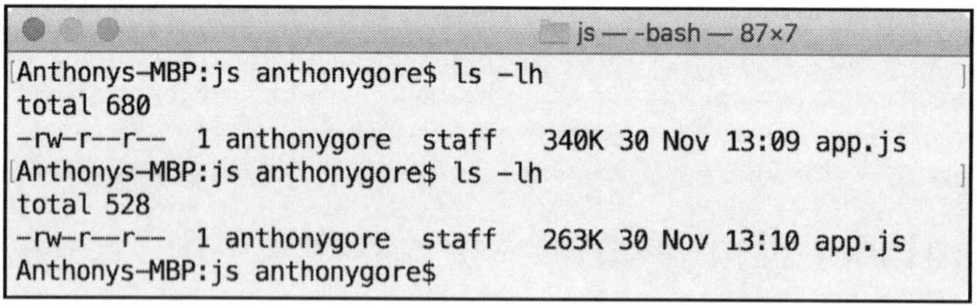

```
● ● ●                          js — -bash — 87×7
[Anthonys-MBP:js anthonygore$ ls -lh                                          ]
total 680
-rw-r--r--  1 anthonygore  staff   340K 30 Nov 13:09 app.js
[Anthonys-MBP:js anthonygore$ ls -lh                                          ]
total 528
-rw-r--r--  1 anthonygore  staff   263K 30 Nov 13:10 app.js
Anthonys-MBP:js anthonygore$
```

Figure 6.17. The difference between bundle sizes after applying the runtime-only build

Keep in mind that without the template compiler we can no longer provide string templates for our components. Doing so will cause an error at runtime. That shouldn't be a problem though since we've got the far more powerful option of SFCs.

Summary

In this chapter, we saw how components are used to create reusable custom elements. We then registered our first Vue.js components, defining them with template strings.

Next, we looked at component communication with props and custom events. We used this knowledge to build an image carousel within the listing page modal window.

In the second half of the chapter, we got an introduction to single-file components, which we used to refactor Vuebnb into a component-based architecture. We then learned how slots can help us make more versatile components by combining parent and child content.

Finally, we saw how the runtime-only build can be used to give a Vue app a smaller size.

In the next chapter, we will make Vuebnb a multi-page app by building a home page, and using Vue Router to allow navigation between pages without reloading.

7

Building a Multi-Page App with Vue Router

In the last chapter, we learned about Vue.js components and converted Vuebnb to a component-based architecture. Now that we've done this, we can easily add new pages to our app using Vue Router.

In this chapter, we'll create a home page for Vuebnb, including a gallery of clickable thumbnails that showcase the full set of mock listings.

Topics covered in this chapter:

- An explanation of what router libraries are and why they are a critical part of single-page applications
- An overview of Vue Router and its main features
- Installation and basic configuration of Vue Router
- Using the `RouterLink` and `RouterView` special components to manage page navigation
- Setting up AJAX with Vue to retrieve data from the web service without a page refresh
- Using route navigation guards to retrieve data before a new page is loaded

Single-page applications

Most websites are broken up into pages in order to make the information they contain easier to consume. Traditionally this is done with a server/client model, where each page must be loaded from the server with a different URL. To navigate to a new page, the browser must send a request to the URL of that page. The server will send the data back and the browser can unload the existing page and load the new one. For the average internet connection, this process will likely take a few seconds, during which the user must wait for the new page to load.

By using a powerful frontend framework and an AJAX utility, a different model is possible: the browser can load an initial web page, but navigating to new pages will not require the browser to unload the page and load a new one. Instead, any data required for new pages can be loaded asynchronously with AJAX. From a user's perspective, such a website would appear to have pages just like any other, but from a technical perspective, this site really only has one page. Hence the name, **Single-Page Application** (**SPA**).

The advantage of the Single-Page Application architecture is that it can create a more seamless experience for the user. Data for new pages must still be retrieved, and will therefore create some small disruption to the user's flow, but this disruption is minimized since the data retrieval can be done asynchronously and JavaScript can continue to run. Also, since SPA pages usually require less data due to the reuse of some page elements, page loading is quicker.

The disadvantage of the SPA architecture is that it makes the client app bulkier due to the added functionality, so gains from speeding up page changes may be negated by the fact that the user must download a large app on the first page load. Also, handling routes adds complexity to the app as multiple states must be managed, URLs must be handled, and a lot of default browser functionality must be recreated in the app.

Routers

If you are going with an SPA architecture and your app design includes multiple pages, you'll want to use a *router*. A router, in this context, is a library that will mimic browser navigation through JavaScript and various native APIs so that the user gets an experience similar to that of a traditional multi-page app. Routers will typically include functionality to:

- Handle navigation actions from within the page
- Match parts of the application to routes
- Manage the address bar
- Manage the browser history
- Manage scroll bar behavior

Vue Router

Some frontend frameworks, such as Angular or Ember, include a router library out-of-the-box. The philosophy guiding these frameworks is that the developer is better served with a complete, integrated solution for their SPA.

Others frameworks/libraries, such as React and Vue.js, do not include a router. Instead, you must install a separate library.

In the case of Vue.js, an official router library is available called *Vue Router*. This library has been developed by the Vue.js core team, so it is optimized for usage with Vue.js and makes full use of fundamental Vue features such as components and reactivity.

With Vue Router, different *pages* of the application are represented by different components. When you set up Vue Router, you will pass in configuration to tell it which URLs map to which component. Then, when a link is clicked in the app, Vue Router will swap the active component so as to match the new URL, for example:

```
let routes = [
  { path: '/', component: HomePage },
  { path: '/about', component: AboutPage },
  { path: '/contact', component: ContactPage }
];
```

Since rendering a component is an almost instantaneous process in normal circumstances, the transition between pages with Vue Router is as well. However, there are asynchronous hooks that can be invoked to give you the opportunity to load new data from the server, if your different pages require it.

Special components

When you install Vue Router, two components are registered globally for use throughout your app: `RouterLink` and `RouterView`.

`RouterLink` is generally used in place of `a` tags and gives your links access to the special features of Vue Router.

As explained, Vue Router will swap designated page components as a way of mimicking browser navigation. `RouterView` is the outlet in which this component swap takes place. Like a slot, you put it somewhere in your main page template. For example:

```
<div id="app">
  <header></header>
  <router-view>
    // This is where different page components display
  </router-view>
  <footer></footer>
</div>
```

Vuebnb routing

It was never a stated goal for Vuebnb to be a single-page application. Indeed, Vuebnb will deviate from pure SPA architecture as we'll see later in the book.

That said, incorporating Vue Router will be very beneficial to the user's experience of navigation in the app, so we'll add it to Vuebnb in this chapter.

Of course, if we're going to add a router, we'll need some extra pages! So far in the project, we've been working on the *listing* page of Vuebnb, but are yet to start work on the front page of the app. So in addition to installing Vue Router, we will start work on the Vuebnb home page, which displays thumbnails and links to all our mock listings:

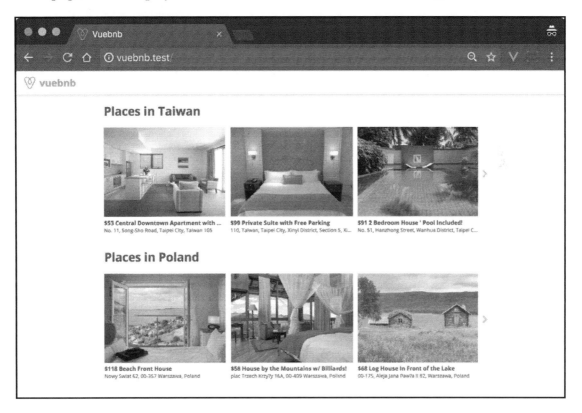

Figure 7.1. Front page of Vuebnb

Installing Vue Router

Vue Router is an NPM package and can be installed on the command line:

```
$  npm i --save-dev vue-router
```

Let's put our router configuration into a new file, `router.js`:

```
$ touch resources/assets/js/router.js
```

To add Vue Router to our project, we must import the library and then use the `Vue.use` API method to make Vue compatible with Vue Router. This will give Vue a new configuration property, `router`, that we can use to connect a new router.

We then create an instance of Vue Router with new `VueRouter()`.

`resources/assets/js/router.js`:

```
import Vue from 'vue';
import VueRouter from 'vue-router';
Vue.use(VueRouter);

export default new VueRouter();
```

By exporting our router instance from this new file, we've made it into a module that can be imported in `app.js`. If we name the imported module `router`, object destructuring can be used to succinctly connect it to our main configuration object.

`resources/assets/js/app.js`:

```
import "core-js/fn/object/assign";
import Vue from 'vue';

import ListingPage from '../components/ListingPage.vue';
import router from './router'

var app = new Vue({
  el: '#app',
  render: h => h(ListingPage),
  router
});
```

Creating routes

The most basic configuration for Vue Router is to provide a `routes` array, which maps URLs to the corresponding page components. This array will contain objects with at least two properties: `path` and `component`.

 Note that by *page components* I'm simply referring to any components that we've designated to represent a page in our app. They are regular components in every other way.

For now, we're only going to have two routes in our app, one for our home page and one for our listing page. The `HomePage` component doesn't exist yet, so we'll keep its route commented out until we create it.

`resources/assets/js/router.js`:

```
import ListingPage from '../components/ListingPage.vue';

export default new VueRouter({
  mode: 'history',
  routes: [
    // { path: '/', component: HomePage }, // doesn't exist yet!
    { path: '/listing/:listing', component: ListingPage }
  ]
});
```

You'll notice that the path for our `ListingPage` component contains a dynamic segment `:listing` so that this route will match paths including `/listing/1, listing/2 ... listing/whatever`.

 There are two modes for Vue Router: *hash* mode and *history* mode. Hash mode uses the URL hash to simulate a full URL so that the page won't be reloaded when the hash changes. History mode has *real* URLs and leverages the `history.pushState` API to change the URL without causing a page reload. The only downside to history mode is that URLs outside of the app, such as `/some/weird/path`, can't be handled by Vue and must be handled by the server. That's no problem for us, so we'll use history mode for Vuebnb.

App component

For our router to work, we need to declare a `RouterView` component somewhere in our page template. Otherwise, there's nowhere for the page components to render.

We'll slightly restructure our app to do this. As it is, the `ListingPage` component is the `root` component of the app, as it is at the top of the component hierarchy and loads all other components that we use.

Since we want the router to switch between `ListingPage` and `HomePage` based on the URL, we need another component to be above `ListingPage` in the hierarchy and handle this work. We'll call this new root component `App`:

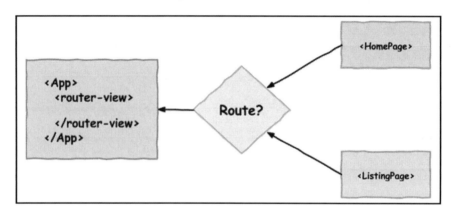

Figure 7.2. The relationship between App, ListingPage, and HomePage

Let's create the `App` component file:

```
$ touch resources/assets/components/App.vue
```

The root instance of Vue should render this to the page when it loads, instead of `ListingPage`.

resources/assets/js/app.js:

```
import App from '../components/App.vue';

...

var app = new Vue({
  el: '#app',
  render: h => h(App),
```

```
    router
});
```

The following is the content of the App component. I've added the
special RouterView component into the template, which is the outlet where either
the HomePage or ListingPage component will render.

You'll also notice I've moved the toolbar from app.blade.php into the template of App.
This is so the toolbar is in the domain of Vue; before it was outside of the mount point and
therefore untouchable by Vue. I've done this so that later we can make the main logo a link
to the home page using RouterLink, as this is a convention for most websites. I've moved
any toolbar related CSS into the style element as well.

resources/assets/components/App.vue:

```
<template>
  <div>
    <div id="toolbar">
      <img class="icon" src="/images/logo.png">
      <h1>vuebnb</h1>
    </div>
    <router-view></router-view>
  </div>
</template>
<style>
  #toolbar {
    display: flex;
    align-items: center;
    border-bottom: 1px solid #e4e4e4;
    box-shadow: 0 1px 5px rgba(0, 0, 0, 0.1);
  }

  #toolbar .icon {
    height: 34px;
    padding: 16px 12px 16px 24px;
    display: inline-block;
  }

  #toolbar h1 {
    color: #4fc08d;
    display: inline-block;
    font-size: 28px;
    margin: 0;
  }
</style>
```

With that done, if you now navigate the browser to a URL like /listing/1, you'll see everything looks the same as it did before. However, if you look at Vue Devtools, you'll see the component hierarchy has changed, reflecting the addition of the App component.

There's also an indicator, which tells us that the ListingPage component is the active page component for Vue Router:

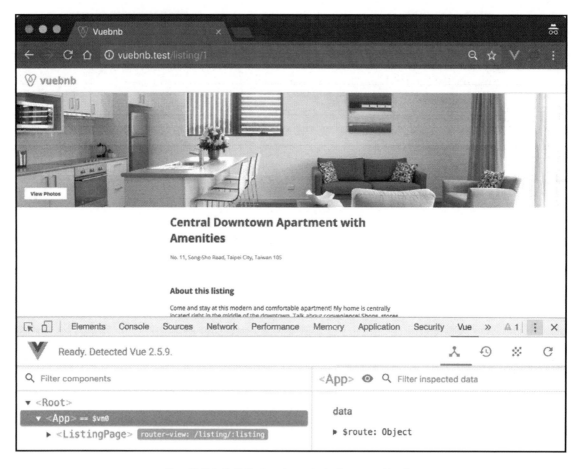

Figure 7.3. /listing/1 with Vue Devtools open, showing the component hierarchy

Home page

Let's start work on our home page now. We'll first create a new component, `HomePage`:

```
$ touch resources/assets/components/HomePage.vue
```

For now, let's add placeholder markup to the component before we set it up properly.

`resources/assets/components/HomePage.vue`:

```
<template>
  <div>Vuebnb home page</div>
</template>
```

Be sure to import this component in the `router` file, and uncomment the route where it's used.

`resources/assets/js/router.js`:

```
....

import HomePage from '../components/HomePage.vue';
import ListingPage from '../components/ListingPage.vue';

export default new VueRouter({
  mode: 'history',
  routes: [
    { path: '/', component: HomePage },
    { path: '/listing/:listing', component: ListingPage }
  ]
});
```

You might be tempted to test this new route out by putting the URL `http://vuebnb.test/` into your browser address bar. You'll find, though, that it results in a 404 error. Remember, we still haven't created a route for this on our server. Although Vue is managing routes from *within* the app, any address bar navigation requests must be served from Laravel.

Let's now create a link to our home page in the toolbar by using the RouterLink component. This component is like an enhanced a tag. For example, if you give your routes a name property, you can simply use the to prop rather than having to supply an href. Vue will resolve this to the correct URL on render.

resources/assets/components/App.vue:

```
<div id="toolbar">
  <router-link :to="{ name: 'home' }">
    <img class="icon" src="/images/logo.png">
    <h1>vuebnb</h1>
  </router-link>
</div>
```

Let's also add name properties to our routes for this to work.

resources/assets/js/app.js:

```
routes: [
  { path: '/', component: HomePage, name: 'home' },
  { path: '/listing/:listing', component: ListingPage, name: 'listing' }
]
```

We'll also have to modify our CSS now since we now have another tag wrapped around our logo. Modify the toolbar CSS rules to match those that follow.

resources/assets/components/App.vue:

```
<template>...</template>
<style>
  #toolbar {
    border-bottom: 1px solid #e4e4e4;
    box-shadow: 0 1px 5px rgba(0, 0, 0, 0.1);
  }

  ...

  #toolbar a {
    display: flex;
    align-items: center;
    text-decoration: none;
  }
</style>
```

Let's now open a listing page, such as /listing/1. If you inspect the DOM, you'll see that our toolbar now has a new a tag inside it with a correctly resolved link back to the home page:

Figure 7.4. The toolbar is a link back to the home page via the RouterLink element

If you click that link, you'll be taken to the home page! Remember, the *page* hasn't actually changed; Vue router simply swapped `ListingPage` for `HomePage` within `RouterView`, and also updated the browser URL via the `history.pushState` API:

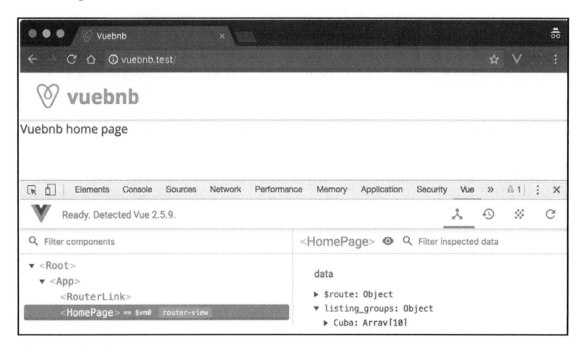

Figure 7.5. Home page with Vue Devtools showing component hierarchy

Home route

Let's now add a server-side route for the home page so that we can load our app from the root path. This new route will point to a `get_home_web` method in our `ListingController` class.

routes/web.php:

```php
<?php

Route::get('/', 'ListingController@get_home_web');

Route::get('/listing/{listing}', 'ListingController@get_listing_web');
```

Going to the controller now, we'll make it so the `get_home_web` method returns the `app` view, just as it does for the listing web route. The `app` view includes a template variable model which we use to pass through the initial application state, as set up in `Chapter 5`, *Integrating Laravel and Vue.js with Webpack*. For now, just assign an empty array as a placeholder.

`app/Http/Controllers/ListingController.php`:

```
public function get_home_web()
{
  return view('app', ['model' => []]);
}
```

With that done, we can now navigate to `http://vuebnb.test/` and it will work! When the Vue app is bootstrapped, Vue Router will check the URL value and, seeing that the path is `/`, will load the `HomePage` component inside the `RouterView` outlet for the first rendering of the app.

Viewing the source of this page, it's exactly the same page as we get when we load the listing route since it's the same view, that is, `app.blade.php`. The only difference is that the initial state is an empty array:

Figure 7.6. Page source of vuebnb.test with empty initial state

Initial state

Just like our listing page, our home page will need initial state. Looking at the finished product, we can see that the home page displays a summary of all our mock listings with a thumbnail image, a title, and short description:

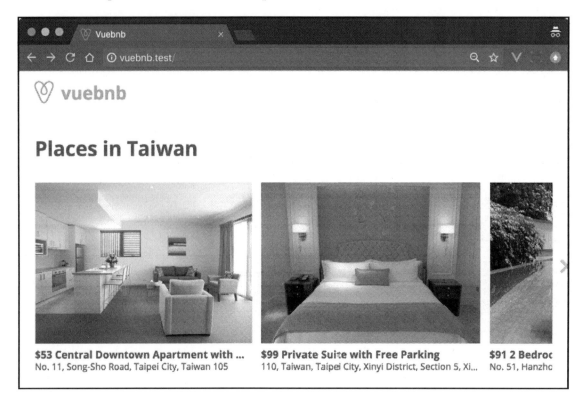

Figure 7.7. Completed home page, focusing on listings

Refactoring

Before we inject the initial state into the home page, let's do a small refactoring of the code including renaming some variables and restructuring some methods. This will ensure that the code semantics reflect the changing requirements and keep our code readable and easy to understand.

Firstly, let's rename our template variable from $model to the more general $data.

resources/views/app.blade.php:

```
<script type="text/javascript">
  window.vuebnb_server_data = "{!! addslashes(json_encode($data)) !!}"
</script>
```

In our listing controller, we're now going to abstract any common logic from our listing route methods into a new helper method called get_listing. In this helper method, we will nest the Listing model inside a Laravel Collection under the listing key. Collection is an array-like wrapper for Eloquent models that offers a bunch of handy methods that we'll be putting to use shortly. get_listing will include logic from the add_image_urls helper method, which can now safely be deleted.

We'll also need to reflect the change to our template variable when we call the view method.

app/Http/Controllers/ListingController.php:

```
private function get_listing($listing)
{
  $model = $listing->toArray();
  for($i = 1; $i <=4; $i++) {
    $model['image_' . $i] = asset(
      'images/' . $listing->id . '/Image_' . $i . '.jpg'
    );
  }
  return collect(['listing' => $model]);
}

public function get_listing_api(Listing $listing)
{
  $data = $this->get_listing($listing);
  return response()->json($data);
}

public function get_listing_web(Listing $listing)
{
  $data = $this->get_listing($listing);
  return view('app', ['data' => $data]);
}

public function get_home_web()
```

```
{
  return view('app', ['data' => []]);
}
```

Finally, we'll need to update our `ListingPage` component to reflect the new name and structure of the server data we're injecting.

`resources/assets/components/ListingPage.vue`:

```
<script>
  let serverData = JSON.parse(window.vuebnb_server_data);
  let model = populateAmenitiesAndPrices(serverData.listing);

  ...
</script>
```

Home page initial state

Using Eloquent ORM, it's trivial to retrieve all our listing entries using the method `Listing::all`. Multiple `Model` instances are returned by this method within a `Collection` object.

Note that we don't need all the fields on the model, for example, `amenities`, `about`, and so on are not used in the listing summaries that populate the home page. To ensure our data is as lean as possible, we can pass an array of fields to the `Listing::all` method that will tell the database to only include those fields explicitly mentioned.

`app/Http/Controllers/ListingController.php`:

```
public function get_home_web()
{
  $collection = Listing::all([
    'id', 'address', 'title', 'price_per_night'
  ]);
  $data = collect(['listings' => $collection->toArray()]);
  return view('app', ['data' => $data]);
}

/*
  [
    "listings" => [
      0 => [
        "id" => 1,
        "address" => "...",
        "title" => "...",
```

```
            "price_per_night" => "..."
        ]
        1 => [ ... ]
        ...
        29 => [ ... ]
    ]
  ]
*/
```

Adding the thumbnail

Each mock listing has a thumbnail version of the first image, which can be used for the listing summary. The thumbnail is much smaller than the image we use for the header of the listing page and is ideal for the listing summaries on the home page. The URL for the thumbnail is public/images/{x}/Image_1_thumb.jpg where {x} is the ID of the listing.

Collection objects have a helper method, transform, that we can use to add the thumbnail image URL to each listing. transform accepts a callback closure function that is called once per item, allowing you to modify that item and return it to the collection without fuss.

app/Http/Controllers/ListingController.php:

```php
public function get_home_web()
{
  $collection = Listing::all([
    'id', 'address', 'title', 'price_per_night'
  ]);
  $collection->transform(function ($listing) {
    $listing->thumb = asset(
      'images/' . $listing->id . '/Image_1_thumb.jpg'
    );
    return $listing;
  });
  $data = collect(['listings' => $collection->toArray()]);
  return view('app', ['data' => $data]);
}

/*
  [
    "listings" => [
      0 => [
        "id" => 1,
        "address" => "...",
```

```
        "title" => "...",
        "price_per_night" => "...",
        "thumb" => "..."
    ]
    1 => [ ... ]
    ...
    29 => [ ... ]
  ]
]
*/
```

Receiving in the client

With the initial state now ready, let's add it to our `HomePage` component. Before we can use it though there's an additional aspect we need to consider: the listing summaries are grouped by *country*. Look again at *Figure 7.7* to see how these groups are displayed.

After we've parsed our injected data, let's modify the object so the listings are grouped by country. We can easily create a function to do this, as every listing object has an `address` property in which the country is always explicitly named, for example, *No. 51, Hanzhong Street, Wanhua District, Taipei City, Taiwan 108*.

To save you having to write this function, I have supplied one in the `helpers` module called `groupByCountry` which can be imported at the top of the component configuration.

`resources/assets/components/HomePage.vue`:

```
...

<script>
  import { groupByCountry } from '../js/helpers';

  let serverData = JSON.parse(window.vuebnb_server_data);
  let listing_groups = groupByCountry(serverData.listings);

  export default {
    data() {
      return { listing_groups }
    }
  }
</script>
```

We'll now see through Vue Devtools that `HomePage` has successfully loaded the listing summaries, grouped by country and ready for display:

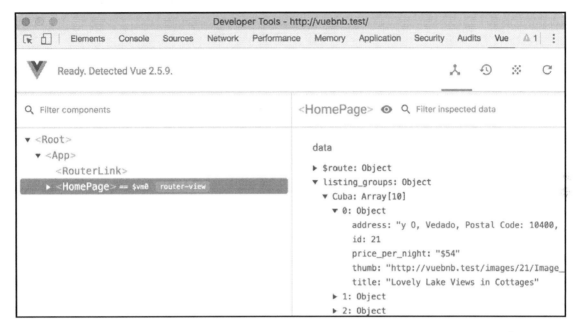

Figure 7.8. Vue Devtools showing the state of the HomePage component

ListingSummary component

Now that the `HomePage` component has data available, we can work on displaying it.

To begin with, clear out the existing content of the component and replace it with a `div`. This `div` will feature a `v-for` directive to iterate through each of our listing groups. Since `listing_groups` is an object with key/value pairs, we'll give our `v-for` two aliases: `group` and `country`, which are the value and key of each object item respectively.

We will interpolate `country` inside a heading. `group` will be used in the next section.

`resources/assets/components/HomePage.vue`:

```
<template>
  <div>
    <div v-for="(group, country) in listing_groups">
      <h1>Places in {{ country }}</h1>
```

```
    <div>
        Each listing will go here
    </div>
  </div>
 </div>
</template>
<script>...</script>
```

This is what the home page will now look like:

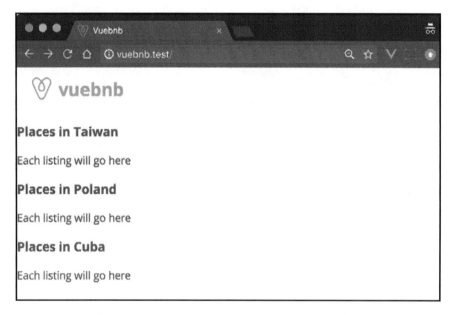

Figure 7.9. Iterating the listing summary groups in the HomePage component

Since each listing summary will be of some complexity, we'll create a separate component, ListingSummary, for displaying them:

```
$ touch resources/assets/components/ListingSummary.vue
```

Let's declare ListingSummary within our HomePage template. We'll again use a v-for directive to iterate group, an array, creating a new instance of ListingSummary for each member. The data for each member will be bound to a single prop, listing.

resources/assets/components/HomePage.vue:

```
<template>
 <div>
```

```
      <div v-for="(group, country) in listing_groups">
        <h1>Places in {{ country }}</h1>
        <div class="listing-summaries">
          <listing-summary
            v-for="listing in group"
            :key="listing.id"
            :listing="listing"
          ></listing-summary>
        </div>
      </div>
    </div>
  </template>
  <script>
    import { groupByCountry } from '../js/helpers';
    import ListingSummary from './ListingSummary.vue';

    let serverData = JSON.parse(window.vuebnb_server_data);
    let listing_groups = groupByCountry(serverData.listings);

    export default {
      data() {
        return { listing_groups }
      },
      components: {
        ListingSummary
      }
    }
  </script>
```

Let's create some simple content for the ListingSummary component, just to test our approach.

resources/assets/components/ListingSummary.vue:

```
  <template>
    <div class="listing-summary">
      {{ listing.address }}
    </div>
  </template>
  <script>
    export default {
      props: [ 'listing' ],
    }
  </script>
```

Refreshing our page, we'll now see this prototype of our listing summaries:

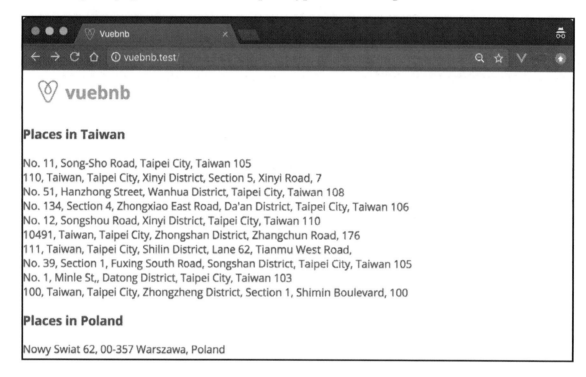

Figure 7.10. Prototype of ListingSummary component

Since this approach is working, let's now complete the structure of
the `ListingSummary` component. To display the thumbnail, we bind it as a background
image for a fixed width/height `div`. We'll also need some CSS rules to get this displaying
nicely.

`resources/assets/components/ListingSummary.vue`:

```
<template>
  <div class="listing-summary">
    <div class="wrapper">
      <div class="thumbnail" :style="backgroundImageStyle"></div>
      <div class="info title">
        <span>{{ listing.price_per_night }}</span>
        <span>{{ listing.title }}</span>
      </div>
      <div class="info address">{{ listing.address }}</div>
    </div>
  </div>
```

```
</template>
<script>
  export default {
    props: [ 'listing' ],
    computed: {
      backgroundImageStyle() {
        return {
          'background-image': `url("${this.listing.thumb}")`
        }
      }
    }
  }
</script>
<style>
  .listing-summary {
    flex: 0 0 auto;
  }

  .listing-summary a {
    text-decoration: none;
  }

  .listing-summary .wrapper {
    max-width: 350px;
    display: block;
  }

  .listing-summary .thumbnail {
    width: 350px;
    height: 250px;
    background-size: cover;
    background-position: center;
  }

  .listing-summary .info {
    color: #484848;
    word-wrap: break-word;
    letter-spacing: 0.2px;
    white-space: nowrap;
    overflow: hidden;
    text-overflow: ellipsis;
  }

  .listing-summary .info.title {
    padding-top: 5px;
    font-weight: 700;
    font-size: 16px;
    line-height: 24px;
```

```
    }

    .listing-summary .info.address {
      font-size: 14px;
      line-height: 18px;
    }
</style>
```

After you add that code, your listing summaries will look like this:

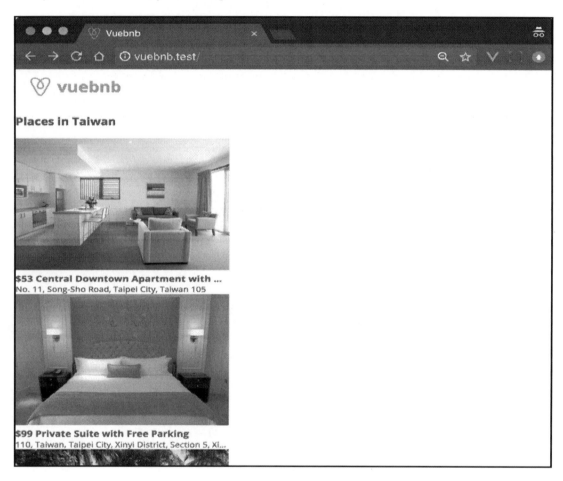

Figure 7.11. Complete listing summaries being displayed

We gave each listing summary a fixed width/height so that we could display them in a neat grid. Currently, they're displaying in one tall column, so let's add some CSS flex rules to the HomePage component to get the summaries into rows.

We'll add a class `listing-summary-group` to the element that wraps the summaries. We'll also add a class `home-container` to the root `div` to constrain the width of the page and center the content.

`resources/assets/components/HomePage.vue`:

```
<template>
  <div class="home-container">
    <div
      v-for="(group, country) in listing_groups"
      class="listing-summary-group"
    >
      ...
    </div>
  </div>
</template>
<script>...</script>
<style>
  .home-container {
    margin: 0 auto;
    padding: 0 25px;
  }

  @media (min-width: 1131px) {
    .home-container {
      width: 1080px;
    }
  }

  .listing-summary-group {
    padding-bottom: 20px;
  }

  .listing-summaries {
    display: flex;
    flex-direction: row;
    justify-content: space-between;
    overflow: hidden;
  }
  .listing-summaries > .listing-summary {
    margin-right: 15px;
  }
  .listing-summaries > .listing-summary:last-child {
```

```
      margin-right: 0;
   }
</style>
```

Finally, we'll need to add a rule to prevent the listings from forcing the edge of the document to exceed the viewport. Add this to the main CSS file.

`resources/assets/css/style.css`:

```
html, body {
  overflow-x: hidden;
}
```

With that, we get a nice looking home page:

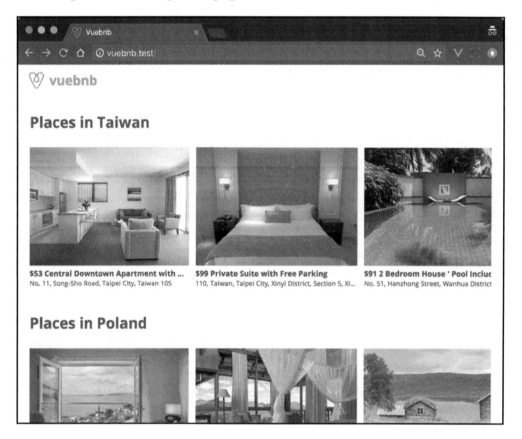

Figure 7.12. Listing summaries in rows

You'll notice that at full page width, we can only see three listings from each country group. The other seven are hidden by the CSS `overflow: hidden` rule. Soon, we'll be adding image slider functionality to each group to allow the user to browse through all the listings.

In-app navigation

If we use the address bar of the browser to navigate to the home page, `http://vuebnb.test/`, it works because Laravel is now serving a page at this route. But, if we navigate to the home page *from the listing page*, there's no longer any page content:

Figure 7.13. Empty home page after navigating from listing page

We currently don't have any links to the listing page from the home page, but if we did, we'd experience a similar issue.

The reason is that our page components currently get their initial state from the data we've injected into the head of the document. If we navigate to a different page using Vue Router, which doesn't invoke a page refresh, the next page component will have the wrong initial state merged in.

We need to improve our architecture so that when a page is navigated to we check if the model injected into the head matches the current page. To facilitate this, we'll add a `path` property to the model and check that it matches the active URL. If not, we'll use AJAX to get the right data from the web service:

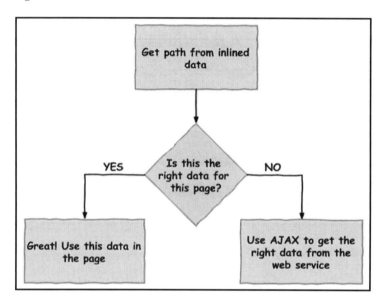

Figure 7.14. How a page decides what data it needs

 If you're interested in reading more about this design pattern, check out the article *Avoid This Common Anti-Pattern In Full-Stack Vue/Laravel Apps* at `https://vuejsdevelopers.com/2017/08/06/vue-js-laravel-full-stack-ajax/`.

Adding a path to the model

Let's go to the listing controller and add a `path` property to the data injected into the head of our view. To do this, we'll add a helper function called `add_meta_data` which will add the path, as well as some other meta properties in later chapters.

Note that the path of the current route can be determined by the Request object. This object can be declared as the last argument of any route-handling functions and is provided in each request by the service container.

app/Http/Controllers/ListingController.php:

```
...

private function add_meta_data($collection, $request)
{
  return $collection->merge([
    'path' => $request->getPathInfo()
  ]);
}

public function get_listing_web(Listing $listing, Request $request)
{
  $data = $this->get_listing($listing);
  $data = $this->add_meta_data($data, $request);
  return view('app', ['data' => $data]);
}

public function get_home_web(Request $request)
{
  $collection = Listing::all([
    'id', 'address', 'title', 'price_per_night'
  ]);
  $collection->transform(function($listing) {
    $listing->thumb = asset(
      'images/' . $listing->id . '/Image_1_thumb.jpg'
    );
    return $listing;
  });
  $data = collect(['listings' => $collection->toArray()]);
  $data = $this->add_meta_data($data, $request);
  return view('app', ['data' => $data]);
}

/*
  [
    "listings" => [ ... ],
    "path" => "/"
  ]
*/
```

Route navigation guards

Similar to lifecycle hooks, *navigation guards* allow you to intercept Vue Router navigations at a particular point in their life cycle. These guards can be applied to a specific component, a specific route, or to all routes.

For example, `afterEach` is the navigation guard called after any route is navigated away from. You might use this hook to store analytics information, for example:

```
router.afterEach((to, from) => {
  storeAnalytics(userId, from.path);
})
```

We can use the `beforeRouteEnter` navigation guard to fetch data from our web service if the data in the head is unsuitable. Consider the following pseudo-code for how we might implement this:

```
beforeRouteEnter(to, from, next) {
  if (to !== injectedData.path) {
    getDataWithAjax.then(data => {
      applyData(data)
    })
  } else {
    applyData(injectedData)
  }
  next()
}
```

next

An important feature of navigation guards is that they will halt navigation until the `next` function is called. This allows asynchronous code to be executed before the navigation is resolved:

```
beforeRouteEnter(to, from, next) {
  new Promise(...).then(() => {
    next();
  });
}
```

You can pass `false` to the `next` function to prevent a navigation, or you can pass a different route to redirect it. If you don't pass anything, the navigation is considered confirmed.

The `beforeRouteEnter` guard is a special case. Firstly, `this` is undefined within it since it is called before the next page component has been created:

```
beforeRouteEnter(to, from, next) {
  console.log(this); // undefined
}
```

However, the `next` function in `beforeRouteEnter` can accept a callback function as an argument, for example, `next(component => { ... });` where `component` is the page component instance.

This callback is not triggered until the route is confirmed and the component instance has been created. Due to how JavaScript closures work, the callback will have access to the scope of the surrounding code where it was called:

```
beforeRouteEnter(to, from, next) {
  var data = { ... }
  next(component => {
    component.$data = data;
  });
}
```

HomePage component

Let's add `beforeRouteEnter` to the `HomePage` component. Firstly, move any logic for retrieving data from the document head into the hook. We then check the `path` property of the data to see if it matches the current route. If so, we call `next` and pass a callback function that applies the data to the component's instance. If not, we'll need to use AJAX to get the right data.

resources/assets/components/HomePage.vue:

```
export default {
  data() {
    return {
      listing_groups: []
    };
  },
  components: {
    ListingSummary
```

```
    },
    beforeRouteEnter(to, from, next) {
      let serverData = JSON.parse(window.vuebnb_server_data);
      if (to.path === serverData.path) {
        let listing_groups = groupByCountry(serverData.listings);
        next(component => component.listing_groups = listing_groups);
      } else {
        console.log('Need to get data with AJAX!')
        next(false);
      }
    }
  }
}
```

 I've added `listing_groups` as a data property. Before, we were applying our data to the component instance as it was created. Now, we're applying the data after the component is created. To set up reactive data, Vue must know the names of the data properties, so we initialize with an empty value and update it when the data needed is available.

Home API endpoint

We'll now implement the AJAX functionality. Before we do, though, we need to add a home page endpoint to our web service.

Let's first add the home API route.

routes/api.php:

```
    ...

    Route::get('/', 'ListingController@get_home_api');
```

Looking now at the `ListingController` class, we'll abstract the bulk of the logic from `get_home_web` into a new function, `get_listing_summaries`. We'll then use this function in the `get_home_api` method and return a JSON response.

app/Http/Controllers/ListingController.php:

```
    private function get_listing_summaries()
    {
      $collection = Listing::all([
        'id', 'address', 'title', 'price_per_night'
      ]);
      $collection->transform(function($listing) {
        $listing->thumb = asset(
```

```
      'images/' . $listing->id . '/Image_1_thumb.jpg'
    );
    return $listing;
  });
  return collect(['listings' => $collection->toArray()]);
}

public function get_home_web(Request $request)
{
  $data = $this->get_listing_summaries();
  $data = $this->add_meta_data($data, $request);
  return view('app', ['data' => $data]);
}

public function get_home_api()
{
  $data = $this->get_listing_summaries();
  return response()->json($data);
}
```

Axios

To perform AJAX requests to the web service, we'll use the Axios HTTP client, which is included with Laravel's default frontend code. Axios has a very simple API allowing us to make requests to a GET URL like this:

```
axios.get('/my-url');
```

Axios is a Promise-based library, so in order to retrieve the response, you can simply chain a then callback:

```
axios.get('/my-url').then(response => {
  console.log(response.data); // Hello from my-url
});
```

As the Axios NPM package is already installed, we can go ahead and import the HomePage component. We can then use it to perform the request to the home API endpoint, /api/. In the then callback, we apply the returned data to the component instance exactly as we did with the inlined model.

resources/assets/components/HomePage.vue:

```
...
import axios from 'axios';
```

```
export default {
  data() { ... },
  components: { ... },
  beforeRouteEnter (to, from, next) {
    let serverData = JSON.parse(window.vuebnb_server_data);
    if (to.path === serverData.path) {
      let listing_groups = groupByCountry(serverData.listings);
      next(component => component.listing_groups = listing_groups);
    } else {
      axios.get(`/api/`).then(({ data }) => {
        let listing_groups = groupByCountry(data.listings);
        next(component => component.listing_groups = listing_groups);
      });
    }
  }
}
```

And with that, we can now navigate to the home page in two ways, either via the address bar, or by going from a link from the listing page. Either way, we get the right data!

Mixins

If you have any functionality that is common between components, you can put it in a mixin to avoid rewriting the same functionality.

A Vue mixin is an object in the same form as a component configuration object. To use it in a component, declare within an array and assign it to the configuration property mixin. When this component is instantiated, any configuration options of the mixin will be merged with what you've declared on the component:

```
var mixin = {
  methods: {
    commonMethod() {
      console.log('common method');
    }
  }
};

Vue.component('a', {
  mixins: [ mixin ]
});

Vue.component('b', {
  mixins: [ mixin ]
  methods: {
```

```
      otherMethod() { ... }
    }
  });
```

You might be wondering what happens if the component configuration has a method or other property that conflicts with the `mixin`. The answer is that `mixins` have a *merging strategy* that determines the priority of any conflicts. Generally, the component's specified configuration will take precedence. The details of the merging strategy are explained in the Vue.js documentation at `http://vuejs.org`.

Moving the solution to a mixin

Let's generalize the solution for getting the right data to the home page so that we can use it on the listing page as well. To do this, we'll move Axios and the `beforeRouteEnter` hook from the `HomePage` component into a mixin that can then be added to both page components:

```
$ touch resources/assets/js/route-mixin.js
```

At the same time, let's improve the code by removing the repetition of the `next` function call. To do this, we'll create a new method, `getData`, which will be responsible for figuring out where to get the right data for the page and also for getting it. Note that this method will be asynchronous since it may need to wait for AJAX to resolve, so it will return a Promise rather than an actual value. This Promise is then resolved within the navigation guard.

resources/assets/js/route-mixin.js:

```
  import axios from 'axios';

  function getData(to) {
    return new Promise((resolve) => {
      let serverData = JSON.parse(window.vuebnb_server_data);
      if (!serverData.path || to.path !== serverData.path) {
        axios.get(`/api${to.path}`).then(({ data }) => {
          resolve(data);
        });
      } else {
        resolve(serverData);
      }
    });
  }

  export default {
```

```
    beforeRouteEnter: (to, from, next) => {
      getData(to).then((data) => {
        next(component => component.assignData(data));
      });
    }
};
```

We don't need a polyfill for Promise as that is already supplied in the
`Axios` library.

assignData

You'll notice that within the `next` callback we call a method on the subject component
called `assignData`, passing the data object as an argument. We'll need to implement
the `assignData` method in any component that uses this `mixin`. We do it this way so that
the component can process the data, if necessary, before it is applied to the component
instance. For example, the `ListingPage` component must process the data via
the `populateAmenitiesAndPrices` helper function.

`resources/assets/components/ListingPage.vue`:

```
...

import routeMixin from '../js/route-mixin';

export default {
  mixins: [ routeMixin ],
  data() {
    return {
      title: null,
      about: null,
      address: null,
      amenities: [],
      prices: [],
      images: []
    }
  },
  components: { ... },
  methods: {
    assignData({ listing }) {
      Object.assign(this.$data, populateAmenitiesAndPrices(listing));
    },
    openModal() {
```

```
                this.$refs.imagemodal.modalOpen = true;
            }
        }
    }
```

We'll also need to add `assignData` to the `HomePage` component.

`resources/assets/components/HomePage.vue`:

```
<script>
  import { groupByCountry } from '../js/helpers';
  import ListingSummary from './ListingSummary.vue';

  import axios from 'axios';
  import routeMixin from '../js/route-mixin';

  export default {
    mixins: [ routeMixin ],
    data() { ... },
    methods: {
      assignData({ listings }) {
        this.listing_groups = groupByCountry(listings);
      },
    },
    components: { ... }
  }
</script>
```

Linking to the listing page

The above should work but we can't test it since there are not yet any in-app links to the listing page!

Each of our `ListingSummary` instances represents a single listing, and should therefore be a clickable link to the page for that listing. Let's use the `RouterLink` component to achieve this. Note that the object we bind to the `to` prop includes the name of the route as well as a `params` object which includes a value for the dynamic segment of the route, the listing ID.

`resources/assets/components/ListingSummary.vue`:

```
<div class="listing-summary">
  <router-link :to="{ name: 'listing', params: { listing: listing.id } }">
    <div class="wrapper">
      <div class="thumbnail" :style="backgroundImageStyle"></div>
      <div class="info title">
```

```
            <span>{{ listing.price_per_night }}</span>
            <span>{{ listing.title }}</span>
          </div>
          <div class="info address">{{ listing.address }}</div>
        </div>
      </router-link>
    </div>
```

With that done, the listing summaries will now be links. Clicking from one to the listing page, we see this:

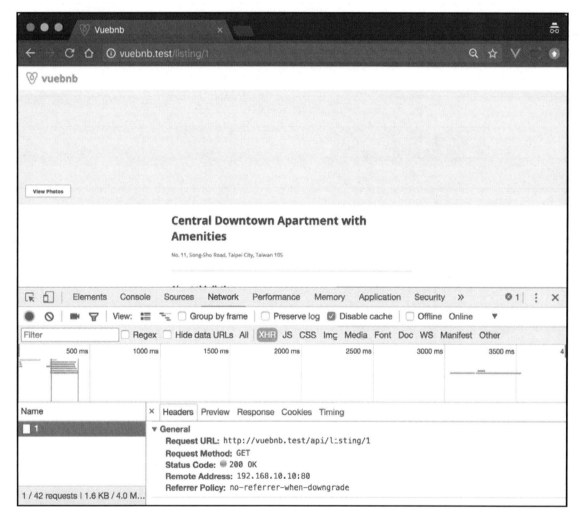

Figure 7.15. Successful AJAX call after navigating to listing page

We can see in *Figure 7.15* that the AJAX call to the listing API was successful and returned the data we wanted. If we also look at the Vue Devtools tab, as well as the Dev Tools console, we can see the correct data in our component instance. The problem is that we now have an unhandled 404 error for the header image:

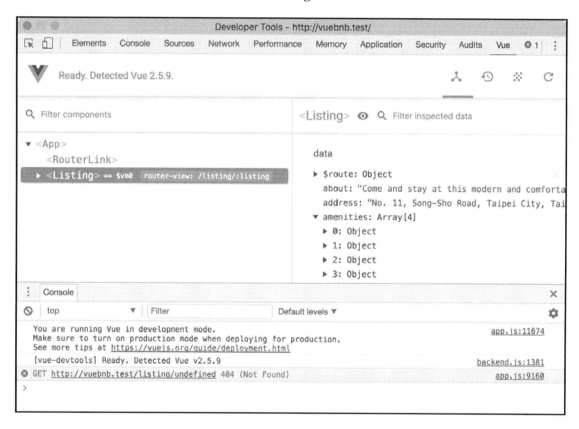

Figure 7.16. Dev Tools console showing error

The reason for this is that the component's first render occurs *before* the callback in the `next` hook is called. This means that the initialization values for the component data are used in the first render.

resources/assets/components/ListingPage.vue:

```
data() {
  return {
    title: null,
    about: null,
    address: null,
```

```
        amenities: [],
        prices: [],
        images: []
     }
  },
```

In the `HeaderImage` declaration, we bind the first image like this: `:image-url="images[0]"`. Since the array is initially empty, this will be an undefined value and results in the unhandled error.

The explanation is complex, but the fix is easy: just add a `v-if` to `header-image`, ensuring it won't render until valid data is available.

`resources/assets/components/ListingPage.vue`:

```
<header-image
  v-if="images[0]"
  :image-url="images[0]"
  @header-clicked="openModal"
></header-image>
```

Scroll behavior

Another aspect of website navigation that the browser automatically manages is *scroll behavior*. For example, if you scroll to the bottom of a page, then navigate to a new page, the scroll position is reset. But if you return to the previous page, the scroll position is remembered by the browser, and you're taken back to the bottom.

The browser can't do this when we've hijacked navigation with Vue Router. So, when you scroll to the bottom of the Vuebnb home page and click a listing in Cuba, let's say, the scroll position is unchanged when the listing page component is loaded. This feels really unnatural to the user, who would expect to be taken to the top of the new page:

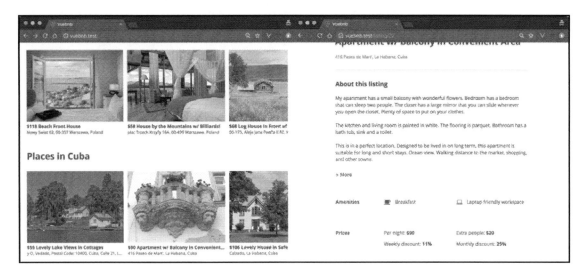

Figure 7.17. Scroll position issue after navigating with Vue Router

Vue Router has a `scrollbehavior` method that allows you to adjust where the page is scrolled when you change routes by simply defining the x and y positions of the horizontal and vertical scroll bars. To keep it simple, and yet to still keep the UX natural, let's make it so we are always at the top of the page when a new page is loaded.

resources/assets/js/router.js:

```
export default new VueRouter({
  mode: 'history',
  routes: [ ... ],
  scrollBehavior (to, from, savedPosition) {
    return { x: 0, y: 0 }
  }
});
```

Adding a footer

To improve the design of Vuebnb, let's add a footer to the bottom of each page. We'll make it a reusable component, so let's begin by creating that:

```
$ touch resources/assets/components/CustomFooter.vue
```

Here is the markup. For now, it's just a stateless component.

resources/assets/js/CustomFooter.vue:

```
<template>
  <div id="footer">
    <div class="hr"></div>
    <div class="container">
      <p>
        <img class="icon" src="/images/logo_grey.png">
        <span>
          <strong>Vuebnb</strong>. A full-stack Vue.js and Laravel demo app
        </span>
      </p>
    </div>
  </div>
</template>
<style>
  #footer {
    margin-bottom: 3em;
  }

  #footer .icon {
    height: 23px;
    display: inline-block;
    margin-bottom: -6px;
  }

  .hr {
    border-bottom: 1px solid #dbdbdb;
    margin: 3em 0;
  }

  #footer p {
    font-size</span>: 15px;
    color: #767676 !important;
    display: flex;
  }
  #footer p img {
    padding-right: 6px;
  }
</style>
```

Let's add the footer to the App component, just below the RouterView where the pages are output.

resources/assets/js/App.vue:

```
<template>
  <div>
    <div id="toolbar">...</div>
    <router-view></router-view>
    <custom-footer></custom-footer>
  </div>
</template>
<script>
  import CustomFooter from './CustomFooter.vue';

  export default {
    components: {
      CustomFooter
    }
  }
</script>
<style>...</style>
```

Here's how it looks on the listing page:

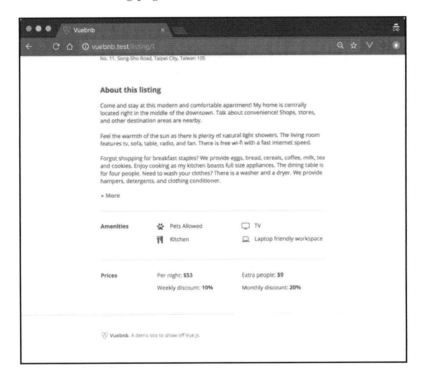

Figure 7.18. Custom footer on listing page

Now here's how it looks on the home page. It doesn't look as good because the text is not aligned left as you'd expect. This is because the container constraints used on this page are different to the `.container` class we've added to the footer:

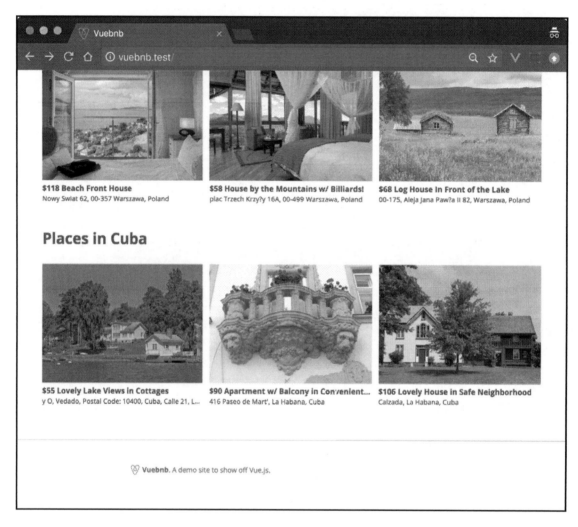

Figure 7.19. Custom footer on home page

In fact, `.container` was specifically designed for the listing page, while `.home-container` was designed for the home page. To fix this, and to make things less confusing, let's firstly rename the `.container` class to `.listing-container`. You'll also need to update the `ListingPage` component to ensure it's using this new class name.

Secondly, let's move `.home-container` to the main CSS file as well, since we'll start to use it globally as well.

`resources/assets/css/style.css`:

```
.listing-container {
  margin: 0 auto;
  padding: 0 12px;
}

@media (min-width: 744px) {
  .listing-container {
    width: 696px;
  }
}

.home-container {
  margin: 0 auto;
  padding: 0 25px;
}

@media (min-width: 1131px) {
  .home-container {
    width: 1080px;
  }
}
```

Now we have `.home-container` and `.listing-container` as two possible containers for our `custom-footer` component. Let's dynamically select the class depending on the route, so the footer is always correctly aligned.

The route object

The *route object* represents the state of the currently active route and can be accessed inside the root instance, or a component instance, as `this.$route`. This object contains parsed information of the current URL and the route records matched by the URL:

```
created() {
  console.log(this.$route.fullPath); // /listing/1
  console.log(this.$route.params); // { listing: "1" }
}
```

Dynamically selecting the container class

In order to select the correct container class in `custom-footer`, we can get the name of the current route from the route object, and use that in a template literal.

`resources/assets/components/CustomFooter.vue`:

```
<template>
  <div id="footer">
    <div class="hr"></div>
    <div :class="containerClass">
      <p>...</p>
    </div>
  </div>
</template>
<script>
  export default {
    computed: {
      containerClass() {
        // this.$route.name is either 'home' or 'listing'
        return `${this.$route.name}-container`;
      }
    }
  }
</script>
<style>...</style>
```

Now the footer will use `.home-container` when displayed on the home page:

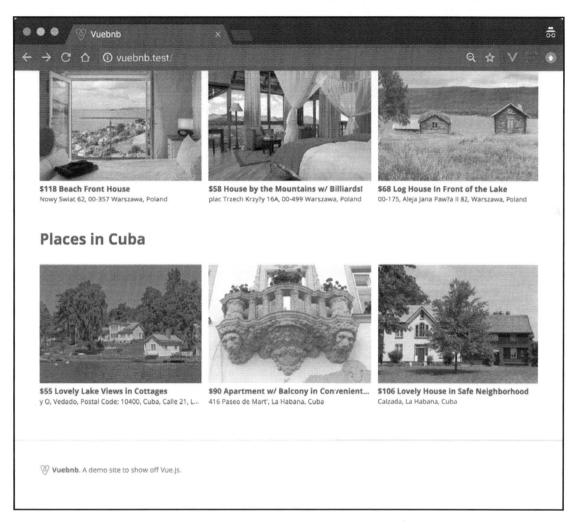

Figure 7.20. Custom footer on home page with the correct container class

Listing summary image slider

On our home page, we need to make it so that a user can see more than just three of the possible 10 listings for each country. To do this, we will turn each listing summary group into an image slider.

Let's create a new component to house each listing summary group. We'll then add arrowheads to the sides of this component, allowing the user to easily step through its listings:

```
$ touch resources/assets/components/ListingSummaryGroup.vue
```

We'll now abstract the markup and logic for displaying listing summaries from HomePage into this new component. Each group will need to know the name of the country and the included listings, so we'll add this data as props.

resources/assets/components/ListingSummaryGroup.vue:

```
<template>
  <div class="listing-summary-group">
    <h1>Places in {{ country }}</h1>
    <div class="listing-summaries">
      <listing-summary
        v-for="listing in listings"
        :key="listing.id"
        :listing="listing"
      ></listing-summary>
    </div>
  </div>
</template>
<script>
  import ListingSummary from './ListingSummary.vue';

  export default {
    props: [ 'country', 'listings' ],
    components: {
      ListingSummary
    }
  }
</script>
<style>
  .listing-summary-group {
    padding-bottom: 20px;
  }

  .listing-summaries {
```

```
    display: flex;
    flex-direction: row;
    justify-content: space-between;
    overflow: hidden;
  }
  .listing-summaries > .listing-summary {
    margin-right: 15px;
  }

  .listing-summaries > .listing-summary:last-child {
    margin-right: 0;
  }
</style>
```

Back in the HomePage, we will declare the ListingSummaryGroup with a v-for, iterating over each country group.

resources/assets/components/HomePage.vue:

```
<template>
  <div class="home-container">
    <listing-summary-group
      v-for="(group, country) in listing_groups"
      :key="country"
      :listings="group"
      :country="country"
      class="listing-summary-group"
    ></listing-summary-group>
  </div>
</template>
<script>
  import routeMixin from '../js/route-mixin';
  import ListingSummaryGroup from './ListingSummaryGroup.vue';
  import { groupByCountry } from '../js/helpers';

  export default {
    mixins: [ routeMixin ],
    data() {
      return {
        listing_groups: []
      };
    },
    methods: {
      assignData({ listings }) {
        this.listing_groups = groupByCountry(listings);
      }
    },
```

```
    components: {
      ListingSummaryGroup
    }
  }
</script>
```

 Most developers will use the terms *image carousel* and *image slider* interchangeably. In this book, I make a slight distinction, a *carousel* contains a single image that gets completely switched out with another, while a *slider* shifts the position of images, with several visible at once.

Adding the slider

We'll now add the slider functionality to ListingSummaryGroup. To do this, we'll reuse the CarouselControl component we made back in Chapter 6, *Composing Widgets with Vue.js Components*. We'll want to display one on either side of the group, so let's put them into the template, remembering to declare the dir attribute. We'll also add some structural markup and CSS for displaying the controls.

resources/assets/components/ListingSummaryGroup.vue:

```
<template>
  <div class="listing-summary-group">
    <h1>Places in {{ country }}</h1>
    <div class="listing-carousel">
      <div class="controls">
        <carousel-control dir="left"></carousel-control>
        <carousel-control dir="right"></carousel-control>
      </div>
      <div class="listing-summaries-wrapper">
        <div class="listing-summaries">
          <listing-summary
            v-for="listing in listings"
            :listing="listing"
            :key="listing.id"
          ></listing-summary>
        </div>
      </div>
    </div>
  </div>
</template>
<script>
  import ListingSummary from './ListingSummary.vue';
  import CarouselControl from './CarouselControl.vue';
```

```
  export default {
    props: [ 'country', 'listings' ],
    components: {
      ListingSummary,
      CarouselControl
    }
  }
</script>
<style>
...

.listing-carousel {
  position: relative;
}

.listing-carousel .controls {
  display: flex;
  justify-content: space-between;
  position: absolute;
  top: calc(50% - 45px);
  left: -45px;
  width: calc(100% + 90px);
}

.listing-carousel .controls .carousel-control{
  color: #c5c5c5;
  font-size: 1.5rem;
  cursor: pointer;
}

.listing-summaries-wrapper {
  overflow: hidden;
}
</style>
```

After adding this code, your home page will look like this:

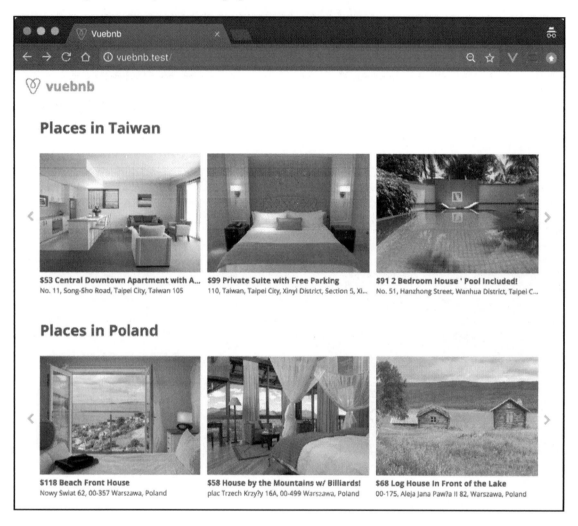

Figure 7.21. Carousel controls on listing summary groups

Translate

In order to *shift* our listing summaries in response to the carousel controls being clicked, we will use a CSS transform called `translate`. This moves an affected element from its current position by an amount specified in pixels.

The total width of each listing summary is 365px (350px fixed width plus 15px margin). This means if we move our group to the left by 365px, it will give the effect of shifting the position of all images by one. You can see here I've added the translate as inline styling to test if it works. Note that we `translate` in a *negative* direction to get the group to move to the left:

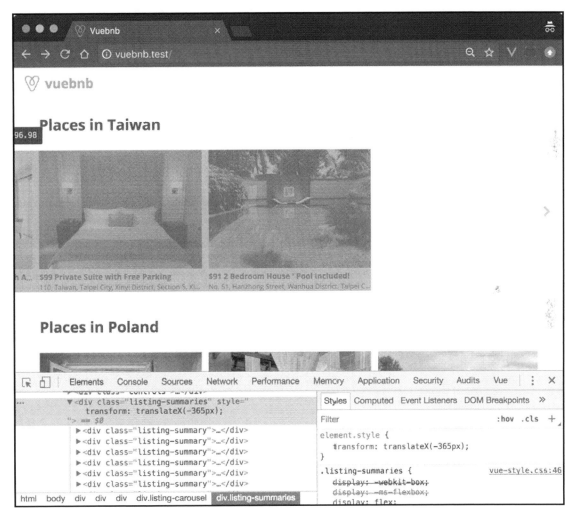

Figure 7.22. Listing group shifted to the left by using translate

By binding inline style to the element with the `listing-summary` class, we can control the translate from JavaScript. Let's do this via a computed property so we can calculate the translate amount dynamically.

`resources/assets/components/ListingSummaryGroup.vue`:

```
<template>
  <div class="listing-summary-group">
    <h1>Places in {{ country }}</h1>
    <div class="listing-carousel">
      <div class="controls">...</div>
      <div class="listing-summaries" :style="style">
        <listing-summary...>...</listing-summary>
      </div>
    </div>
  </div>
</template>
<script>
  export default {
    props: [ 'country', 'listings' ],
    computed: {
      style() {
        return { transform: `translateX(-365px)` }
      }
    },
    components: { ... }
  }
</script>
```

Now all of our summary groups will be shifted:

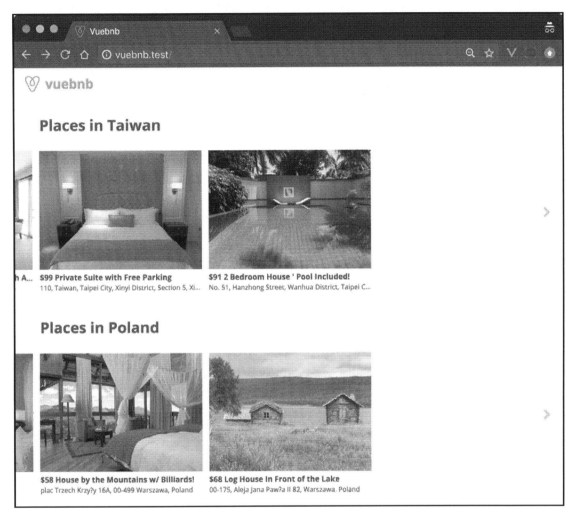

Figure 7.23. Shifted listing groups with translate controlled by JavaScript

The problem evident in *Figure 7.23* is that we can only see three images at once and that they're overflowing out of the container into the other parts of the page.

To fix this, we'll move the CSS rule `overflow: hidden` from `listing-summaries` to `listing-summaries-wrapper`.

`resources/assets/components/ListingSummaryGroup.vue`:

```
...

.listing-summaries-wrapper {
  overflow: hidden;
}

.listing-summaries {
  display: flex;
  flex-direction: row;
  justify-content: space-between;
}

...
```

Carousel controls

We now need the carousel controls to change the value of the translate. To do so, let's add a data property, `offset`, to `ListingSummaryGroup`. This will track how many images we've shifted along, that is, it will start at zero, and go up to a maximum of seven (not 10 because we don't want to shift so far along that all of the images are off-screen).

We'll also add a method `change`, which will serve as an event handling function for the custom event that the carousel control components emit. This method accepts one argument, `val`, which will either be −1 or 1, depending on whether the left or right carousel control was triggered.

`change` will step the value of `offset`, which is then multiplied by the width of each listing (365px) to calculate the translate.

`resources/assets/components/ListingSummaryGroup.vue`:

```
...

const rowSize = 3;
const listingSummaryWidth = 365;

export default {
  props: [ 'country', 'listings' ],
  data() {
```

```
      return {
        offset: 0
      }
    },
    methods: {
      change(val) {
        let newVal = this.offset + parseInt(val);
        if (newVal >= 0 && newVal <= this.listings.length - rowSize) {
          this.offset = newVal;
        }
      }
    },
    computed: {
      style() {
        return {
          transform: `translateX(${this.offset * -listingSummaryWidth}px)`
        }
      }
    },
    components: { ... }
}
```

Lastly, we must use a v-on directive in the template to register a listener for the change-image event of the CarouselControl components.

resources/assets/components/ListingSummaryGroup.vue:

```
<div class="controls">
  <carousel-control dir="left" @change-image="change"></carousel-control>

  <carousel-control dir="right" @change-image="change"></carousel-control>
</div>
```

With that done, we have a working image slider for each listing group!

Finishing touches

There are two more small features to add to these image sliders to give Vuebnb users the best possible experience. Firstly, let's add a CSS transition to animate the translate change over a period of half a second and give a nice *sliding* effect.

resources/assets/components/ListingSummaryGroup.vue:

```
.listing-summaries {
  display: flex;
  flex-direction: row;
```

```
  justify-content: space-between;
  transition: transform 0.5s;
}
```

Sadly you can't see the effects of this in a book, so you'll have to try it for yourself!

Finally, unlike our image carousel, these sliders are not continuous; they have a minimum and maximum value. Let's hide the appropriate arrow if that minimum or maximum is reached. For example, when the sliders load, the left arrow should be hidden because the user cannot decrement the offset further below zero.

To do this, we'll use style bindings to dynamically add a `visibility: hidden` CSS rule.

resources/assets/components/ListingSummaryGroup.vue:

```
<div class="controls">
  <carousel-control
    dir="left"
    @change-image="change"
    :style="leftArrowStyle"
  ></carousel-control>
  <carousel-control
    dir="right"
    @change-image="change"
    :style="rightArrowStyle"
  ></carousel-control>
</div>
```

And the computed properties.

resources/assets/components/ListingSummaryGroup.vue:

```
computed: {
  ...
  leftArrowStyle() {
    return { visibility: (this.offset > 0 ? 'visible' : 'hidden') }
  },
  rightArrowStyle() {
    return {
      visibility: (
        this.offset < (this.listings.length - rowSize)
        ? 'visible' : 'hidden'
      )
    }
  }
}
```

With that done, we can see the left arrow is hidden when the page loads, as expected:

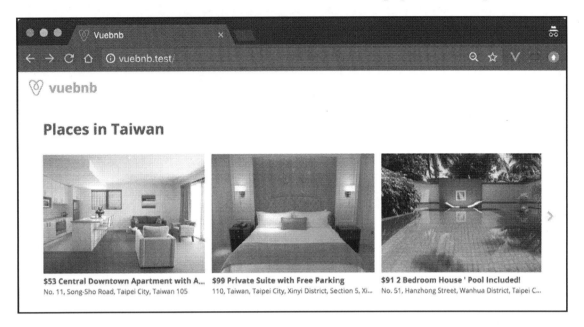

Figure 7.24. Hidden left arrow on page load

Summary

In this chapter, we learned how router libraries work and why they are a crucial addition to SPAs. We then got familiar with the key features of Vue Router including the route object, navigation guards, and the `RouterLink` and `RouterView` special components.

Putting this knowledge into practice, we installed Vue Router and configured it for use in our app. We then built a home page for Vuebnb, including a gallery of listing summaries organized within image sliders.

Finally, we implemented an architecture for correctly matching pages with either available local data or new data retrieved from the web service via AJAX.

Now that we have a substantial number of components in our app, many of which communicate data between one another, it's time to investigate another key Vue.js tool: Vuex. Vuex is a Flux-based library that offers a superior way of managing application state.

8
Managing Your Application State with Vuex

In the last chapter, you learned how Vue Router can be used to add virtual pages to a Vue.js single-page app. We will now add components to Vuebnb that share data across pages and therefore can't rely on transient local state. To do this, we will utilize Vuex, a Flux-inspired library for Vue.js that offers a robust means of managing global application state.

Topics covered in this chapter:

- An introduction to the Flux application architecture and why it is useful for building user interfaces
- An overview of Vuex and its key features, including state and mutations
- How to install Vuex and set up a global store that can be accessed by Vue.js components
- How Vuex allows for superior debugging with Vue Devtools via mutation logging and time-travel debugging
- The creation of a save feature for Vuebnb listings and a saved listings page
- Moving page state into Vuex to minimize unnecessary data retrieval from the server

Flux application architecture

Imagine you've developed a multi-user chat app. The interface has a user list, private chat windows, an inbox with chat history and a notification bar to inform users of unread messages.

Millions of users are chatting through your app on a daily basis. However, there are complaints about an annoying problem: the notification bar of the app will occasionally give false notifications; that is, a user will be notified of a new unread message, but when they check to see what it is, it's just a message they've already seen.

What I've described is a real scenario that Facebook developers had with their chat system a few years ago. The process of solving this inspired their developers to create an application architecture they named *Flux*. Flux forms the basis of Vuex, Redux and other similar libraries.

Facebook developers struggled with this *zombie notification* bug for some time. They eventually realized that its persistent nature was more than a simple bug; it pointed to an underlying flaw in the architecture of the app.

The flaw is most easily understood in the abstract: when you have multiple components in an application that share data, the complexity of their interconnections will increase to a point where the state of the data is no longer predictable or understandable. When bugs like the one described inevitably arise, the complexity of the app data makes them near impossible to resolve:

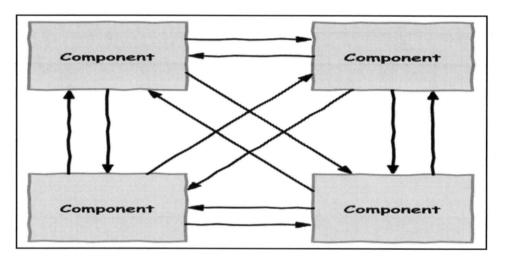

Figure 8.1. The complexity of communication between components increases with every extra component

Flux is not a library. You can't go to GitHub and download it. Flux is a set of guiding principles that describe a scalable frontend architecture that sufficiently mitigates this flaw. It is not just for a chat app, but for any complex UI with components which share state, like Vuebnb.

Let's now explore the guiding principles of Flux.

Principle #1 – Single source of truth

Components may have *local data* that only they need to know about. For example, the position of the scroll bar in the user list component is probably of no interest to other components:

```
Vue.component('user-list', {
  data() {
    scrollPos: ...
  }
});
```

But any data that is to be shared between components, for example *application data*, needs to be kept in a single place, separate from the components that use it. This location is referred to as the *store*. Components must read application data from this location and not keep their own copy to prevent conflict or disagreement:

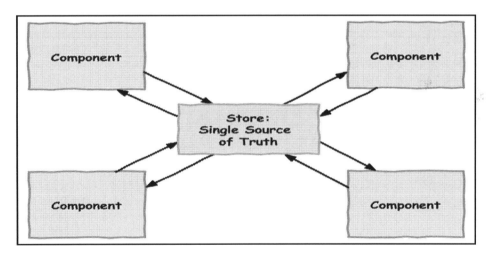

Figure 8.2. Centralized data simplifies application state

Principle #2 – Data is read-only

Components can freely read data from the store. But they cannot change data in the store, at least not directly.

Instead, they must inform the store of their intent to change the data and the store will be responsible for making those changes via a set of defined functions called *mutator methods*.

Why this approach? If we centralize the data-altering logic then we don't have to look far if there are inconsistencies in the state. We're minimizing the possibility that some random component (possibly in a third party module) has changed the data in an unexpected fashion:

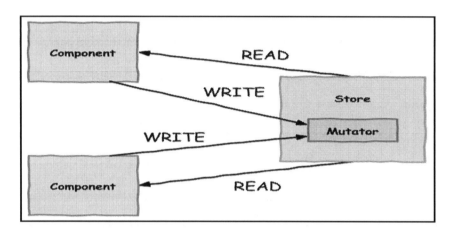

Figure 8.3. State is read-only. Mutator methods are used to write to the store

Principle #3 – Mutations are synchronous

It's much easier to debug state inconsistencies in an app that implements the above two principles in its architecture. You could log commits and observe how the state changes in response (which automatically happens with Vue Devtools, as we'll see).

But this ability would be undermined if our mutations were applied *asynchronously*. We'd know the order our commits came in, but we would not know the order in which our components committed them. Synchronous mutations ensure state is not dependent on the sequence and timing of unpredictable events.

Vuex

Vuex (usually pronounced *veweks*) is the official Vue.js implementation of the Flux architecture. By enforcing the principles described previously, Vuex keeps your application data in a transparent and predictable state even when that data is being shared across many components.

Vuex includes a store with state and mutator methods, and will reactively update any components that are reading data from the store. It also allows for handy development features like hot module reloading (updating modules in a running application) and time-travel debugging (stepping back through mutations to trace bugs).

In this chapter, we will add a *save* feature to our Vuebnb listings so that a user can keep track of the listings that they like best. Unlike other data in our app so far, the saved state must persist across pages; for example, when a user changes from one page to another, the app must remember which items the user has already saved. We will use Vuex to achieve this:

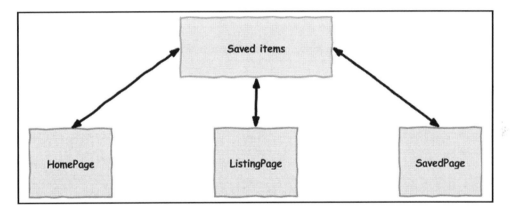

Figure 8.4. Saved state is available to all page components

Installing Vuex

Vuex is an NPM package that can be installed from the command line:

```
$ npm i --save-dev vuex
```

We will put our Vuex configuration into a new module file `store.js`:

```
$ touch resources/assets/js/store.js
```

We need to import Vuex in this file and, like Vue Router, install it with `Vue.use`. This gives special properties to Vue that make it compatible with Vuex, such as allowing components to access the store via `this.$store`.

resources/assets/js/store.js:

```
import Vue from 'vue';
import Vuex from 'vuex';
Vue.use(Vuex);

export default new Vuex.Store();
```

We will then import the store module in our main app file, and add it to our Vue instance.

resources/assets/js/app.js:

```
...

import router from './router';
import store from './store';

var app = new Vue({
  el: '#app',
  render: h => h(App),
  router,
  store
});
```

Save feature

As mentioned, we'll be adding a *save* feature to our Vuebnb listings. The UI of this feature is a small, clickable icon that is overlaid on the top right of a listing summary's thumbnail image. It acts similarly to a checkbox, allowing the user to toggle the saved status of any particular listing:

Figure 8.5. The save feature shown on listing summaries

The save feature will also be added as a button in the header image on the listing page:

Figure 8.6. The save feature shown on the listing page

ListingSave component

Let's begin by creating the new component:

```
$ touch resources/assets/components/ListingSave.vue
```

The template of this component will include a Font Awesome *heart* icon. It will also include a click handler which will be used to toggle the saved state. Since this component will always be a child of a listing or listing summary, it will receive a listing ID as a prop. This prop will be used shortly to save the state in Vuex.

resources/assets/components/ListingSave.vue:

```
<template>
  <div class="listing-save" @click.stop="toggleSaved()">
    <i class="fa fa-lg fa-heart-o"></i>
  </div>
</template>
<script>
  export default {
    props: [ 'id' ],
    methods: {
      toggleSaved() {
        // Implement this
      }
    }
  }
</script>
<style>
  .listing-save {
    position: absolute;
    top: 20px;
    right: 20px;
    cursor: pointer;
  }

  .listing-save .fa-heart-o {
    color: #ffffff;
  }
</style>
```

 Note that the click handler has a `stop` modifier. This modifier prevents the click event from bubbling up to ancestor elements, especially any anchor tags which might trigger a page change!

We'll now add `ListingSave` to the `ListingSummary` component. Remember to pass the listing's ID as a prop. While we're at it, let's add a `position: relative` to the `.listing-summary` class rules so that `ListingSave` can be positioned absolutely against it.

resources/assets/components/ListingSummary.vue:

```
<template>
  <div class="listing-summary">
    <router-link :to="{ name: 'listing', params: {listing: listing.id}}">
      ...
    </router-link>
    <listing-save :id="listing.id"></listing-save>
  </div>
</template>
<script>
  import ListingSave from './ListingSave.vue';

  export default {
    ...
    components: {
      ListingSave
    }
  }
</script>
<style>
  .listing-summary {
    ...
    position: relative;
  }
  ...

  @media (max-width: 400px) {
    .listing-summary .listing-save {
      left: 15px;
      right: auto;
    }
  }
</style>
```

With that done, we will now see the `ListingSave` heart icon rendered on each summary:

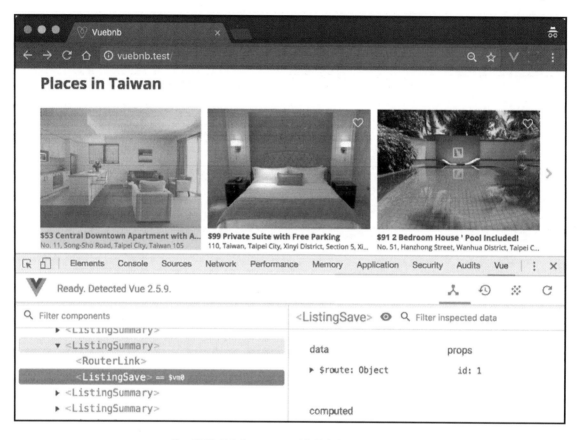

Figure 8.7. The ListingSave component within ListingSummary components

Saved state

The `ListingSave` component does not have any local data; we will instead keep any saved listings in our Vuex store. To do this, we will create an array in the store called `saved`. Each time the user toggles the saved state of a listing its ID will be either added or removed from this array.

To begin, let's add a `state` property to our Vuex store. This object will hold any data we want to be globally available to the components of our app. We will add the `saved` property to this object and assign it an empty array.

`resources/assets/js/store.js`:

```
...

export default new Vuex.Store({
  state: {
    saved: []
  }
});
```

Mutator method

We created the stub for a `toggleSaved` method in our `ListingSave` component. This method should add or remove the listing's ID from the `saved` state in the store. Components can access the store as `this.$store`. More specifically, the `saved` array can be accessed at `this.$store.state.saved`.

`resources/assets/components/ListingSave.vue`:

```
methods: {
  toggleSaved() {
    console.log(this.$store.state.saved);
    /* Currently an empty array.
      []
    */
  }
}
```

Remember that in the Flux architecture state is read-only. That means we cannot directly modify `saved` from a component. Instead, we must create a mutator method in the store which does the modification for us.

Let's create a `mutations` property in our store configuration, and add a function property `toggleSaved`. Vuex mutator methods receive two arguments: the store state and a payload. This payload can be anything you want to pass from the component to the mutator. For the current case, we will send the listing ID.

The logic for `toggleSaved` is to check if the listing ID is already in the `saved` array and if so, remove it, or if not, add it.

`resources/assets/js/store.js:`

```
export default new Vuex.Store({
  state: {
    saved: []
  },
  mutations: {
    toggleSaved(state, id) {
      let index = state.saved.findIndex(saved => saved === id);
      if (index === -1) {
        state.saved.push(id);
      } else {
        state.saved.splice(index, 1);
      }
    }
  }
});
```

We now need to commit this mutation from `ListingSave`. *Commit* is Flux jargon that is synonymous with *call* or *trigger*. A commit looks like a custom event with the first argument being the name of the mutator method and the second being the payload.

`resources/assets/components/ListingSave.vue:`

```
export default {
  props: [ 'id' ],
  methods: {
    toggleSaved() {
      this.$store.commit('toggleSaved', this.id);
    }
  }
}
```

The main point of using mutator methods in the store architecture is that state is changed consistently. But there is an additional benefit: we can easily log these changes for debugging. If you check the Vuex tab in Vue Devtools after clicking one of the save buttons, you will see an entry for that mutation:

Figure 8.8: Mutation log

Each entry in the log can tell you the state after the change was committed, as well as the particulars of the mutation.

> If you double-click a logged mutation, Vue Devtools will revert the state of the app to what it was directly after that change. This is called *time-travel debugging* and can be useful for fine-grained debugging.

Changing the icon to reflect the state

Our `ListingSave` component's icon will appear differently, depending on whether or not the listing is saved; it will be opaque if the listing is saved, and transparent if it is not. Since the component doesn't store its state locally, we need to retrieve state from the store to implement this feature.

Vuex store state should generally be retrieved via a computed property. This ensures that the component is not keeping its own copy, which would violate the *single source of truth* principle, and that the component is re-rendered when the state is mutated by this component or another. Reactivity works with Vuex state, too!

Let's create a computed property `isListingSaved`, which will return a Boolean value reflecting whether or not this particular listing has been saved.

`resources/assets/components/ListingSave.vue`:

```
export default {
  props: [ 'id' ],
  methods: {
    toggleSaved() {
      this.$store.commit('toggleSaved', this.id);
    }
  },
  computed: {
    isListingSaved() {
      return this.$store.state.saved.find(saved => saved === this.id);
    }
  }
}
```

We can now use this computed property to change the icon. Currently we're using the Font Awesome icon `fa-heart-o`. This should represent the *unsaved* state. When the listing is saved we should instead use the icon `fa-heart`. We can implement this with a dynamic class binding.

`resources/assets/components/ListingSave.vue`:

```
<template>
  <div class="listing-save" @click.stop="toggleSaved()">
    <i :class="classes"></i>
  </div>
</template>
<script>
  export default {
    props: [ 'id' ],
    methods: { ... },
    computed: {
      isListingSaved() { ...},
      classes() {
        let saved = this.isListingSaved;
        return {
          'fa': true,
          'fa-lg': true,
          'fa-heart': saved,
          'fa-heart-o': !saved
        }
      }
    }
  }
```

```
  }
</script>
<style>
  ...

  .listing-save .fa-heart {
    color: #ff5a5f;
  }
</style>
```

Now the user can visually identify which listings have been saved and which haven't. Thanks to reactive Vuex data, the icon will instantly be updated when a change to the `saved` state is made from anywhere in the app:

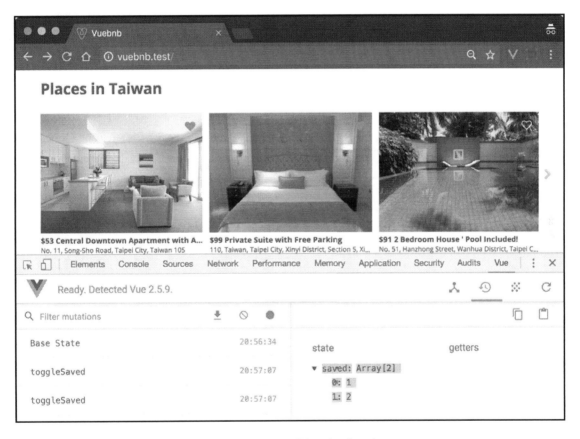

Figure 8.9. The ListingSave icon will change depending on the state

Adding to ListingPage

We also want the save feature to appear on the listing page. It will go inside the HeaderImage component alongside the **View Photos** button so that, like with the listing summaries, the button is overlaid on the listing's main image.

resources/assets/components/HeaderImage.vue:

```
<template>
  <div class="header">
    <div
      class="header-img"
      :style="headerImageStyle"
      @click="$emit('header-clicked')"
    >
      <listing-save :id="id"></listing-save>
      <button class="view-photos">View Photos</button>
    </div>
  </div>
</template>
<script>
  import ListingSave from './ListingSave.vue';

  export default {
    computed: { ... },
    props: ['image-url', 'id'],
    components: {
      ListingSave
    }
  }
</script>
<style>...</style>
```

Note that HeaderImage does not have the listing ID in its scope, so we'll have to pass this down as a prop from ListingPage. id is not currently a data property of ListingPage either, but, if we declare it, it will simply work.

This is because the ID is already a property of the initial state/AJAX data the component receives, therefore `id` will automatically be populated by the `Object.assign` when the component is loaded by the router.

resources/assets/components/ListingPage.vue:

```
<template>
  <div>
    <header-image
      v-if="images[0]"
      :image-url="images[0]"
      @header-clicked="openModal"
      :id="id"
    ></header-image>
    ...
  </div>
</template>
<script>
  ...
  export default {
    data() {
      ...
      id: null
    },
    methods: {
      assignData({ listing }) {
        Object.assign(this.$data, populateAmenitiesAndPrices(listing));
      },
      ...
    },
    ...
  }
</script>
<style>...</style>
```

With that done, the save feature will now appear on the listing page:

Figure 8.10. The listing save feature on the listing page

 If you save a listing via the listing page, then return to the home page, the equivalent listing summary will be saved. This is because our Vuex state is global and will persist across page changes (though not page refreshes...yet).

Making ListingSave a button

As it is, the `ListingSave` feature appears too small in the listing page header and will be easily overlooked by a user. Let's make it a proper button, similar to the **View Photos** button in the bottom left of the header.

To do this, we'll modify `ListingSave` to allow parent components to send a prop `button`. This Boolean prop will indicate if the component should include a `button` element wrapped around the icon or not.

The text for this button will be a computed property `message` which will change from **Save** to **Saved** depending on the value of `isListingSaved`.

resources/assets/components/ListingSave.vue:

```
<template>
  <div class="listing-save" @click.stop="toggleSaved()">
    <button v-if="button">
      <i :class="classes"></i>
      {{ message }}
    </button>
    <i v-else :class="classes"></i>
  </div>
</template>
<script>
  export default {
    props: [ 'id', 'button' ],
    methods: { ... },
    computed: {
      isListingSaved() { ... },
      classes() { ... },
      message() {
          return this.isListingSaved ? 'Saved' : 'Save';
      }
    }
  }
</script>
<style>
  ...

  .listing-save i {
    padding-right: 4px;
  }

  .listing-save button .fa-heart-o {
    color: #808080;
  }
</style>
```

We will now set the `button` prop to `true` within `HeaderImage`. Even though the value is not dynamic, we use a `v-bind` to ensure the value is interpreted as a JavaScript value, not a string.

`resources/assets/components/HeaderImage.vue`:

```
<listing-save :id="id" :button="true"></listing-save>
```

With that, the `ListingSave` will appear as a button on our listing pages:

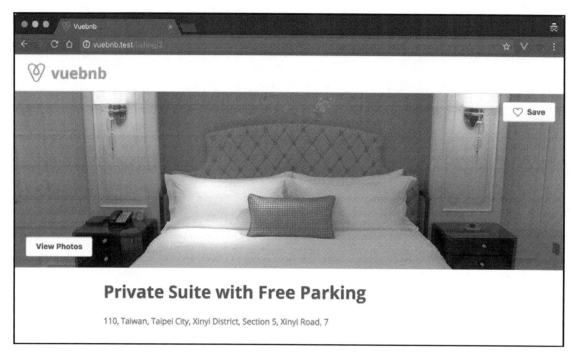

Figure 8.11. The listing save feature appears as a button on the listing page

Moving page state into the store

Now that the user can save any listings that they like, we will need a *saved* page where they can view those saved listings together. We will build this new page shortly, and it will look like this:

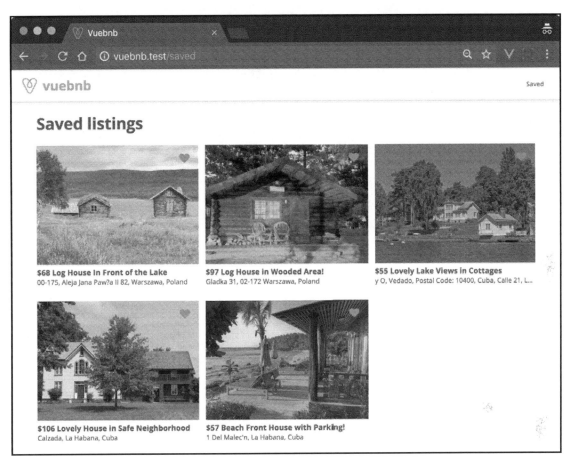

Figure 8.12: Saved page

Implementing the saved page will require an enhancement to our app architecture, however. Let's do a quick recap of how data is retrieved from the server to understand why.

All the pages in our app require a route on the server to return a view. This view includes the data for the relevant page component inlined in the document head. Or, if we navigate to that page via in-app links, an API endpoint will instead supply that same data. We set up this mechanism in Chapter 7, *Building A Multi-Page App With Vue Router*.

The saved page will require the same data as the home page (the listing summary data), as the saved page is really just a slight variation on the home page. It makes sense, then, to share data between the home page and saved page. In other words, if a user loads Vuebnb from the home page, then navigates to the saved page, or vice versa, it would be a waste to load the listing summary data more than once.

Let's decouple our page state from our page components and move it into Vuex. That way it can be used by whichever page needs and it and avoid unnecessary reloading:

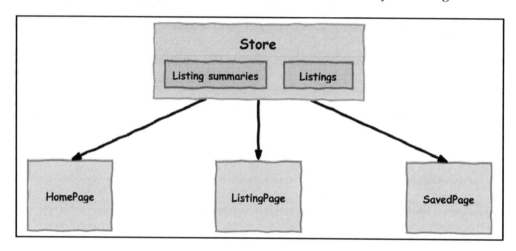

Figure 8.13. Page state in store

State and mutator methods

Let's add two new state properties to our Vuex store: `listings` and `listing_summaries`. These will be arrays that store our listings and listing summaries respectively. When the page first loads, or when the route changes and the API is called, the loaded data will be put into these arrays rather than being assigned directly to the page components. The page components will instead retrieve this data from the store.

We'll also add a mutator method, `addData`, for populating these arrays. It will accept a payload object with two properties: `route` and `data`. `route` is the name of the route, for example, *listing*, *home*, and so on. `data` is the listing or listing summary data retrieved from the document head or the API.

`resources/assets/js/store.js`:

```
import Vue from 'vue';
```

```
import Vuex from 'vuex';
Vue.use(Vuex);

export default new Vuex.Store({
  state: {
    saved: [],
    listing_summaries: [],
    listings: []
  },
  mutations: {
    toggleSaved(state, id) { ... },
    addData(state, { route, data }) {
      if (route === 'listing') {
        state.listings.push(data.listing);
      } else {
        state.listing_summaries = data.listings;
      }
    }
  }
});
```

Router

The logic for retrieving page state is in the mixin file `route-mixin.js`. This mixin adds a `beforeRouteEnter` hook to a page component which applies the page state to the component instance when it becomes available.

Now that we're storing page state in Vuex we will utilize a different approach. Firstly, we won't need a mixin anymore; we'll put this logic into `router.js` now. Secondly, we'll use a different navigation guard, `beforeEach`. This is not a component hook, but a hook that can be applied to the router itself, and it is triggered before every navigation.

You can see in the following code block how I've implemented this in `router.js`. Note that before `next()` is called we commit the page state to the store.

`resources/assets/js/router.js`:

```
...

import axios from 'axios';
import store from './store';

let router = new VueRouter({
  ...
});
```

```
router.beforeEach((to, from, next) => {
  let serverData = JSON.parse(window.vuebnb_server_data);
  if (!serverData.path || to.path !== serverData.path) {
    axios.get(`/api${to.path}`).then(({data}) => {
      store.commit('addData', {route: to.name, data});
      next();
    });
  }
  else {
    store.commit('addData', {route: to.name, data: serverData});
    next();
  }
});

export default router;
```

With that done, we can now delete the route mixin:

```
$ rm resources/assets/js/route-mixin.js
```

Retrieving page state from Vuex

Now that we've moved page state into Vuex we'll need to modify our page components to retrieve it. Starting with `ListingPage`, the changes we must make are:

- Remove local data properties.
- Add a computed property `listing`. This will find the right listing data from the store based on the route.
- Remove the mixin.
- Change template variables so they're properties of `listing`: an example is `{{ title }}`, which will become `{{ listing.title }}`. Unfortunately, all variables are now properties of `listing` which makes our template slightly more verbose.

resources/assets/components/ListingPage.vue:

```
<template>
  <div>
    <header-image
      v-if="listing.images[0]"
      :image-url="listing.images[0]"
      @header-clicked="openModal"
      :id="listing.id"
    ></header-image>
```

```
    <div class="listing-container">
      <div class="heading">
        <h1>{{ listing.title }}</h1>
        <p>{{ listing.address }}</p>
      </div>
      <hr>
      <div class="about">
        <h3>About this listing</h3>
        <expandable-text>{{ listing.about }}</expandable-text>
      </div>
      <div class="lists">
        <feature-list title="Amenities" :items="listing.amenities">
          ...
        </feature-list>
        <feature-list title="Prices" :items="listing.prices">
          ...
        </feature-list>
      </div>
    </div>
    <modal-window ref="imagemodal">
      <image-carousel :images="listing.images"></image-carousel>
    </modal-window>
  </div>
</template>
<script>
  ...

  export default {
    components: { ... },
    computed: {
      listing() {
        let listing = this.$store.state.listings.find(
          listing => listing.id == this.$route.params.listing
        );
        return populateAmenitiesAndPrices(listing);
      }
    },
    methods: { ... }
  }
</script>
```

Changes to `HomePage` are much simpler; just remove the mixin and the local state, and replace it with a computed property, `listing_groups`, which will retrieve all the listing summaries from the store.

`resources/assets/components/HomePage.vue`:

```
export default {
  computed: {
    listing_groups() {
      return groupByCountry(this.$store.state.listing_summaries);
    }
  },
  components: { ... }
}
```

After making these changes, reload the app and you should see no obvious change in behavior. However, inspecting the Vuex tab of Vue Devtools, you will see that page data is now in the store:

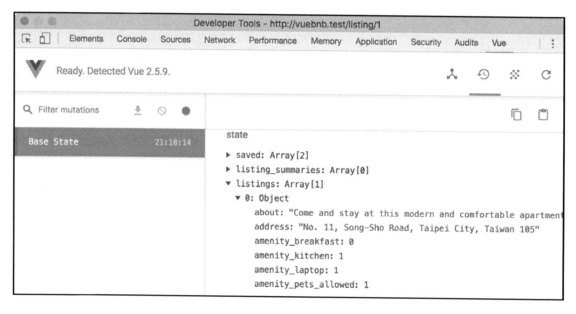

Figure 8.14. Page state is now in the Vuex store

Getters

Sometimes what we want to get from the store is not a direct value, but a derived value. For example, say we wanted to get only those listing summaries that were saved by the user. To do this, we can define a *getter*, which is like a computed property for the store:

```
state: {
  saved: [5, 10],
  listing_summaries: [ ... ]
},
getters: {
  savedSummaries(state) {
    return state.listing_summaries.filter(
      item => state.saved.indexOf(item.id) > -1
    );
  }
}
```

Now, any component that needs the getter data can retrieve it from the store as follows:

```
console.log(this.$store.state.getters.savedSummaries);

/*
[
  5 => [ ... ],
  10 => [ ... ]
]
*/
```

Generally, you define a getter when several components need the same derived value, to save repeating code. Let's create a getter which retrieves a specific listing. We've already created this functionality in `ListingPage`, but since we're going to need it in our router as well, we'll refactor it as a getter.

One thing about getters is that they don't accept a payload argument like mutations do. If you want to pass a value to a getter, you need to return a function where the payload is an argument of that function.

`resources/assets/js/router.js`:

```
getters: {
  getListing(state) {
    return id => state.listings.find(listing => id == listing.id);
  }
}
```

Let's now use this getter in our `ListingPage` to replace the previous logic.

`resources/assets/components/ListingPage.vue`:

```
computed: {
  listing() {
    return populateAmenitiesAndPrices(
      this.$store.getters.getListing(this.$route.params.listing)
    );
  }
}
```

Checking if page state is in the store

We've successfully moved page state into the store. Now in the navigation guard, we will check to see if the data a page needs is already stored to avoid retrieving the same data twice:

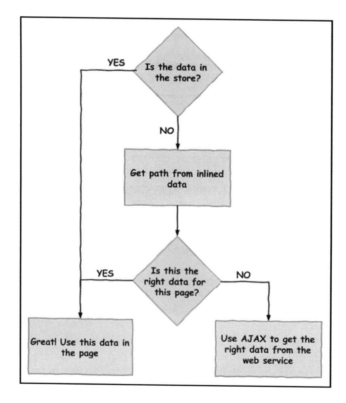

Figure 8.15. Decision logic for getting page data

Let's implement this logic in the `beforeEach` hook in `router.js`. We'll add an `if` block at the start that will instantly resolve the hook if the data is already present. The `if` uses a ternary function with the following logic:

- If the route name is *listing*, use the `getListing` getter to see if that particular listing is available (this getter returns `undefined` if it is not)
- If the route name is *not listing*, check to see if the store has listing summaries available. Listing summaries are always retrieved all at once, so if there's at least one, you can assume they're all there

`resources/assets/js/router.js`:

```
router.beforeEach((to, from, next) => {
  let serverData = JSON.parse(window.vuebnb_server_data);
  if (
    to.name === 'listing'
      ? store.getters.getListing(to.params.listing)
      : store.state.listing_summaries.length > 0
  ) {
    next();
  }
  else if (!serverData.path || to.path !== serverData.path) {
    axios.get(`/api${to.path}`).then(({data}) => {
      store.commit('addData', {route: to.name, data});
      next();
    });

  }
  else {
    store.commit('addData', {route: to.name, data: serverData});
    next();
  }
});
```

With that done, if the in-app navigation is used to navigate from the home page to listing 1, then back to the home page, then back to listing 1, the app will retrieve listing 1 from the API just the once. It would have done it twice under the previous architecture!

Saved page

We will now add the saved page to Vuebnb. Let's begin by creating the component file:

```
$ touch resources/assets/components/SavedPage.vue
```

Next, we'll create a new route with this component at the path /saved.

resources/assets/js/router.js:

```
...

import SavedPage from '../components/SavedPage.vue';

let router = new VueRouter({
  ...
  routes: [
    ...
    { path: '/saved', component: SavedPage, name: 'saved' }
  ]
});
```

Let's also add some server-side routes to the Laravel project. As discussed above, the saved page uses exactly the same data as the home page. This means that we can just call the same controller methods used for the home page.

routes/web.php:

```
Route::get('/saved', 'ListingController@get_home_web');
```

routes/api.php:

```
Route::get('/saved', 'ListingController@get_home_api');
```

Now we will define the SavedPage component. Beginning with the script tag, we will import the ListingSummary component we created back in Chapter 6, *Composing Widgets with Vue.js Components*. We'll also create a computed property, listings, that will return the listing summaries from the store, filtered by whether or not they're saved.

resources/assets/components/SavedPage.vue:

```
<template></template>
<script>
  import ListingSummary from './ListingSummary.vue';

  export default {
```

```
    computed: {
      listings() {
        return this.$store.state.listing_summaries.filter(
          item => this.$store.state.saved.indexOf(item.id) > -1
        );
      }
    },
    components: {
      ListingSummary
    }
  }
</script>
<style></style>
```

Next, we will add to the template tag of SavedPage. The main content includes a check for the length of the array returned by the listings computed property. If it is 0, no items have been saved yet. In this case, we display a message to inform the user. If there are listings saved, however, we'll iterate through them and display them with the ListingSummary component.

resources/assets/components/SavedPage.vue:

```
<template>
  <div id="saved" class="home-container">
    <h2>Saved listings</h2>
    <div v-if="listings.length" class="listing-summaries">
      <listing-summary
        v-for="listing in listings"
        :listing="listing"
        :key="listing.id"
      ></listing-summary>
    </div>
    <div v-else>No saved listings.</div>
  </div>
</template>
<script>...</script>
<style>...</style>
```

Lastly, we'll add to the `style` tag. The main thing to note here is that we're utilizing the `flex-wrap: wrap` rule and justifying to the left. This ensures that our listing summaries will organize themselves in rows without gaps.

`resources/assets/components/SavedPage.vue`:

```
<template>...</template>
<script>...</script>
<style>
  #saved .listing-summaries {
    display: flex;
    flex-wrap: wrap;
    justify-content: left;
    overflow: hidden;
  }

  #saved .listing-summaries .listing-summary {
    padding-bottom: 30px;
  }

  .listing-summaries > .listing-summary {
    margin-right: 15px;
  }
</style>
```

Let's also add the `.saved-container` CSS rules in our global CSS file. This ensures that our custom footer has access to these rules as well.

`resources/assets/css/style.css`:

```
.saved-container {
  margin: 0 auto;
  padding: 0 25px;
}

@media (min-width: 1131px) {
  .saved-container {
    width: 1095px;
    padding-left: 40px;
    margin-bottom: -10px;
  }
}
```

The final task is to add some default saved listings to the store. I've chosen 1 and 15 at random, but you can add any you want. We'll remove these again in the next chapter when we use Laravel to persist saved listings to the database.

`resources/assets/js/store.js`:

```
state: {
  saved: [1, 15],
  ...
},
```

With that done, here's what our saved page looks like:

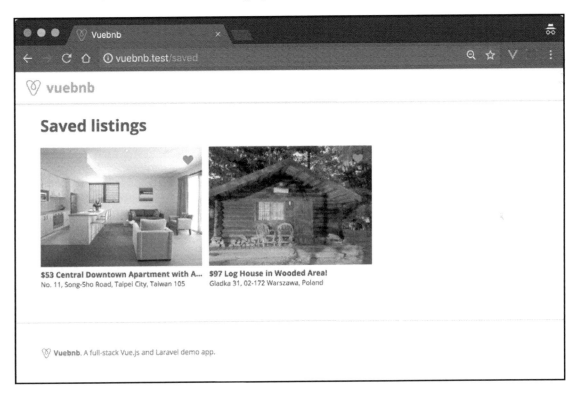

Figure 8.16. Saved page

If we remove all our saved listings, this is what we see:

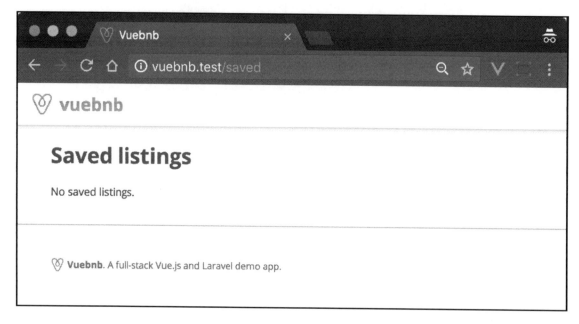

Figure 8.17. Saved page without listings

Toolbar links

The last thing we'll do in this chapter is to add a link to the saved page in the toolbar so that the saved page is accessible from any other page. To do this, we'll add an inline `ul` where links are enclosed within a child `li` (we'll add more links to the toolbar in `Chapter 9`, *Adding a User Login and API Authentication with Passport*).

`resources/assets/components/App.vue`:

```
<div id="toolbar">
  <router-link :to="{ name: 'home' }">
    <img class="icon" src="/images/logo.png">
    <h1>vuebnb</h1>
  </router-link>
  <ul class="links">
    <li>
      <router-link :to="{ name: 'saved' }">Saved</router-link>
    </li>
  </ul>
</div>
```

To display this correctly, we'll have to add some extra CSS. Firstly, we'll modify the `#toolbar` declaration so that the toolbar uses flex for display. We'll also add some new rules below that for displaying the links.

`resources/assets/components/App.vue`:

```
<style>
  #toolbar {
    display: flex;
    justify-content: space-between;
    border-bottom: 1px solid #e4e4e4;
    box-shadow: 0 1px 5px rgba(0, 0, 0, 0.1);
  }

  ...

  #toolbar ul {
    display: flex;
    align-items: center;
    list-style: none;
    padding: 0 24px 0 0;
    margin: 0;
  }

  @media (max-width: 373px) {
    #toolbar ul  {
      padding-right: 12px;
    }
  }

  #toolbar ul li {
    padding: 10px 10px 0 10px;
  }

  #toolbar ul li a {
    text-decoration: none;
    line-height: 1;
    color: inherit;
    font-size: 13px;
    padding-bottom: 8px;
    letter-spacing: 0.5px;
    cursor: pointer;
  }

  #toolbar ul li a:hover {
    border-bottom: 2px solid #484848;
    padding-bottom: 6px;
```

```
    }
</style>
```

We now have a link to the saved page in the toolbar:

Figure 8.18: Saved link in toolbar

Summary

In this chapter, we learned about Vuex, Vue's official state management library, which is based on the Flux architecture. We installed Vuex in Vuebnb and set up a store where global state could be written and retrieved.

We then learned the main features of Vuex including state, mutator methods and getters, and how we can debug Vuex using Vue Devtools. We used this knowledge to implement a listing save component, which we then added to our main pages.

Lastly, we married Vuex and Vue Router to allow page state to be more efficiently stored and retrieved when the route changes.

In the next chapter, we'll cover one of the trickiest topics of full-stack apps - authentication. We'll add a user profile to Vuebnb so a user can persist their saved items to the database. We'll also continue to add to our knowledge of Vuex by utilizing some of its more advanced features.

9

Adding a User Login and API Authentication with Passport

In the last chapter, we allowed the user to save their favorite Vuebnb listings. This feature was only implemented in the frontend app though, so if the user reloaded the page their selections would be lost.

In this chapter, we'll create a user login system and persist saved items to the database so they can be retrieved after a page refresh.

Topics covered in this chapter:

- Setting up a user login system utilizing Laravel's built-in authentication features
- Creating a login form with CSRF protection
- Using Vuex actions for asynchronous operations in the store
- A brief introduction to the OAuth protocol for API authentication
- Setting up Laravel Passport to allow authenticated AJAX requests

User model

In order to save listing items to the database, we first need a user model, as we want each user to have their own unique list. Adding a user model means we'll also need an authentication system so that users can sign in and out. Fortunately, Laravel provides a full-featured user model and authentication system out-of-the-box.

Let's now take a look at the user model boilerplate files to see what modifications will be needed to fit them for our purposes.

Migration

Looking first at the database migration, the user table schema already includes ID, name, email, and password columns.

database/migrations/2014_10_12_000000_create_users_table.php:

```php
<?php

use Illuminate\Support\Facades\Schema;
use Illuminate\Database\Schema\Blueprint;
use Illuminate\Database\Migrations\Migration;

class CreateUsersTable extends Migration
{
  public function up()
  {
    Schema::create('users', function (Blueprint $table) {
      $table->increments('id');
      $table->string('name');
      $table->string('email')->unique();
      $table->string('password');
      $table->rememberToken();
      $table->timestamps();
    });
  }

  public function down()
  {
    Schema::dropIfExists('users');
  }
}
```

This schema will be sufficient for our needs if we add an additional column for storing the saved listing IDs. Ideally, we'd store these in an array, but since relational databases don't have an array column type, we will instead store them as a serialized string, for example, [1, 5, 10] within a `text` column.

database/migrations/2014_10_12_000000_create_users_table.php:

```php
Schema::create('users', function (Blueprint $table) {
    ...
    $table->text('saved');
});
```

Model

Let's now take a look now at the `User` model class that Laravel provides.

app/User.php:

```php
<?php

namespace App;

use Illuminate\Notifications\Notifiable;
use Illuminate\Foundation\Auth\User as Authenticatable;

class User extends Authenticatable
{
    use Notifiable;

    protected $fillable = [
        'name', 'email', 'password',
    ];

    protected $hidden = [
        'password', 'remember_token',
    ];
}
```

The default configuration is fine, but let's allow the `saved` attribute to be mass assignable by adding it to the `$fillable` array.

We'll also get our model to serialize and deserialize the `saved` text when we read it or write it. To do this we can add a `$casts` attribute to the model and cast `saved` as an array.

app/User.php:

```
class User extends Authenticatable
{
  ...

  protected $fillable = [
    'name', 'email', 'password', 'saved'
  ];

  ...

  protected $casts = [
    'saved' => 'array'
  ];
}
```

Now we can treat the `saved` attribute as an array, even though it's stored as a string in the database:

```
echo gettype($user->saved());

// array
```

Seeder

In a normal web app with a login system, you'd have a registration page so users can create their own accounts. To ensure this book doesn't get too long, we'll skip that feature and instead generate user accounts with a database seeder:

```
$ php artisan make:seeder UsersTableSeeder
```

 You can implement a registration page for Vuebnb yourself if you want. The Laravel documentation covers it quite thoroughly at `https:// laravel.com/docs/5.5/authentication`.

Let's create at least one account with a name, email, password, and an array of saved listings. Note that I've used the `make` method of the `Hash` facade to hash the password rather than storing it as plain-text. Laravel's default `LoginController` will automatically verify plain-text passwords against the hash during the login process.

database/seeds/UsersTableSeeder.php:

```php
<?php

use Illuminate\Database\Seeder;
use App\User;
use Illuminate\Support\Facades\Hash;

class UsersTableSeeder extends Seeder
{
  public function run()
  {
    User::create([
      'name'     => 'Jane Doe',
      'email'    => 'test@gmail.com',
      'password' => Hash::make('test'),
      'saved'    => [1,5,7,9]
    ]);
  }
}
```

To run the seeder we need to call it from the main `DatabaseSeeder` class.

database/seeds/DatabaseSeeder.php:

```php
<?php

use Illuminate\Database\Seeder;

class DatabaseSeeder extends Seeder
{
  public function run()
  {
    $this->call(ListingsTableSeeder::class);
    $this->call(UsersTableSeeder::class);
  }
}
```

Let's now rerun our migrations and seeder to install the user table and data with the following command:

```
$ php artisan migrate:refresh --seed
```

To confirm that our user table and data were created correctly, we'll use Tinker to query the table. You should get an output similar to the following:

```
$ php artisan tinker

>>> DB::table('users')->get();

/*
{
  "id": 1,
  "name": "Jane Doe",
  "email": "test@gmail.com",
  "password": "...",
  "remember_token": null,
  "created_at": "2017-10-27 02:30:31",
  "updated_at": "2017-10-27 02:30:31",
  "saved": "[1,5,7,9]"
}
*/
```

Login system

Now that we have our user model created, we can implement the rest of the login system. Again, Laravel includes this as an out-of-the-box feature, so there is only a small amount of configuration for us to do.

Here's an overview of how the login system works:

1. The user provides their email and password in a login form. We'll create this form with Vue
2. The form is submitted to the /login POST route
3. The LoginController will then verify the user's credentials against the database

4. If the login is successful, the user is redirected to the home page. A session cookie is attached to the response, which is then passed to all outgoing requests to verify the user

Here's a diagrammatic representation of the login system for further clarity:

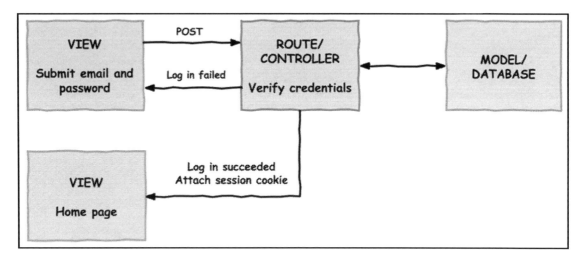

Figure 9.1. Login flow

LoginPage component

We will need a login page for our app, so let's create a new page component:

```
$ touch resources/assets/components/LoginPage.vue
```

We'll begin by defining the template markup, which includes a form with fields for email and password, and a submit button. The form uses the HTTP POST method and is sent to the /login path. I've wrapped the form elements in a div with the .form-controller class to help with styling.

resources/assets/components/LoginPage.vue:

```
<template>
  <div id="login" class="login-container">
    <form role="form" method="POST" action="/login">
      <div class="form-control">
        <input id="email" type="email" name="email"
          placeholder="Email Address" required autofocus>
```

```
      </div>
      <div class="form-control">
        <input id="password" type="password" name="password"
          placeholder="Password" required>
      </div>
      <div class="form-control">
        <button type="submit">Log in</button>
      </div>
    </form>
  </div>
</template>
```

We don't need any JavaScript functionality just yet, so let's add our CSS rules now.

`resources/assets/components/LoginPage.vue`:

```
<template>...</template>
<style>
  #login form {
    padding-top: 40px;
  }

  @media (min-width: 744px) {
    #login form {
      padding-top: 80px;
    }
  }

  #login .form-control {
    margin-bottom: 1em;
  }

  #login input[type=email],
  #login input[type=password],
  #login button,
  #login label {
    width: 100%;
    font-size: 19px !important;
    line-height: 24px;
    color: #484848;
    font-weight: 300;
  }

  #login input {
    background-color: transparent;
    padding: 11px;
    border: 1px solid #dbdbdb;
    border-radius: 2px;
```

```
      box-sizing:border-box
    }

    #login button {
      background-color: #4fc08d;
      color: #ffffff;
      cursor: pointer;
      border: #4fc08d;
      border-radius: 4px;
      padding-top: 12px;
      padding-bottom: 12px;
    }
  </style>
```

We'll add a `login-container` class to our global CSS file so the footer for this page aligns correctly. We'll also add a CSS rule to ensure text inputs display correctly on iPhone. The login page will be the only place we'll have a text input, but let's add it as a global rule in case you decide to add other forms later.

`resources/assets/css/style.css:`

```
  ...

  .login-container {
    margin: 0 auto;
    padding: 0 12px;
  }

  @media (min-width: 374px) {
    .login-container {
      width: 350px;
    }
  }

  input[type=text] {
    -webkit-appearance: none;
  }
```

Finally, let's add this new page component to our router. We'll first import the component then add it to our `routes` array in the router configuration.

Note that the login page does not require any data from the server like the other pages of Vuebnb do. This means that we can skip the data-fetching step by modifying the logic of the first `if` statement in the navigation guard. It should now resolve straightaway if the name of the route is `login`.

`resources/assets/js/router.js`:

```
...

import LoginPage from '../components/LoginPage.vue';

let router = new VueRouter({
  ...
  routes: [
    ...
    { path: '/login', component: LoginPage, name: 'login' }
  ],
  ...
});

router.beforeEach((to, from, next) => {
  ...
  if (
    to.name === 'listing'
      ? store.getters.getListing(to.params.listing)
      : store.state.listing_summaries.length > 0
    || to.name === 'login'
  ) {
    next();
  }
  ...
});

export default router;
```

Server routes

Now that we've added a login page at the `/login` route, we will need to create a matching server-side route. We will also need a route for the login form that posts to the same `/login` path.

In fact, both of these routes are provided out-of-the-box by Laravel as part of its default login system. All we have to do to activate the routes is add the following line to the bottom of our web route file.

`routes/web.php`:

```
...

Auth::routes();
```

To see the effect of this code, we can use Artisan to show a list of the routes in our app:

```
$ php artisan route:list
```

Output:

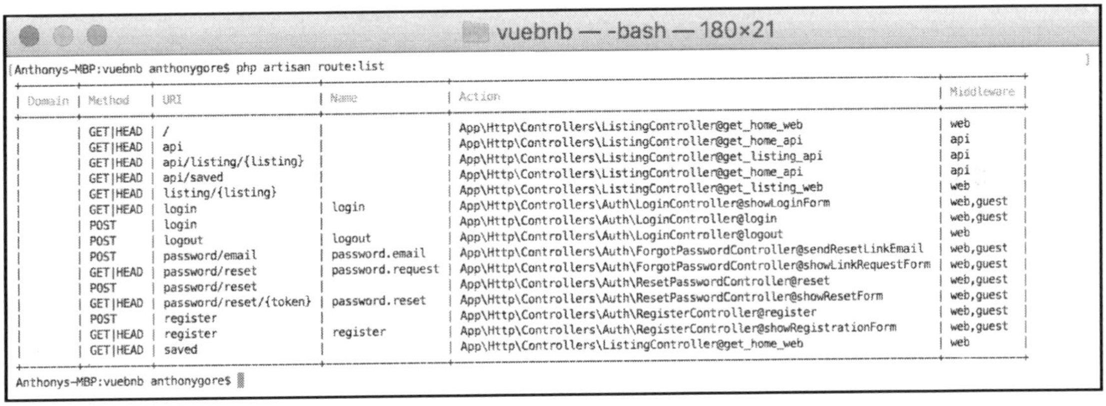

```
vuebnb — -bash — 180×21
Anthonys-MBP:vuebnb anthonygore$ php artisan route:list
+--------+----------+-------------------------+------------------+-------------------------------------------------------------------------+------------+
| Domain | Method   | URI                     | Name             | Action                                                                  | Middleware |
+--------+----------+-------------------------+------------------+-------------------------------------------------------------------------+------------+
|        | GET|HEAD | /                       |                  | App\Http\Controllers\ListingController@get_home_web                     | web        |
|        | GET|HEAD | api                     |                  | App\Http\Controllers\ListingController@get_home_api                     | api        |
|        | GET|HEAD | api/listing/{listing}   |                  | App\Http\Controllers\ListingController@get_listing_api                  | api        |
|        | GET|HEAD | api/saved               |                  | App\Http\Controllers\ListingController@get_home_api                     | api        |
|        | GET|HEAD | listing/{listing}       |                  | App\Http\Controllers\ListingController@get_listing_web                  | web        |
|        | GET|HEAD | login                   | login            | App\Http\Controllers\Auth\LoginController@showLoginForm                 | web,guest  |
|        | POST     | login                   |                  | App\Http\Controllers\Auth\LoginController@login                         | web,guest  |
|        | POST     | logout                  | logout           | App\Http\Controllers\Auth\LoginController@logout                        | web        |
|        | POST     | password/email          | password.email   | App\Http\Controllers\Auth\ForgotPasswordController@sendResetLinkEmail   | web,guest  |
|        | GET|HEAD | password/reset          | password.request | App\Http\Controllers\Auth\ForgotPasswordController@showLinkRequestForm  | web,guest  |
|        | POST     | password/reset          |                  | App\Http\Controllers\Auth\ResetPasswordController@reset                 | web,guest  |
|        | GET|HEAD | password/reset/{token}  | password.reset   | App\Http\Controllers\Auth\ResetPasswordController@showResetForm         | web,guest  |
|        | POST     | register                |                  | App\Http\Controllers\Auth\RegisterController@register                   | web,guest  |
|        | GET|HEAD | register                | register         | App\Http\Controllers\Auth\RegisterController@showRegistrationForm       | web,guest  |
|        | GET|HEAD | saved                   |                  | App\Http\Controllers\ListingController@get_home_web                     | web        |
+--------+----------+-------------------------+------------------+-------------------------------------------------------------------------+------------+
Anthonys-MBP:vuebnb anthonygore$
```

Figure 9.2. Terminal output showing routes list

You'll see all the routes that we've manually created, plus a few that we didn't, for example, *login*, *logout*, and *register*. These are the routes used by Laravel's authentication system that we just activated.

Looking at the GET/HEAD /login route, you'll see that it points to the LoginController controller. Let's take a look at that file.

App\Http\Controllers\Auth\LoginController.php:

```php
<?php

namespace App\Http\Controllers\Auth;

use App\Http\Controllers\Controller;
use Illuminate\Foundation\Auth\AuthenticatesUsers;

class LoginController extends Controller
{
  use AuthenticatesUsers;

  protected $redirectTo = '/home';

  public function __construct()
  {
    $this->middleware('guest')->except('logout');
  }
}
```

This class uses an AuthenticatesUsers trait that defines the showLoginForm method that the /login route handler refers to. Let's overwrite that method so it simply returns our app view. Since this instance of the view doesn't need any data to be inlined in the head (the login form has no state), we will pass an empty array to the data template variable.

App\Http\Controllers\Auth\LoginController.php:

```php
class LoginController extends Controller
{
  ...

  public function showLoginForm()
  {
    return view('app', ['data' => []]);
  }
}
```

With that done, we can now see our complete login page by navigating the browser to /login:

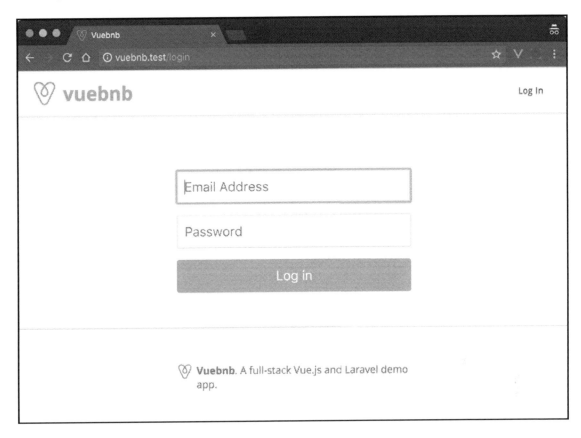

Figure 9.3. Login page

CSRF protection

CSRF (cross-site request forgery) is a type of malicious exploit where an attacker gets a user to unknowingly perform an action on a server that they're currently logged in to. This action will change something on the server that is advantageous to the attacker, for example, transfer money, change the password to one the attacker knows, and so on.

For example, an attacker might hide a script in a web page or email and direct the user to it somehow. When it executes, this script could make a POST request to `importantwebsite.com/updateEmailAndPassword`. If the user is logged in to this site, the request may be successful.

One way to prevent this kind of attack is to embed a special token, essentially a random string, in any form that a user might submit. When the form is submitted, the token is checked against the user's session to make sure it matches. An attacker won't be able to forge this token in their script and should, therefore, be thwarted by this feature.

In Laravel, CSRF token creation and verification is managed by the `VerifyCsrfToken` middleware that is added to the web routes by default:

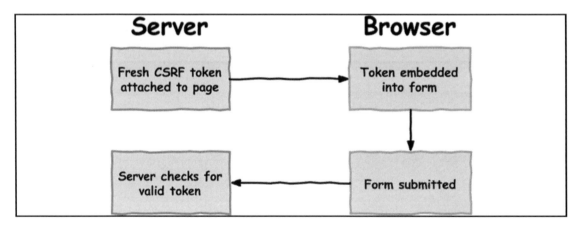

Figure 9.4. CSRF prevention process

To include the CSRF token in a form you can simply add `{{ csrf_field() }}` within the `form` tag. This will generate a hidden input field containing a valid CSRF token, for example:

```
<input type="hidden" name="_token" value="3B08L3fj...">
```

This won't work in our scenario, though, as our form is not inside a Blade view but inside a single-file component that will not get processed by Blade. As an alternative, we can add the CSRF token to the head of the page and assign it to the `window` object.

`resources/views/app.blade.php`:

```
<script type="text/javascript">
  window.vuebnb_server_data = "{!! addslashes(json_encode($data)) !!}"
  window.csrf_token = "{{ csrf_token() }}"
</script>
```

We can now retrieve this from within our Vue.js app and manually add it to the login form. Let's modify `LoginPage` to include a hidden `input` field in the form. We'll add some state to this component now, in which the token is included as a data property and bound to the hidden field.

`resources/assets/js/components/LoginPage.vue`:

```
<template>
  <div id="login" class="login-container">
    <form role="form" method="POST" action="/login">
      <input type="hidden" name="_token" :value="csrf_token">
      ...
    </form>
  </div>
</template>
<script>
  export default {
    data() {
      return {
        csrf_token: window.csrf_token
      }
    }
  }
</script>
<style>...</style>
```

If we now try to log in to our app using the credentials of the user we created in the seeder, we'll get served this error page. Looking in the address bar, you'll see that the route we're on is /home, which is not a valid route within our app, hence the NotFoundHttpException:

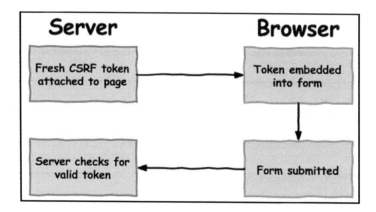

Figure 9.5. Invalid route

Post-login redirection

When a user logs in, Laravel will redirect them to a page defined by the $redirectTo attribute in the login controller. Let's change this from /home to /.

app/Http/Auth/Controllers/LoginController.php:

```
class LoginController extends Controller
{
    ...

    protected $redirectTo = '/';

    ...
}
```

Let's also update the RedirectIfAuthenticated middleware class so that if a logged-in user attempts to view the login page, they're redirect to / (instead of the default /home value.)

app/Http/Middleware/RedirectIfAuthenticated.php:

```
    ...
```

```
if (Auth::guard($guard)->check()) {
  return redirect('/');
}
```

With that done, our login process will now work correctly.

Adding authentication links to the toolbar

Let's now add login and logout links in the toolbar so Vuebnb users can easily access these features.

The login link is simply a `RouterLink` pointing to the `login` route.

The logout link is a bit more interesting: we capture the click event from this link and trigger the submission of a hidden form. This form sends a POST request to the `/logout` server route, which logs the user out and redirects them back to the home page. Note that we must include the CSRF token as a hidden input for this to work.

`resources/assets/components/App.vue`:

```
<template>
  ...
  <ul class="links">
    <li>
      <router-link :to="{ name: 'saved' }">
        Saved
      </router-link>
    </li>
    <li>
      <router-link :to="{ name: 'login' }">
        Log In
      </router-link>
    </li>
    <li>
      <a @click="logout">Log Out</a>
      <form
        style="display: hidden"
        action="/logout"
        method="POST"
        id="logout"
      >
        <input type="hidden" name="_token" :value="csrf_token"/>
      </form>
    </li>
  </ul>
```

```
    ...
  </template>
  <script>
    ...

    export default {
      components: { ... },
      data() {
        return {
          csrf_token: window.csrf_token
        }
      },
      methods: {
        logout() {
          document.getElementById('logout').submit();
        }
      }
    }
  </script>
```

Protecting the saved route

We can use our login system now to protect certain routes from guests, that is, unauthenticated users. Laravel provides the auth middleware, which can be applied to any route and will redirect a guest user to the login page if they attempt to access it. Let's apply this to our saved page route.

routes/web.php:

```
Route::get('/saved', 'ListingController@get_home_web')->middleware('auth');
```

If you log out of the application and attempt to access this route from the navigation bar of your browser, you'll find it redirects you back to /login.

Passing authentication state to the frontend

We now have a complete mechanism for logging users in and out of Vuebnb. However, the frontend app is not yet aware of the user's authentication state. Let's remedy that now so we can add authentication-based features to the frontend.

auth meta property

We'll begin by adding the authentication state to the meta information we pass through in the head of each page. We'll utilize the `Auth` facade `check` method, which returns `true` if the user is authenticated, and assign this to a new `auth` property.

app/Http/Controllers/ListingController.php:

```
...
use Illuminate\Support\Facades\Auth;

class ListingController extends Controller
{
  ...

  private function add_meta_data($collection, $request)
  {
    return $collection->merge([
      'path' => $request->getPathInfo(),
      'auth' => Auth::check()
    ]);
  }
}
```

We'll also add an `auth` property to our Vuex store. We'll mutate it from the `addData` method which, as you'll recall from the previous chapter, is where we retrieve data from the document head or API. Since the API does not include meta data, we'll conditionally mutate the `auth` property to avoid accessing a potentially undefined object property.

resources/assets/js/store.js:

```
...

export default new Vuex.Store({
  state: {
    ...
    auth: false
  },
  mutations: {
    ...
    addData(state, { route, data }) {
      if (data.auth) {
        state.auth = data.auth;
      }
      if (route === 'listing') {
```

```
          state.listings.push(data.listing);
      } else {
          state.listing_summaries = data.listings;
      }
   }
  },
  getters: { ... }
});
```

With that done, Vuex is now tracking the authentication state of the user. Be sure to test this out by logging in and out and noticing the value of auth in the Vuex tab of Vue Devtools:

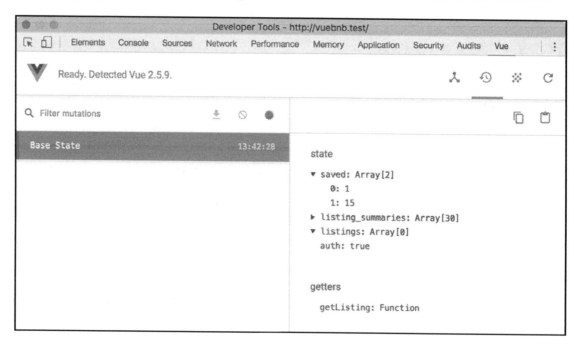

Figure 9.6. Value of auth in Vue Devtools

Responding to authenticated state

Now that we're tracking the authentication state of the user, we can get Vuebnb to respond to it. For one, let's make it so that a user can't save a listing unless they're logged in. To do this, we'll modify the behavior of the toggleSaved mutator method so that if the user is logged in they can save an item, but if not they are redirected to the login page via the push method of Vue Router.

Note that we'll have to import our router module at the top of the file to access its features.

`resources/assets/js/store.js`:

```
...
import router from './router';

export default new Vuex.Store({
  ...
  mutations: {
    toggleSaved(state, id) {
      if (state.auth) {
        let index = state.saved.findIndex(saved => saved === id);
        if (index === -1) {
          state.saved.push(id);
        } else {
          state.saved.splice(index, 1);
        }
      } else {
        router.push('/login');
      }
    },
    ...
  },
  ...
});
```

We'll also make it so that either the login link or the logout link is shown in the toolbar, never both. This can be achieved by using `v-if` and `v-else` directives in the toolbar that depend on the `$store.state.auth` value.

It would also make sense to hide the saved page link unless the user is logged in, so let's do that as well.

`resources/assets/components/App.vue`:

```
<ul class="links">
  <li v-if="$store.state.auth">
    <router-link :to="{ name: 'saved' }">
      Saved
    </router-link>
  </li>
  <li v-if="$store.state.auth">
    <a @click="logout">Log Out</a>
    <form
      style="display: hidden"
      action="/logout"
```

```
      method="POST"
      id="logout"
   >
      <input type="hidden" name="_token" :value="csrf_token"/>
   </form>
</li>
<li v-else>
   <router-link :to="{ name: 'login' }">
      Log In
   </router-link>
</li>
</ul>
```

This is how the toolbar will look now, depending on whether the user is logged in or out:

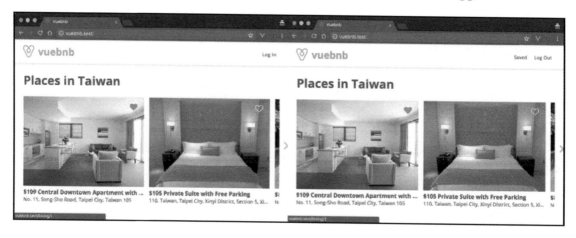

Figure 9.8. Comparison of the logged in and logged out state in toolbar

Retrieving saved items from the database

Let's now work on retrieving the saved items from the database and displaying them in the frontend. To begin with, we'll add a new `saved` property to the metadata we put in the document head. This will be an empty array if the user is logged out, or the array of saved listing IDs associated with that user, if they're logged in.

app/Http/Controllers/ListingController.php:

```
   private function add_meta_data($collection, $request)
   {
      return $collection->merge([
```

```
        'path' => $request->getPathInfo(),
        'auth' => Auth::check(),
        'saved' => Auth::check() ? Auth::user()->saved : []
    ]);
}
```

Back in the frontend, we'll put the logic for retrieving the saved items in
the beforeEach router navigation guard. The reason we put it here and not in
the addData mutation is that we don't want to directly assign the data to the store state, but
instead call the toggleSaved mutation for each of the listings. You can't commit a mutation
from another mutation, so this must be done outside the store.

resources/assets/js/router.js:

```
router.beforeEach((to, from, next) => {
    let serverData = JSON.parse(window.vuebnb_server_data);
    if ( ... ) { ... }
    else if ( ... ) { ... }
    else {
        store.commit('addData', {route: to.name, data: serverData});
        serverData.saved.forEach(id => store.commit('toggleSaved', id));
        next();
    }
});
```

Let's also remove the placeholder listing IDs we added to saved in the previous chapter so
the store is empty upon initialization.

resources/assets/js/store.js:

```
state: {
    saved: [],
    listing_summaries: [],
    listings: [],
    auth: false
}
```

With that done, we should find that the saved listings in the database now match those in the frontend if we check with Vue Devtools:

```
$ php artisan tinker
>>> DB::table('users')->select('saved')->first();
# "saved": "[1,5,7,9]"
```

Figure 9.8. Vuex tab of Vue Devtools shows saved listings match database

Persisting saved listings

The mechanism for persisting saved listings is as follows: when a listing is toggled in the frontend app, we trigger an AJAX request that POSTs the ID to a route on the backend. This route calls a controller that will update the model:

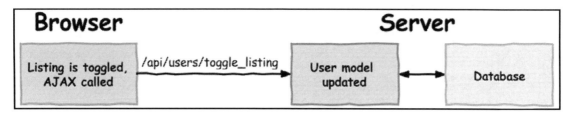

Figure 9.9. Persisting saved listings

Let's now implement this mechanism.

Creating an API route

We'll begin on the server side and add a route for the frontend to POST listing IDS to. We'll need to add the auth middleware so that only authenticated users can access this route (we'll discuss the meaning of :api shortly).

routes/api.php:

```
    ...

    Route::post('/user/toggle_saved', 'UserController@toggle_saved')
        ->middleware('auth:api')
    ;
```

Since this is an API route, its full path will be /api/user/toggle_saved. We haven't yet created the controller that this route calls, UserController, so let's do that now:

```
$ php artisan make:controller UserController
```

In this new controller, we'll add the toggled_saved handling method. Since this is an HTTP POST route, this method will have access to the form data. We'll make it so that the frontend AJAX call to this route includes an id field, which will be the listing ID we want to toggle. To access this field, we can use the Input facade, that is, Input::get('id');.

Since we're using the `auth` middleware on this route, we can retrieve the user model associated with the request by using the `Auth::user()` method. We can then either add or remove the ID from the user's `saved` listings, just as we do in the `toggledSaved` method in our Vuex store.

Once the ID is toggled, we can then use the model's `save` method to persist the update to the database.

app/Http/Controllers/UserController.php:

```php
<?php

...

use Illuminate\Support\Facades\Auth;
use Illuminate\Support\Facades\Input;

class UserController extends Controller
{
  public function toggle_saved()
  {
    $id = Input::get('id');
    $user = Auth::user();
    $saved = $user->saved;
    $key = array_search($id, $saved);
    if ($key === FALSE) {
        array_push($saved, $id);
    } else {
        array_splice($saved, $key, 1);
    }
    $user->saved = $saved;
    $user->save();
    return response()->json();
  }
}
```

Vuex actions

In Chapter 8, *Managing Your Application State With Vuex*, we discussed the key principles of the Flux pattern, including the principle that mutations must be synchronous to avoid race conditions that make our application data unpredictable.

If you have a need to include asynchronous code in a mutator method, you should instead create an *action*. Actions are like mutations, but instead of mutating the state, they commit mutations. For example:

```
var store = new Vuex.Store({
  state: {
    val: null
  },
  mutations: {
    assignVal(state, payload) {
      state.val = payload;
    }
  },
  actions: {
    setTimeout(() => {
      commit('assignVal', 10);
    }, 1000)
  }
});


store.dispatch('assignVal', 10);
```

By abstracting asynchronous code into actions we can still centralize any state-altering logic in the store without tainting our application data through race conditions.

AJAX request

Let's now use AJAX to make the request to `/api/user/toggle_saved` when a listing is saved. We'll put this logic into a Vuex action so that the `toggleSaved` mutation is not committed until the AJAX call resolves. We'll import the Axios HTTP library into the store to facilitate this.

Also, let's move the authentication check from the mutation to the action, as it makes sense to do this check before the AJAX call is initiated.

`resources/assets/js/store.js`:

```
import axios from 'axios';

export default new Vuex.Store({
  ...
  mutations: {
    toggleSaved(state, id) {
      let index = state.saved.findIndex(saved => saved === id);
```

```
            if (index === -1) {
              state.saved.push(id);
            } else {
              state.saved.splice(index, 1);
            }
        },
        ...
    },
    ...
    actions: {
      toggleSaved({ commit, state }, id) {
        if (state.auth) {
          axios.post('/api/user/toggle_saved', { id }).then(
            () => commit('toggleSaved', id)
          );
        } else {
          router.push('/login');
        }
      }
    }
  }
});
```

We now need to call the `toggledSaved` action, not the mutation, from our `ListingSave` component. Calling an action is done in exactly the same way as a mutation, only the terminology changes from `commit` to `dispatch`.

`resources/assets/components/ListingSave.vue`:

```
toggleSaved() {
  this.$store.dispatch('toggleSaved', this.id);
}
```

The code for this feature in the frontend is correct, but if we test it out and try and save an item we get a *401 Unauthenticated* error from the server:

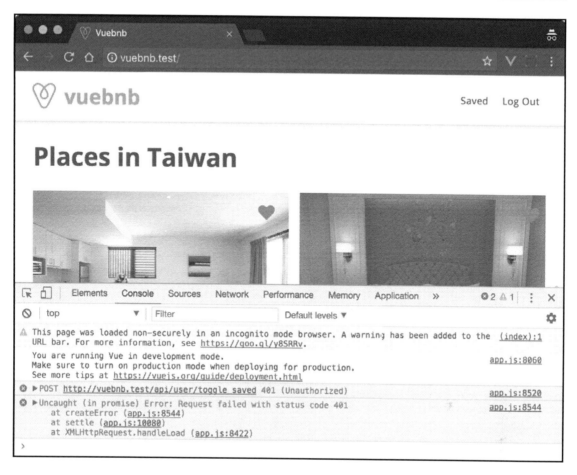

Figure 9.10. AJAX call results in a 401 Unauthenticated error

API authentication

We added the `auth` middleware to our `/api/user/toggle_saved` route to protect it from guest users. We also specified the `api` guard for this middleware, that is, `auth:api`.

Guards define how users are authenticated and are configured in the following file.

`config/auth.php`:

```
<?php
```

```
return [
  ...
  'guards' => [
    'web' => [
       'driver' => 'session',
       'provider' => 'users',
    ],
    'api' => [
       'driver' => 'token',
       'provider' => 'users',
    ],
  ],
  ...
];
```

Our web routes use the *session* driver which maintains authentication state using session cookies. The session driver ships with Laravel and works out-of-the-box. API routes, though, use the *token* guard by default. We have not yet implemented this driver, hence our AJAX calls are unauthorized.

We could use the session driver for API routes as well, but this is not recommended, as session authentication is not sufficient for AJAX requests. We're instead going to use the passport guard, which implements the OAuth protocol.

You may see auth used as a shorthand for auth:web, as the web guard is the default.

OAuth

OAuth is an authorization protocol that allows third-party applications to access a user's data on a server without exposing their password. Access to this protected data is given in exchange for a special token that is granted to the application once it, and the user, have identified themselves to the server. A typical use case for OAuth is *social login*, for example, when you utilize a Facebook or Google login for your own website.

One challenge of making secure AJAX requests is that you can't store any credentials in the frontend source code, as it's trivial for an attacker to find these. A simple implementation of OAuth, where the third-party application is actually your own frontend app, is a good solution to the issue. This is the approach we'll be taking now for Vuebnb.

While OAuth is a great solution for API authentication, it is also quite an in-depth topic that I can't fully cover in this book. I recommend you read this guide to get a better understanding: `https://www.oauth.com/`.

Laravel Passport

Laravel Passport is an implementation of OAuth that can easily be set up in a Laravel application. Let's install it now for use in Vuebnb.

First, install Passport with Composer:

```
$ composer require laravel/passport
```

Passport includes new database migrations that generate the tables needed to store OAuth tokens. Let's run the migration:

```
$ php artisan migrate
```

The following command will install the encryption keys needed to generate secure tokens:

```
$ php artisan passport:install
```

After running this command, add the `Laravel\Passport\HasApiTokens` trait to the user model.

app/User.php:

```
<?php

...

use Laravel\Passport\HasApiTokens;

class User extends Authenticatable
{
  use HasApiTokens, Notifiable;

  ...
}
```

Finally, in the `config/auth.php` configuration file, let's set the driver option of the API guard to `passport`. This ensures the `auth` middleware will use Passport as a guard for API routes.

`config/auth.php`:

```
'guards' => [
  'web' => [
    'driver' => 'session',
    'provider' => 'users',
  ],

  'api' => [
    'driver' => 'passport',
    'provider' => 'users',
  ],
],
```

Attaching tokens

OAuth requires an access token to be sent to the frontend app when the user logs in. Passport includes a middleware that can handle this for you. Add the `CreateFreshApiToken` middleware to the web middleware group and the `laravel_token` cookie will be attached to outgoing responses.

`app/Http/Kernel.php`:

```
protected $middlewareGroups = [
  'web' => [
    ...
    \Laravel\Passport\Http\Middleware\CreateFreshApiToken::class,
  ],
  ...
```

For outgoing requests, we need to add some headers to our AJAX calls. We can make it so Axios automatically attaches these by default. `'X-Requested-With'`: `'XMLHttpRequest'` ensures that Laravel knows the request was from AJAX, while `'X-CSRF-TOKEN'`: `window.csrf_token` attaches the CSRF token.

`resources/assets/js/store.js`:

```
    ...

    axios.defaults.headers.common = {
```

```
    'X-Requested-With': 'XMLHttpRequest',
    'X-CSRF-TOKEN': window.csrf_token
};

export default new Vuex.Store({
    ...
});
```

With that done, our API requests should now be properly authenticated. To test this, let's use Tinker to see which items we have saved for our first seeded user:

```
$ php artisan tinker

>>> DB::table('users')->select('saved')->first();

# "saved": "[1,5,7,9]"
```

Make sure you're logged in as that user and load Vuebnb in the browser. Toggle a few of your saved listing selections and rerun the query above. You should find that the database is now persisting the saved listing IDs.

Summary

In this chapter, we learned about authentication in full-stack Vue/Laravel apps, including session-based authentication for web routes, and token-based authentication for API routes using Laravel Passport.

We used this knowledge to set up a login system for Vuebnb, and to allow saved room listings to be persisted to the database.

Along the way, we also learned how to utilize CSRF tokens for securing forms, and about Vuex actions for adding asynchronous code to the store.

In the next, and final, chapter, we will learn how to deploy a full-stack Vue and Laravel app to production by deploying Vuebnb to a free Heroku PHP server. We will also begin serving images and other static content from a free CDN.

10

Deploying a Full-Stack App to the Cloud

Now that the functionality of Vuebnb is complete, the final step is to deploy it to production. We'll use two free services, Heroku and KeyCDN, to share Vuebnb with the world.

Topics covered in this chapter:

- An introduction to the Heroku cloud platform service
- Deploying Vuebnb to Heroku as a free app
- How CDNs improve the performance of full-stack apps
- Integrating a free CDN with Laravel
- Building assets in production-mode for performance and security

Heroku

Heroku is a cloud platform service for web applications. It's immensely popular among developers due to the simplicity and affordability it offers for getting apps online.

Heroku applications can be made in a variety of languages including PHP, JavaScript, and Ruby. In addition to a web server, Heroku offers a variety of add-ons, such as databases, email services, and application monitoring.

Heroku apps can be deployed for free, though there are certain limitations, for example, the app will *sleep* after periods of inactivity, making it slow to respond. These limitations are lifted if you upgrade to a paid service.

We will now deploy Vuebnb to the Heroku platform. The first step is to create an account by visiting the following URL: `https://signup.heroku.com`.

CLI

The most convenient way to use Heroku is from the command line. Visit the following URL and follow the steps for installation: `https://devcenter.heroku.com/articles/heroku-cli`.

Once you've installed the CLI, log in to Heroku from the Terminal. After verifying your credentials you'll be able to use the CLI to create and manage your Heroku apps:

```
$ heroku login

# Enter your Heroku credentials:
# Email: anthony@vuejsdevelopers.com
# Password: ************
# Logged in as anthony@vuejsdevelopers.com
```

Creating an app

Let's now create a new Heroku app. New apps require a unique name, so replace `vuebnbapp` in the command below with your own choice. The name will be part of the app's URL, so make sure it's short and memorable:

```
$ heroku create vuebnbapp
```

Once the app is created you will be given the URL, for example: `https://vuebnbapp.herokuapp.com/`. Put it in the browser and you'll see this default message:

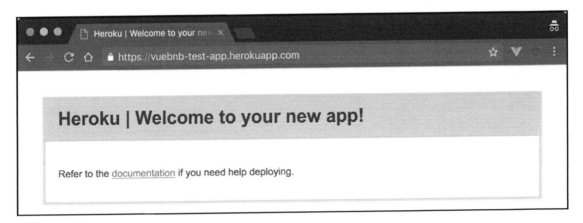

Figure 10.1. Heroku default message

 New Heroku apps are assigned a free domain name, for example: `appname.herokuapp.com`, but you can also use your own custom domain. See the Heroku Dev Center for more information at `https://devcenter.heroku.com`.

Source code

To deploy code to your Heroku app you can use Heroku's Git server. When you created your app with the CLI, a new remote repository was automatically added to your Git project. Confirm this with the following command:

```
$ git remote -v

heroku   https://git.heroku.com/vuebnbapp.git (fetch)
heroku   https://git.heroku.com/vuebnbapp.git (push)
origin   git@github.com:fsvwd/vuebnb.git (fetch)
origin   git@github.com:fsvwd/vuebnb.git (push)
```

Once we've completed the configuration of our app we'll make our first push. Heroku will use this code to build the app.

Environment variables

Heroku apps have an ephemeral filesystem that only includes code from the most recent Git push. This means Vuebnb will not have its `.env` file present since this file is not committed to the source code.

Environment variables are instead set by Heroku CLI, with the `heroku config` command. Let's begin by setting the app key. Replace the following value with your own app key:

```
$ heroku config:set APP_KEY=base64:mDZ51QnC2Hq+M6G2iesFzxRxpr+vKJS1+8bbGs=
```

Creating a database

We need a database for our production app. The ClearDB add-on for Heroku provides a MySQL cloud database that is easy to set up and connect.

This add-on is free for a limited number of transactions each month. However, you will need to verify your Heroku account before you can add a database, which means you'll need to supply credit card details, even if you use the free plan.

To verify your Heroku account, go to this URL: `https://heroku.com/verify`.

Once you've done that, create a new ClearDB database with this command:

```
$ heroku addons:create cleardb:ignite
```

Default string length

At the time of writing, ClearDB uses MySQL version 5.5, while our Homestead database is MySQL 5.7. The default string length in MySQL 5.5 is too short for Passport authorization keys, so we need to manually set the default string length in the app service provider before we run the database migrations in our production app.

`app/Providers/AppServiceProvider.php`:

```php
<?php

...
```

```
use Illuminate\Support\Facades\Schema;

class AppServiceProvider extends ServiceProvider
{
  ...

  public function boot()
  {
    Schema::defaultStringLength(191);
  }

  ...
}
```

Configuration

When you installed the ClearDB add-on, a new environment
variable, CLEARDB_DATABASE_URL, was automatically set. Let's read its value using
the heroku config:get command:

```
$ heroku config:get CLEARDB_DATABASE_URL

# mysql://b221344377ce82c:398z940v@us-cdbr-iron-
east-03.cleardb.net/heroku_n0b30ea856af46f?reconnect=true
```

In a Laravel project, the database is connected by setting values
for DB_HOST and DB_DATABASE. We can extract the values for these from
the CLEARDB_DATABASE_URL variable, which is in the form:

```
mysql://[DB_USERNAME]:[DB_PASSWORD]@[DB_HOST]/[DB_DATABASE]?reconnect=true
```

Once you've extracted the values, set the applicable environment variables in the Heroku
app:

```
$ heroku config:set \
DB_HOST=us-cdbr-iron-east-03.cleardb.net \
DB_DATABASE=heroku_n0b30ea856af46f \
DB_USERNAME=b221344377ce82c \
DB_PASSWORD=398z940v
```

Configuring a web server

Web server configuration for Heroku is done via a special file called `Procfile` (no file extension) that lives in the root of your project directory.

Let's now create that file:

```
$ touch Procfile
```

Each line of the `Procfile` is a declaration that tells Heroku how to run various pieces of your app. Let's create a `Procfile` for Vuebnb now and add this single declaration.

Procfile:

```
web: vendor/bin/heroku-php-apache2 public/
```

The part to the left of the colon is the process type. The `web` process type defines where HTTP requests are sent in the app. The part to the right is the command to run or start that process. We will route requests to an Apache server that points to the *public* directory of our app.

Passport keys

In Chapter 9, *Adding a User Login and API Authentication with Passport*, we created encryption keys for Passport with the `php artisan passport:install` command. These keys are stored in text files that can be found in the `storage` directory.

Encryption keys should not be under version control, as this would make them insecure. Instead, we need to regenerate these keys on each deploy. We can do this by adding a post-install script to our composer file.

composer.json:

```
"scripts": {
  ...
  "post-install-cmd": [
    "Illuminate\\Foundation\\ComposerScripts::postInstall",
    "php artisan optimize",
```

```
      "php artisan passport:install"
   ],
}
```

Deployment

We've done all the necessary set up and configuration, so we're ready now to deploy Vuebnb. Make sure you commit any file changes to your Git repository and push to the master branch of the Heroku Git server:

```
$ git add --all
$ git commit -m "Ready for deployment!"
$ git push heroku master
```

During the push you'll see the output similar to the following:

```
● ● ●                        vuebnb — -bash — 87×24
Anthonys-MBP:vuebnb anthonygore$ git push heroku master
Counting objects: 3, done.
Delta compression using up to 4 threads.
Compressing objects: 100% (3/3), done.
Writing objects: 100% (3/3), 298 bytes | 99.00 KiB/s, done.
Total 3 (delta 2), reused 0 (delta 0)
remote: Compressing source files... done.
remote: Building source:
remote:
remote: -------> PHP app detected
remote: -------> Bootstrapping...
remote: -------> Installing platform packages...
remote:          - php (7.1.11)
remote:          - ext-mbstring (bundled with php)
remote:          - nginx (1.8.1)
remote:          - apache (2.4.29)
remote: -------> Installing dependencies...
remote:          Composer version 1.5.2 2017-09-11 16:59:25
remote:          Loading composer repositories with package information
remote:          Installing dependencies from lock file
remote:          Package operations: 49 installs, 0 updates, 0 removals
remote:            - Installing doctrine/inflector (v1.2.0): Loading from cache
remote:            - Installing doctrine/lexer (v1.0.1): Loading from cache
remote:            - Installing erusev/parsedown (1.6.3): Loading from cache
```

Figure 10.2. Git output after a push to Heroku

Something wrong with your Heroku app that needs debugging? `heroku logs --tail` will show you the Terminal output from your Heroku app. You can also set the `APP_DEBUG=true` environment variable to debug Laravel. Remember to set it back to `false` when you've finished, though.

Migration and seed

Once the deploy completes, we will migrate our tables and seed the database. You can run Artisan and other app commands on the production app via Heroku CLI by preceding them with `heroku run`:

```
$ heroku run php artisan migrate --seed
```

Once the migration and seeding are complete, we can attempt to view the app via the browser. The page should be served but you'll see these mixed content errors:

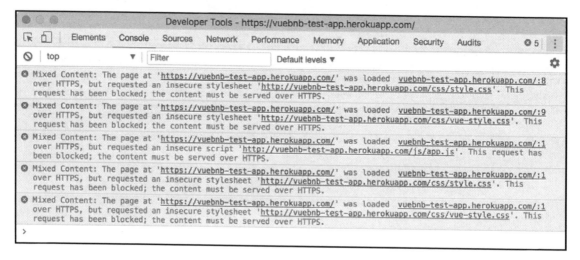

Figure 10.3. Console errors

Fixing these errors won't help much, as the files referred to are not on the server anyway. Let's deal with that issue first.

Serving static assets

Since our static assets, that is, CSS, JavaScript and image files, are not in version control, they have not been deployed to our Heroku app server.

This is okay, though, as a better option is to serve them via a CDN. In this part of the chapter, we'll set up an account with KeyCDN and serve our static assets from there.

Content distribution networks

When a server receives an incoming HTTP request, it usually responds with one of two types of content: dynamic or static. Dynamic content includes web pages or AJAX responses containing data specific to that request, for example, a web page with user data inserted via Blade.

Static content includes images, JavaScript, and CSS files that do not change between requests. It's inefficient to use a web server for serving static content since it unnecessarily engages the server resources to simply return a file.

A **Content Delivery Network (CDN)** is a network of servers, usually in different locations around the world, that are optimized for delivering static assets more quickly and cheaply than your typical web server.

KeyCDN

There are many different CDN services available, but in this book we'll use KeyCDN as it offers an easy-to-use service with a free usage tier.

Let's sign up for an account by visiting this link and following the instructions: `https://app.keycdn.com/signup`.

Once you have created and confirmed a new KeyCDN account, add a new zone by visiting the following link. *Zones* are simply collections of assets; you'd probably have a different zone for each website you're managing with KeyCDN. Call your new zone *vuebnb* and make sure it's a *Push* zone type, which will allow us to add files with FTP: `https://app.keycdn.com/zones/add`.

Uploading files with FTP

We will now push our static assets to the CDN with FTP. You could use an FTP utility such as Filezilla to do this, but I've included a Node script with the project, `scripts/ftp.js`, that allows you to do it with a simple command.

The script requires a few NPM packages, so install those first:

```
$ npm i --save-dev dotenv ftp recursive-readdir
```

Environment variables

In order to connect to your KeyCDN account, the FTP script requires a few environment variables to be set. Let's create a new file called `.env.node` to keep this configuration separate from the main Laravel project:

```
$ touch .env.node
```

The URL used for FTP-ing to KeyCDN is `ftp.keycdn.com`. The username and password will be the same as those you created an account with, so be sure to replace those in the values in the following code. The remote directory will be the same as the name of the zone you created.

`.env.node`:

```
FTP_HOST=ftp.keycdn.com
FTP_USER=anthonygore
FTP_PWD=*********
FTP_REMOTE_DIR=vuebnb
FTP_SKIP_IMAGES=0
```

Skipping images

The files we need to transfer to the CDN are in the `public/css`, `public/js`, `public/fonts`, and `public/images` directories. The FTP script has been configured to recursively copy these.

If you set the `FTP_SKIP_IMAGES` environment variable to true, however, the script will ignore any files in `public/images`. You'll want to do this after you've run the script the first time, as the images don't change and take quite a while to transfer.

`.env.node`:

```
FTP_SKIP_IMAGES=1
```

You can see how this takes effect in `scripts/ftp.js`:

```
let folders = [
  'css',
  'js',
  'fonts'
];

if (process.env.FTP_SKIP_IMAGES == 0) {
  folders.push('images');
}
```

NPM scripts

To make it easy to use the FTP script, add the following script definitions to your `package.json` file.

`package.json`:

```
"ftp-deploy-with-images": "cross-env node ./ftp.js",
"ftp-deploy": "cross-env FTP_SKIP_IMAGES=1 node ./ftp.js"
```

Production build

Before you run the FTP script, be sure to first build your app for production with the npm `run prod` command. This runs a Webpack build with the `NODE_ENV=production` environment variable set.

A production build ensures your assets are optimized for a production environment. For example, when Vue.js is bundled in production mode, it will not include warnings and tips, and will disable Vue Devtools. You can see how this is achieved from this snippet of the `vue.runtime.common.js` module.

`node_modules/vue/dist/vue.runtime.common.js`:

```
/**
 * Show production mode tip message on boot?
 */
productionTip: process.env.NODE_ENV !== 'production',

/**
 * Whether to enable devtools
 */
devtools: process.env.NODE_ENV !== 'production',
```

Webpack will also run certain production-only plugins during a production build to ensure your bundle files are as small and secure as possible.

Running the FTP script

The first time you run the FTP script you will need to copy all the files, including images. This will take some time, probably 20 to 30 minutes depending on your Internet connection speed:

```
$ npm run prod && npm run ftp-deploy-with-images
```

Once the transfer completes, uploaded files will be available at the zone URL, for example, `http://vuebnb-9c0f.kxcdn.com`. The path to a file will be relative to the `public` folder, for example, `public/css/vue-style.css` will be available at `[ZONE_URL]/css/vue-style.css`.

Test a few files to ensure the transfer was successful:

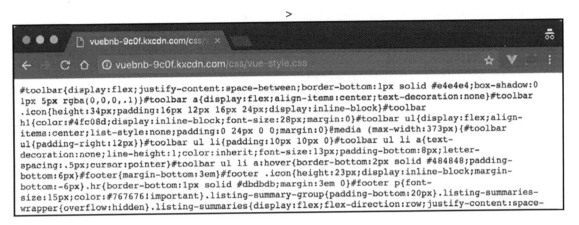

Figure 10.4. Testing CDN files

Subsequent transfers can skip the images by using this command:

```
$ npm run prod && npm run ftp-deploy
```

Reading from the CDN

We now want Vuebnb to load any static assets from the CDN instead of the web server when in production. To do this, we're going to create our own Laravel helper method.

Currently, we reference assets in our app using the `asset` helper. This helper returns a fully-qualified URL for that asset's location on the web server. For example, in our app view we link to the JavaScript bundle file like this:

```
<script type="text/javascript" src="{{ asset('js/app.js') }}"></script>
```

Our new helper, which we'll call `cdn`, will instead return a URL that points to the asset's location on the CDN:

```
<script type="text/javascript" src="{{ cdn('js/app.js') }}"></script>
```

CDN helper

Let's begin by creating a file called `helpers.php`. This will declare a new `cdn` method which, for now, won't do anything but return the `asset` helper method.

`app/helpers.php`:

```php
<?php

if (!function_exists('cdn'))
{
  function cdn($asset)
  {
    return asset($asset);
  }
}
```

To ensure this helper is available to be used anywhere in our app, we can use Composer's *autoload* feature. This makes a class or file available to all other files without them having to manually `include` or `require` it.

`composer.json`:

```json
. . .

"autoload": {
  "classmap": [ ... ],
  "psr-4": { ... },
  "files": [
    "app/helpers.php"
  ]
},

. . .
```

Each time you modify Composer's autoload declaration you need to run `dump-autoload`:

```
$ composer dump-autoload
```

With that done, the `cdn` helper will be available for use within our app. Let's test it with Tinker:

```
$ php artisan tinker
>>>> cdn('js/app.js')
=> "http://vuebnb.test/js/app.js"
```

Setting the CDN URL

The cdn helper method will need to know the URL of the CDN. Let's set an CDN_URL environment variable that will be assigned the zone URL for Vuebnb, minus the protocol prefix.

While we're at it, let's add another variable, CDN_BYPASS, that can be used to bypass the CDN in our local development environment where we won't need it.

.env:

```
...

CDN_URL=vuebnb-9c0f.kxcdn.com
CDN_BYPASS=0
```

Let's now register these new variables in the app configuration file.

config/app.php:

```php
<?php

return [
  ...
  // CDN

  'cdn' => [
    'url' => env('CDN_URL'),
    'bypass' => env('CDN_BYPASS', false),
  ],
];
```

Now we can complete the logic of our cdn helper.

app/helpers.php:

```php
<?php

use Illuminate\Support\Facades\Config;

if (!function_exists('cdn'))
{
  function cdn($asset)
  {
    if (Config::get('app.cdn.bypass') || !Config::get('app.cdn.url')) {
      return asset($asset);
    } else {
```

```
        return  "//" . Config::get('app.cdn.url') . '/' . $asset;
      }
    }
  }
```

If you still have Tinker open, exit and re-enter, and test the changes work as expected:

```
>>>> exit
$ php artisan tinker
>>>> cdn('js/app.js')
=> "//vuebnb-9c0f.kxcdn.com/js/app.js"
```

Using the CDN in Laravel

Let's now replace usages of the `asset` helper in our Laravel files with the `cdn` helper.

app/Http/Controllers/ListingController.php:

```
<?php

...

class ListingController extends Controller
{
  private function get_listing($listing)
  {
    ...
    for($i = 1; $i <=4; $i++) {
      $model['image_' . $i] = cdn(
        'images/' . $listing->id . '/Image_' . $i . '.jpg'
      );
    }
    ...
  }

  ...

  private function get_listing_summaries()
  {
    ...
    $collection->transform(function($listing) {
      $listing->thumb = cdn(
        'images/' . $listing->id . '/Image_1_thumb.jpg'
      );
      return $listing;
    });
```

```
        ...
    }

    ...
}
```

resources/views/app.blade.php:

```
<html>
  <head>
      ...
      <link rel="stylesheet" href="{{ cdn('css/style.css') }}"
type="text/css">
      <link rel="stylesheet" href="{{ cdn('css/vue-style.css') }}"
type="text/css">
      ...
  </head>
  <body>
      ...
      <script src="{{ cdn('js/app.js') }}"></script>
  </body>
</html>
```

Using the CDN in Vue

In our Vue app, we're loading some static assets as well. For example, in the toolbar we use the logo.

resources/assets/components/App.vue:

```
<img class="icon" src="/images/logo.png">
```

As this is a relative URL it will, by default, point to the web server. If we make it an absolute URL instead, we'd have to hard-code the CDN URL, which is not ideal either.

Let's instead get Laravel to pass the CDN URL in the head of the document. We can do this by simply calling the cdn helper with an empty string.

resources/views/app.blade.php:

```
<head>
    ...
    <script type="text/javascript">
        ...
```

```
        window.cdn_url = "{{ cdn('') }}";
      </script>
  </head>
```

We'll now use a computed property to construct the absolute URL using this global value.

`resources/assets/components/App.vue`:

```
    <template>
      ...
      <router-link :to="{ name: 'home' }">
        <img class="icon" :src="logoUrl">
        <h1>vuebnb</h1>
      </router-link>
      ...
    </template>
    <script>
      export default {
        computed: {
          logoUrl() {
            return `${window.cdn_url || ''}images/logo.png`;
          }
        },
        ...
      }
    </script>
    <style>...</style>
```

We'll use the same concept in the footer where the grey logo is used.

`resources/assets/components/CustomFooter.vue`:

```
    <template>
    ...
      <img class="icon" :src="logoUrl">
    ...
    </template>
    <script>
      export default {
        computed: {
          containerClass() { ... },
          logoUrl() {
            return `${window.cdn_url || ''}images/logo_grey.png`;
          }
        },
      }
    </script>
```

Deploying to Heroku

With that done, commit any file changes to Git and push again to Heroku to trigger a new deploy. You'll also need to rebuild your frontend assets and transfer these to the CDN.

Finally, set the CDN environment variables:

```
$ heroku config:set \
CDN_BYPASS=0 \
CDN_URL=vuebnb-9c0f.kxcdn.com
```

Finale

You have now completed the case-study project for this book, a sophisticated full-stack Vue.js and Laravel application. Congratulations!

Be sure to show Vuebnb off to your friends and colleagues, as they'll no doubt be impressed with your new skills. I'd also appreciate if you tweeted me the link to your project so I can admire your work too. My Twitter handle is `@anthonygore`.

Recap

We've come a long way in this book, let's recap some of what we've achieved:

- In `Chapter 1`, *Hello Vue – An Introduction to Vue.js*, we were introduced to Vue.js
- In `Chapter 2`, *Prototyping Vuebnb, Your First Vue.js Project*, we learned the basics of Vue.js including installation, data binding, directives, and lifecycle hooks. We built a prototype of the listing page of Vuebnb including the image modal
- In `Chapter 3`, *Setting Up a Laravel Development Environment*, we installed the main Vuebnb project and set up the Homestead development environment
- In `Chapter 4`, *Building a Web Service with Laravel*, we created a Laravel web service to supply data for Vuebnb
- In `Chapter 5`, *Integrating Laravel and Vue.js with Webpack*, we migrated the prototype into the main project and used Laravel Mix to compile our assets into bundle files
- In `Chapter 6`, *Composing Widgets with Vue.js Components*, we learned about components. We used this knowledge to add an image carousel to the modal on the listing page and refactored the frontend to incorporate single-file components

- In Chapter 7, *Building a Multi-Page App With Vue Router,* we added Vue Router to the project, allowing us to add a home page with the listing summary sliders
- In Chapter 8, *Managing Your Application State With Vuex,* we introduced the Flux architecture and added Vuex to our app. We then created a save feature and moved page state into Vuex
- In Chapter 9, *Adding a User Login and API Authentication With Passport,* we added a user login to the project. We sent the user's saved listings back to the database with an authenticated AJAX call
- In Chapter 10, *Deploying a Full-Stack App to the Cloud,* we deployed the app to a Heroku cloud server and transferred static assets to a CDN

Next steps

You may have reached the end of the book, but your journey as a full-stack Vue developer has only just begun! What should you move on to next?

Firstly, there are still plenty more features you can add to Vuebnb. Designing and implementing these yourself will increase your skill and knowledge immensely. Here are a few ideas to get you started:

- Complete the user authentication flow. Add a registration page and functionality for resetting passwords
- Add a user profile page. Here, users can upload an avatar that will display in the toolbar when they're logged in
- Create a form on the listing page that allows the room to be booked. Include a drop-down datepicker widget for selecting start and end dates
- Server render the app by running Vue from a JavaScript sandbox on the server. This way users get a complete page with visible content when they load the site

Secondly, I invite you to check out *Vue.js Developers,* an online community for Vue.js enthusiasts that I founded. Here you can read articles on Vue.js, stay up-to-date with Vue.js news through our newsletter, and share tips and tricks with other developers in our Facebook group.

Check it out at this URL: `https://vuejsdevelopers.com`.

Summary

In this chapter, we learned how to deploy a full-stack app to a Heroku cloud server. To do this, we used the Heroku CLI to set up a new Heroku app, and then deployed it using Heroku's Git server.

We also created a CDN with KeyCDN, and used FTP to deploy our static assets to the CDN.

Finally, we learned why it's important for performance and security to build our JavaScript assets in production-mode ahead of deployment.

This is the final chapter of the book. Thank you for reading and good luck on your web development journey!

Index

Made in the USA
San Bernardino, CA
15 March 2019